COMPUTER-ASSISTED INSTRUCTION

LHBEC

COMPUTER-ASSISTED INSTRUCTION

A SYNTHESIS OF THEORY, PRACTICE, AND TECHNOLOGY

Esther R. Steinberg

Computer-based Education Research
Laboratory and College of Education
University of Illinois at Urbana-Champaign

LEA LAWRENCE ERLBAUM ASSOCIATES, PUBLISHERS
1991   Hillsdale, New Jersey   Hove and London

Lawrence Erlbaum Associates, Inc., Publishers
365 Broadway
Hillsdale, New Jersey 07642

Library of Congress Cataloging-in-Publication Data

Steinberg, Esther R.
    Computer-assisted instruction: a synthesis of theory, practice, and technology / Esther R.
Steinberg.
        p.   cm.
    Includes bibliographical references and index.
    ISBN 0-89859-830-3. — ISBN 0-8058-0865-5 (pbk.)
    1. Computer-assisted instruction.   I. Title.
LB1028.5.S72   1990
371.3'34 — dc20   90-43494
                                                        CIP

Printed in the United States of America
10 9 8 7 6 5 4 3 2 1

Contents

Preface

This book is for designers of computer-assisted instruction (CAI) and computer-based training (CBT). It is for practitioners and for students learning how to become instructional designers. Instructors and administrators who select CAI lessons for their curricula will also find this book helpful. It will enable them to better understand the potential and the limitations of computers as tutors.

The purpose of this book is to lay a foundation for designing CAI. It is the second of a two-volume series about CAI design. The first, *Teaching Computers to Teach* (Steinberg, 1984), is a "how to" book. It presents procedures and principles for designing instruction delivered by computer. This volume is a "why" book. It presents a theoretical framework and background for designing CAI. While there are parallel chapters in the two books, each stands alone. Each can be read without the other.

Designers of CAI draw on research from many disciplines and on practical experience. While some of the current research is published in CAI-specific journals such as the *Journal of Computer-Based Instruction,* some studies appear in educational journals devoted to a specific subject, such as the *Journal of Chemical Education.* Topics critical to instructional design, such as motivation and learning processes, are discussed in journals such as the *Journal of Educational Psychology* and *Cognitive Psychology,* but the focus is rarely CAI. Thus the implications of the research for CAI are not discussed. Information gained from experience with pioneering systems and early research are not readily accessible. Results often appear only in conference proceedings and in institutional technical reports, some of which are no longer available. The goal of this book is to synthesize the findings from these many sources.

The first chapter establishes two themes. The first is that instructional interactions between human beings and computers make CAI a distinctive form of instruction. CAI is not merely the application of computer technology to known instructional principles. CAI is the synthesis rather than the sum of many disciplines.

The second theme is that CAI shares many features with other instructional modes, such as traditional classrooms and programmed instruction, but also differs from them in fundamental ways. The development of a theory or model for CAI design should begin with what is already known. Knowledge that is inappropriate for CAI should be modified or discarded. Where information is lacking because of the unique features of CAI, new knowledge should be sought. We can learn from both early and current theories and practice, from behavioral as well as educational and cognitive psychology, and from pioneering CAI systems as well as from intelligent tutoring systems.

Chapters 2 and 3 flow directly from these themes. Chapter 2 proposes a framework for CAI that is a synthesis and extension of established theories and models of learning and instruction. The central theme is that effective CAI is the result of the interaction of six components: the Target Population, the Goals, the Task, Instruction, appropriate Computer Application, and Environmental Implementation. The key word here is interaction.

Chapter 3 presents the Three-Phase Plan, a procedure for designing CAI. The plan attends to all six components of the CAI framework and fosters attention to their interaction. The procedure draws on lessons learned from two pioneering CAI systems, incorporates modifications of known instructional design procedures, and adds features specific to CAI.

Each of the succeeding four chapters discusses an aspect of the design of instruction per se: Instructional Presentations, Interactions, Human Factors, and Displays and Interactive Videos. Each chapter reviews relevant research and discusses the implications for CAI. A recurring theme is that each of these aspects of instruction interacts with other components of the CAI framework to influence the effectiveness of a lesson.

Individualization is a hallmark of computer-presented instruction and it is the topic of Chapters 8 and 9. Chapter 8 begins with a summary of nonCAI individualized instructional systems and the implications for CAI. This is followed by a discussion of individualized instruction in CAI and individualized CAI systems that are based on mathematical and statistical models of learning.

Chapter 9 presents an overview of intelligent tutoring systems (ITS) and adaptive techniques employed by various systems. CAI and ITS are compared in some detail.

The book concludes with a chapter about evaluation. The purpose of generating CAI is to promote learning. Evaluation is essential to determine whether the lesson and the learners achieve their goals. The theme of the chapter is that evaluation is essential both during the development of the lesson and in the assessment of students' performance after the lesson is completed.

Esther R. Steinberg

Chapter 1

CAI: DISTINCTIVE INSTRUCTION

Computer-assisted instruction (CAI) has now been with us for more than a quarter of a century. People everywhere are studying CAI lessons. Medical students are diagnosing illnesses of simulated patients. Factory workers are getting oriented to their jobs. Fifth graders are developing thinking skills, and kindergartners are learning the alphabet.

What makes these lessons attractive to learners? What makes them instructionally effective? The answers come from many sources. Computer systems, videodiscs, expert systems, and other technologies make possible innovative and sophisticated presentations. Research in the psychology of learning and of instruction help us understand how people learn and how to apply that knowledge to instruction. Practice in real classrooms adds information not present in laboratory environments.

Although CAI draws on many disciplines, it is not merely the sum total of this knowledge. Technology interacts with learners and with presentations to generate issues unique to computer-presented instruction. In traditional classrooms, for example, students get meaning not only from the subject matter content but also from cues such as facial expressions and the context of discussions. The cues that are present in interpersonal communication are not present in communication between a person and a computer. A message displayed on a computer screen does not contain the same information as the identical message presented in a classroom. In addition, technology affords new instructional techniques. Simulations in CAI, for instance, can provide learning experiences that are not possible with other media.

1

Thus, CAI is more than the application of technology to instruction. Effective CAI is a synthesis of technology, theory, and practice. The purpose of this text is to present such a synthesis.

DEFINING CAI

To date there is no established definition for the term CAI. Computers can assist instruction in many ways. They can actually present instruction, interacting with students in tutor-like fashion, individually or in small groups. Computer-presented instruction embraces a wide range of techniques and can vary in complexity from simple drills to decision making tasks. Drills in foreign language vocabulary can be written to retire items a student has learned and repeat items missed. Simulations allow students to make life threatening decisions and observe their consequences without danger to themselves or others.

Computers can also assist instruction by providing tools for learning. One geometry program, for example, draws constructions specified by the students, makes measurements, and computes values such as areas. Thus it frees students from physical requirements and enables them to make conjectures, explore relationships, and "behave like geometers" (Yerushalmy & Houde, 1986). Databases can serve as resources for implementing innovative instruction in social studies (Elder & White, 1989). Word processors and outliners facilitate instruction in language arts.

Communications capabilities of computer networks make it possible for students in different locations, even in different countries, to engage in cooperative science experiments (Waugh & Levin, 1988/89). Networks allow students to engage in lively dialogues, expressing views and "listening" to others and developing critical thinking skills (Bresler, 1989).

Some definitions of CAI encompass all of these applications of computers to instruction; some include only computer-presented applications. In this text CAI means computer-presented instruction that is individualized, interactive, and guided.

Individualized

Instruction is individualized because the computer serves as a tutor for one individual rather than as an instructor for a group. CAI need not be confined to individual users and can be effective for students working in pairs or small groups. In this text the focus is on individualized instruction.

Interactive

CAI is interactive in that it involves two-way communication between a learner and a computer system. In some lessons the computer poses questions, the learner responds, and the computer presents feedback. In other lessons the user initiates the interaction and the computer responds. For example, the goal of a lesson might be to find the faulty component in an engine. The student might ask whether there is fuel in the gas tank or whether the electrical system is functioning correctly and the computer supplies the answers. This interaction continues until the student solves the problem.

Guided

Because CAI is instruction, some element of guidance is implied. Consider a physics lesson in which a student observes how the path of a projectile varies with the angle of projection. The student specifies the angle at which the projectile should be fired and then watches as the computer traces the path of the projectile on the display screen. By entering different values for the angle, the student can observe how changes in the angle of elevation affect the height and horizontal distance of the projectile. Such a program provides interaction and offers an opportunity for self-instruction. Some learners enter a reasonable range of values and make correct inferences about the laws of physics while others do not. Some students even make incorrect deductions while still others have no idea of what values to enter.

To be CAI as defined here, the lesson should guide the student by suggesting an appropriate range of values to select if the range she selected is too narrow or otherwise inadequate. To help her make the desired inferences, the program might summarize her work by presenting a table showing the height and horizontal value for each of the angles of elevation she entered. The program might ask questions to help the student understand the underlying concepts and principles.

A Medium, Not a Method

Computers are an instructional medium. CAI is instruction presented via this medium. CAI is not a method of instruction. Many methods are implemented in CAI, including direct and exploratory lessons, drills, games, and simulations.

PAST EXPERIENCE AND NEW TECHNOLOGY

Developing CAI involves becoming familiar with a new instructional medium and learning how it is both like and unlike other media. In many ways the application of computers to instruction parallels past experiences of applying new technology in other fields. The transitions from handwritten manuscripts to printed, and from radio shows to television shows can provide some useful insights about the processes involved.

Resistance to Change

We tend to apply new technology within the constraints of past experiences. For example, books that were printed between 1450 and 1480, were almost indistinguishable from manuscripts of that period (Steinberg, 1966). Printers replicated what scribes did. Rather than striving for legibility and clarity, printers accepted and copied scribes' compact lines, closely woven pages and other conventions. Similarly in the early years of television, advertisements were written in a radio format, with a video component tacked on. Announcers would read the advertisement off camera while signs containing the message were held in front of a television camera (Sterling & Kittross, 1978).

Reasons for Resistance

Why do we limit uses of new technology to old methods? The answers lie with both producers and consumers. Producers are conservative and prefer to work with familiar methods even though new technology can make their work easier and/or more efficient. Consumers resist changes offered by producers. Steinberg (1966) cites a study of five centuries of printing in which the author states that "for a new fount (sic) to be successful it has to be so good that only very few recognize its novelty."

Preference for the familiar is not restricted to earlier times. When reading print materials, people prefer mixed text (upper and lower case). The same is true of computer-presented text (Henney, 1983). Many people, when learning to use a word processor, find it more comfortable to backspace one letter at a time (as with a typewriter) than to learn how to use a feature that erases the entire word with one keystroke.

Application of Past Experience

Developers, like consumers, may view new technology as merely a different or a more convenient tool to accomplish old tasks. They may transfer a task directly from the old technology to the new, with little or no attention to differences between the two. They consider neither the impact of the new technology on the consumer nor its potential for change. Many CAI "lessons," for instance, resemble books. One display screen after another is filled with text. No interaction is required other than to press a key (like turning a page) to advance through the program. Authors of such programs have not taken notice of the differences between learning from printed materials and learning through meaningful interaction with a computer lesson.

Add-ons to Past Experience

Sometimes producers are aware of the distinctive features of the new technologies but use them merely as additions to the old. They fail to consider the possibility that the interaction of the new characteristics with the old might warrant modifications of the customary methods. For example, during the early years of television much of the "programming was radio material with the addition of limited visual elements" (Sterling & Kittross, 1978, p. 278).

The mentality of add-ons can be seen in the remedial sequences of some CAI lessons. The author uses the computer's capability to individualize instruction by sequencing a student through remediation if she does not meet performance standards. Unfortunately "remediation" is a repeat of all of the same instruction that she did not understand initially. The author did not take advantage of the ability to present alternative explanations or instruction specific to her error.

Synthesis and Integration

Ultimately, exploring new technologies increases our understanding of the differences between the old and the new and the implications for the most effective application. A deeper understanding also leads to new and creative implementations. Advertising on television, for example, evolved from simply adding signs or slides to messages read off-camera by announcers to producing "sound film, especially with animation and other visual sleights of hand" (Sterling & Kittross, p. 272). Television sportscasters use split screens, instant replays, and other enhancements to get their audiences more intimately involved in the game.

Similarly, as computers become more sophisticated and as we explore their potential, we can expect to see more effective and creative computer-presented lessons. While many of the early commercially produced CAI lessons resembled flashcard-like drills, an increasing number of lessons today present sophisticated drills. Many lessons now go beyond drills and provide an opportunity to acquire concepts and to develop critical thinking and problem-solving skills.

Value of Past Experience

Should past experience be discarded when new tools and mechanisms are available? Not at all. We can transfer much from past experience. Television, during the years of transition from radio, used many of the same shows that were broadcast on radio. Detective drama appealed to audiences whether on radio or television. Shows aimed at young people such as the Lone Ranger and Roy Rogers continued to interest viewers when transferred to television.

In the same way much of the experience and information gained from traditional instruction and the instructional design literature can be applied to CAI. Wherever this knowledge is applicable to CAI, why not use it? Why not apply instructional techniques that have proved successful? Drill and practice is an effective technique for some instructional goals and for some groups of learners. Why reject it simply because it is associated with limited but important aspects of education? Of course, CAI has potential far beyond drill and practice, and may even have its greatest benefit in lessons that help meet new goals, such as learning how to learn. Nonetheless, students still need to acquire basic skills, concepts, and principles. If we can learn from other disciplines how CAI can achieve these goals, why not take advantage of that knowledge? Past experience can provide guidelines for the future and prevent repetition of mistakes made in the past.

Attention to Differences

Old technologies often have limitations that have since been surpassed. Assumptions underlying implementation of the old technology are no longer valid for implementation of the new. Furthermore, new technology is accompanied by new issues. An unexpected impact of television, for instance, was that performers and speakers appear more human than on radio. Viewers, particularly children, feel more involved in the events. Violence on television, for example, has raised considerable controversy about its potential for inciting violence in children, whereas violence was not a big issue with the radio. Political candidates used radio to reach the public, but their radio image was not nearly as significant a factor in elections as their television image is today.

CAI

An understanding of the differences between CAI and other modes of instruction will enable us to draw appropriately from past experience. The next section anlayzes those differences and the limitations of other instructional modes for CAI.

DIFFERENCES BETWEEN CAI AND OTHER MODES OF INSTRUCTION

Learning in group-paced situations such as listening to lectures, participating in discussions, and viewing films is different than learning from CAI lessons. Even learning with individually paced print media such as books and programmed instruction is significantly different than with CAI.

Classroom and CAI

Classroom instruction differs from CAI in three ways. They are (1) modes of communication, (2) instructor-learner interactions, and (3) environment.

Modes of communication. One major difference between classrooms and CAI is communication between a learner and an instructor (Figure 1.1). In traditional classrooms, instructors talk much of the time. They also write on the board, draw diagrams, and display illustrations. In addition, instructors communicate by their nonverbal, physical actions. They point to an item to draw attention to it, smile to reward or to encourage correct responses, shake their heads, raise an eyebrow, or otherwise use body language to indicate approval or disapproval. The point is that instructors use several modes of communication, much of it oral and physical. In CAI, the computer/instructor communicates almost exclusively in one mode: visual. At present oral communication in CAI is rather limited. Ear training lessons in music include sound (Hofstetter, 1981). Lessons in other fields include pleasant musical tones for correct responses and "beeps" for incorrect ones. However, these sounds are not the equivalent of oral instruction.

As new technology becomes economically feasible CAI will be able to include oral presentations. Interactive videodiscs (which have both audio and video) are already gaining popularity. Technology that allows for randomly accessible human (i.e., not synthesized) speech is now commer-

MODE OF COMMUNICATION	INSTRUCTIONAL MODE	
	CAI	TRADITIONAL
Instruction	Primarily visual Verbal and graphic	Oral and visual Verbal, graphic, and physical
Learner	Reads Observes Sometimes listens	Reads Observes Listens
Response mode	Types Touches Manipulates tools	Speaks Writes Uses body movements
	May be familiar	Familiar

FIG 1.1. Comparison of modes of communication in CAI and traditional instruction.

cially available. Nonetheless, at present, most CAI lessons are primarily visual.

In the classroom, learners listen, read, and observe. In CAI, learners only read and observe; they are rarely expected to listen. In the classroom, students communicate by speaking or by writing. In CAI, they type, touch a display screen, or manipulate a tool such as a "mouse." Students know how to speak and they know how to write, but many do not know how to type. Not all of them are adept at manipulating tools for pointing.

Instructor-learner interaction. An important aspect of classroom instruction is the interaction between an instructor and a learner (Figure 1.2). An instructor tries to monitor students' understanding by asking questions. Usually only one student at a time responds overtly. The others respond covertly, if at all. All learners except one are supposed to "think" the answer. Instructors can also judge progress in learning by observing students' behavior. If they are staring out of the window or dropping pencils, it's easy to tell that they are not paying attention and probably not learning. If learners are waving their hands or scowling, the instructor can infer they are confused or would like additional information. In either case, the instructor can take action to remedy the situation.

Not so in CAI. A computer/instructor cannot see a learner. The only way a computer/instructor can monitor understanding is by asking questions

INSTRUCTOR – LEARNER INTERACTION	INSTRUCTIONAL MODE	
	CAI	TRADITIONAL
How learning is monitored	Questions	Questions Observations
Nature of each learner's response	Overt	Overt or covert
Judging learners' responses	Limited or flexible Automatic or student initiated	Flexible Automatic
Potential for feedback to learners' questions	Limited	Broad
Locus of control of learning	Learner, computer, or both	Instructor, or both learner and instructor
Sequence of instruction	Individualized	Group-based

FIG 1.2. Comparison of instructor-learner interactions in CAI and traditional instruction.

and evaluating responses. To accomplish this, a computer lesson must require overt responses.

Judging learners' responses is also different in classrooms than it is in CAI. Human instructors can be flexible in judging a student's response because they can draw on their large store of knowledge ad hoc. They can accept an answer that is correct even if it is not the one that they anticipated. Instructors know if an answer is partially correct and can provide appropriate feedback. In CAI, answer judging can be very flexible, but it is not an innate part of computer systems. Flexible response judging has to be specifically written into a CAI lesson. For example, a computer has to be programmed to accept synonyms or to ignore extra words. It does not judge "His name was Lincoln," "Abe Lincoln," and "Lincoln" as equally acceptable responses to a question about who freed the slaves unless it is programmed to do so.

An instructor knows that when a student quits talking, she has finished responding and is waiting to have her answer judged. Unless a response of fixed length is anticipated, a computer does not know when to begin judging it until the learner somehow signals readiness, as by pressing a prespecified key.

Another difference between CAI and traditional instruction is that a computer cannot answer just any question posed by a learner. Instructors, on the other hand, can usually answer learners' questions. If not, they can suggest resources for finding the answers.

Teacher-learner interaction also differs from CAI in the source of responsibility for managing instruction. Classroom learning is, for the most part, group-paced. Therefore it is basically teacher-controlled even in small group instruction. The teacher determines the sequence of instruction, when to continue to discuss a topic, when to remediate, and when to move on. Instruction is not only group-paced but usually also linear. It moves along the same path for everybody. In contrast, CAI can be individually paced and can allow multiple instructional paths. The flow of instruction can be controlled by the computer, the learner, the teacher, or some combination. The computer can direct the flow of instruction by following a set of rules that specifies the action to take under particular conditions. Alternatively, a lesson can be written to allow the learner to make decisions about the sequence of instruction, or to share control of these decisions with the computer. Some lessons are even written to allow an instructor to specify and thus control sequence.

Environmental factors.   A third category of CAI-classroom differences can be classified as environmental (Figure 1.3). Most of these factors are self-evident or common knowledge in one instructional mode but not in the

ENVIRONMENTAL FACTORS	INSTRUCTIONAL MODE	
	CAI	TRADITIONAL
Knowing how well you're doing	Depends on lesson design	Often self-evident
Learner's expectations		
Response time	2 seconds or less	Not known
How to start, when to start, how to get help, how to get around, how to correct errors	Not known to learner unless present in lesson	Known from past experience
Opportunity to respond	Every person, every question	Not every person to every question
Acknowledgement of responses	Not innate	Innate
Learner–learner interaction	Not common	Common
Opportunity to observe the instructor	Not innate	Innate
Pacing	Individualized	Group or individualized
Repetition of identical lesson	Available	Not available
Delivery vehicle	Display screen, sometimes audio	Person, chalkboard, slides, transparencies
Capacity of delivery vehicle	Limited	Extensive

FIG 1.3. Comparison of environmental factors in CAI and traditional instruction.

other. A good example is information about progress and achievement. In the classroom the quality of your performance is often self-evident. You can measure your progress toward your goals by glancing ahead in printed material to see how much remains to be done. The status of your knowledge and performance relative to the performance of others is generally self-evident. In CAI, information about your performance is self-evident only in some lessons (e.g., game formats, problem solving). Knowing how you compare to others is not self-evident. Nor is it generally easy or even possible to flip through a CAI lesson to see how much remains to be done. That information is usually available only if the lesson designer presents it on the display screen.

Students are familiar with the mechanical aspects of learning in the classroom from previous experiences. They know how much time they have to make responses, how to get help, and how to correct answers. This is not necessarily so in CAI. Even if a student has experience with CAI lessons, that experience may not transfer to other lessons or other computer systems.

Students know from a teacher's verbal responses or from a nod of the head that she heard an oral response. They can tell from checkmarks, grades, and other red pencil marks on a paper that written responses were noticed. Based on this experience, students expect overt evidence from a computer lesson that their responses have been received. If incorrect answers are erased by a computer program, without comment and before learners see it, they may think that the answer was not received and enter it again.

Students learn by observing and interacting with others in a classroom. A student who is unable to answer a question posed by the teacher can learn by listening to another student's response. A student who does not understand a concept can learn from a teacher's responses to other students' questions. The give and take of classroom learning is not present in CAI. Although some CAI lessons are intended to be studied by two or more students working together, most are intended for an individual learner.

Because CAI is individualized instruction, lessons can allow each learner to progress at a self-determined pace, moving quickly through topics that are easily understood and slowly through more difficult ones. A concept missed or not thoroughly understood can be repeated. In contrast, students in a classroom move along more or less at the same pace. Faster students have to wait for slower ones and slower ones may be unable to keep up with the group.

There are obviously considerable physical differences between a computer and a classroom environment in capacity for delivering instruction. A computer display screen is limited in size. Sometimes both the illustration and the explanatory text cannot be presented simultaneously on the display screen. In contrast, an instructor can illustrate on the chalkboard or show an overhead transparency while providing extensive oral explanations. Advances in technology such as videodiscs and digitized speech may soon help to overcome or minimize these differences.

Programmed Instruction and CAI

Programmed instruction is an educational application of Skinner's principles of human behavior (Skinner, 1953). The general idea is that programmed instruction is individualized instruction in which brief sections of information are presented followed by questions. The student responds to the questions and receives immediate feedback about the correctness of the responses.

Programmed textbooks have been prepared for many subjects and at all levels of education. Unfortunately, Skinner's techniques "were frequently disseminated in superficial forms for practical exploitation" (Glaser, 1978, p. 222). Many of the programmed materials did not apply Skinner's principles as intended. The following discussion addresses programmed texts as they came to be generally applied.

Learner interaction.   Like CAI, presentations in programmed instruction present information interspersed with questions and can provide immediate feedback about correctness of responses. A major difference between programmed instruction and CAI is learner interaction with the lesson. In programmed instruction, a student may find that his answer is wrong. However, there is not necessarily any feedback about why this is so. A student's response may be correct, but not the same as the one provided by the program. The student must decide if his answer is equivalent to the one provided. If he is a novice in the subject matter, he may not have the background to make such a judgment. In contrast, a CAI lesson can be programmed to judge answers flexibly, accept all correct responses, and provide informative feedback specific to the nature of the learner's misconception.

Given the interactive attribute of CAI, a program can assess students' knowledge and arrange instructional paths accordingly. A CAI lesson can branch a student around material that he has mastered or provide further instruction if he needs remediation. Branching is theoretically possible in programmed instruction but is generally not provided because implementation is cumbersome.

Physical differences.   In programmed instruction, a student can peek at the correct answer before he formulates a response. In CAI, an author has the option of allowing a student to do so or of requiring him to enter a response before displaying the correct one.

Books

Not all instruction is externally managed. Some media, such as books, provide a tool for self-instruction. This instructional mode is also different from CAI.

Individualization.   A book presents the identical information to every reader. In that sense books are not individualized instruction. However, every learner reads at her own pace and learns what she is capable of and motivated to learn. In that sense books are individualized self-instruction.

Interaction. Clearly there is no interaction between a reader and a book. Questions may be inserted in the text, answers provided, and helpful learning hints presented. Nevertheless, it is one-way instruction. A book does not respond to a reader's activities.

Physical differences. One difference between the printed page and the computer is that diagrams can be created dynamically on the display screen. Textual information can be interspersed as a diagram is created in much the same fashion as an instructor makes comments as he creates a diagram on the board. In addition, illustrations are all "stills" on printed pages whereas they may be either stills or animations on computer displays.

In CAI it is possible to focus on a specific concept by physically isolating it and presenting it on a separate display. It is also possible to do this in books, but it is not common practice. An entire page is usually filled with print.

Sometimes a person wants to glance at information that is presented on two separate pages. He can do this in a book by keeping a finger on one page or perhaps even turning the page back while looking up information on another. Interdisplay continuity is difficult to achieve in CAI. On some computer systems it is possible to display information from more than one source using "windows." The problem is that even when this is possible, there may be too much information for the size of the display or the information may be presented in such small print that it is too hard to read.

Film and Television

Like books, films and television can be a form of self-instruction. All viewers see and hear the same presentation. What they learn is a function of their goals, their background knowledge, and their motivation.

Interaction. Films and television are one-way instruction. They present, but do not interact with learners.

Realism. Films and television can be realistic. Until recently, only a limited amount of realism was possible in CAI. At present both videodiscs and high resolution computer screens enable realism in CAI. This is not to say that realism in visuals is always essential in instruction. It may even interfere with learning in some situations (see Chapter 7).

WHAT WE CAN TRANSFER TO CAI FROM OTHER INSTRUCTIONAL MODES

Many aspects of instruction are universal and apply to all instructional modes. Elements that are generic to all instruction can be transferred to CAI even though the methods of implementation may be different. Among these elements are events that prepare students for learning, instructional techniques, and procedures for producing instruction.

Preparation for Learning

Gaining a learner's attention is an example of a generic construct. It is the first event in preparing students for instruction (Gagné & Briggs, 1974). The need to gain learners' attention is an obvious, but often overlooked element in computer implementations of instruction. It is still too common to find CAI lessons that do not begin with instruction, but rather with long delays while programs are transferred from storage (e.g. disks) to the computer or while extended graphics and animations appear on the display screen. The most wonderful lesson is of little value if students' attention is lost before the lesson even begins.

Instructional Techniques

Many well known techniques for presenting instruction are also applicable to CAI, either directly or with some modification. These include successful instructional models, principles for writing good questions, and motivational factors in learning.

Presentations. Instructional techniques specific to a subject can frequently transfer directly to CAI. For example, students often have difficulty understanding that a unit fraction such as 1/5 implies division into five equal parts. Teachers are able to get across the idea by appealing to children's understanding of equality in terms of getting one's "fair share." Children can divide candy bars equally among five people whether in the classroom or in CAI (Seiler & Weaver, 1976).

Interactions. Question-response-feedback sequences are an integral part of instruction. Guidelines for writing good questions are as applicable to CAI as to other instructional modes.

One principle is that students should be required to respond actively to questions. Experienced teachers apply this concept when they ask a question and then hesitate a few seconds before calling on a specific student to respond. They know that students will more likely try to formulate an answer if they think they might be called on. Significant effects for active responding have also been documented in studies of instructional television (Barbatsis, 1978).

Feedback, a critical event in instruction, (Gagné & Briggs, 1974), may be motivational or informative. Selection of appropriate feedback in CAI can be guided by research in programmed instruction.

Motivation.   Motivation is obviously an important factor in learning. Classroom experience provides knowledge about motivators that are appropriate for particular student populations. Some students are adequately motivated by praise while others require more tangible motivators, such as raisins and nuts. Some games are motivating and others are not. A CAI arithmetic game that is motivating when one child plays against another may not be at all motivating when a child plays against the computer (B. A. Seiler, personal communication, 1976).

Systems for Producing Instruction

Educational psychologists and developers of programmed instruction have generated procedural models for producing instruction. The components of these models are also important to producing CAI. We have learned, for example, that evaluation is a critical element in the instructional design process, and is conducted in all its phases. Many of the steps in the design process can also be implemented in CAI, although they need to be modified for CAI (see Chapter 3).

LIMITATION OF PAST INSTRUCTIONAL RESEARCH FOR CAI

In every instructional medium there are some underlying assumptions, both explicit and implicit, that influence the effectiveness of the techniques that are employed. Before transferring techniques directly from one medium to another, it is important to first determine whether any of the underlying assumptions will be violated. One of the implicit assumptions in the classroom, for instance, is that students learn primarily by listening, although they also learn by "doing" and by reading. This is different from the implicit assumption in CAI that students learn primarily by reading. This difference affects the validity of some teaching techniques.

Learning by Listening Versus Learning by Reading

Learning by listening is different from learning by reading in two ways that are relevant to CAI. The first is human development. Listening skills develop before reading skills (Sticht, 1984). An individual may be able to comprehend information when it is spoken, but not necessarily when it is presented in written form. Until about sixth grade (11-year-olds), there seems to be an advantage to learning by listening. From the seventh through the twelfth grades, an increasing amount of research reports an advantage for reading or else no differences between the two learning modes (Pearson & Fielding, 1982).

The second difference between listening and reading is that people automatically take cues from the speaker's intonation, the rising and falling of his pitch, and stress or emphasis on certain words. Intonation provides cues about differences between declarations, questions, and commands. Pearson and Fielding (1982, p. 618) present the following example:

1. *You* are going to buy a new hat.
2. You are going to *buy* a new hat?
3. You are going to buy a new *hat*!

Stress tends to focus attention on important parts of the message. Emphasizing the first word in the sentence, you, indicates that WHO gets the hat is important. Emphasis on the word, buy, signals that the ACTION is important and on the word hat, that WHAT you are going to buy is important.

While it is true that typographical features and punctuation marks provide these cues in print, they are not as striking as the oral cues. Likewise there are print equivalents of stress, such as italics or underlining, but they are rarely employed.

Implication for CAI.. These findings affect the selection of appropriate topics of instruction for CAI. A subject that is appropriate for a given group of students in a classroom is not necessarily suitable as a CAI lesson for this same group of students. For immature readers, the most appropriate topics for CAI lessons might be those that depend primarily on nonverbal information (e.g. illustrations) that is not affected by reading skills. This suggestion is contingent on the assumption that the learners have the necessary skills to learn from the nonverbal information.

The manner in which text is displayed on the computer screen is also critically important for immature readers. For such students, text should provide comprehension cues and focus on salient information. This can be accomplished with techniques such as underlining and large-size type.

Interpersonal vs. Human-Machine Communication

A related though implicit assumption about classroom instruction is that if students don't understand the teacher's explanations, they can ask questions and expect further clarification. Likewise, a teacher can frequently figure out what a student has in mind even though the student does not state her message precisely. Verbal ambiguity is accommodated in a classroom because people interpret oral communication partly in terms of the context of interaction. In written communication, that interaction is missing, so there may be more ambiguity in written language than in oral. Thus, although it is important to be explicit and specific in oral classroom instruction, it is even more critical in computer-presented instruction. "Computers never understand ambiguous utterances and they never read between the lines, whereas humans are able to, or do, just that" (Olson, 1985, p. 7).

Group vs. Individualized Instruction

Some components of group instruction are the same in CAI as in the classroom, but their significance and their application is different. For instance, good instruction involves asking meaningful and relevant questions. Techniques for generating good questions are applicable to both group and individualized instruction. However, there are differences in the roles of questions in the two instructional modes, as well as differences in the opportunity to individualize the questions to each learner's understanding. There are also differences in the ability of the teacher/instructor to respond appropriately to all questions.

Some classroom techniques are either inappropriate for CAI or must be modified for transfer. Guided discovery learning for instance, is a method in which a teacher leads learners to infer a principle by asking a series of questions rather than by just stating it. The questions by which teachers guide the discovery are contingent on on their estimate of learners' collective knowledge. Some students who are unable to make the discovery by themselves learn from the responses of others. Simulations provide a powerful format for discovery learning in CAI, but the computer/tutor must replace both the human teacher AND the other students in the classroom.

If instructing an individual rather than a group is the issue, why not apply principles of programmed instruction to CAI? Here again, as in the case of classroom, many of the techniques are appropriate but others are not.

Unique Issues in CAI

Displays.   In CAI, students often view each display as a separate entity and fail to perceive the continuity between displays. Consequently, the physical scheduling of related information must be planned with special care.

Design techniques.   Creative designs can be generated for every instructional method, including tutorials, drills, guided discovery, simulations, and games. Many innovative options can be implemented, even for drills, which can be designed to present items randomly, to repeat missed items at prespecified intervals, to remove items a student has learned, to change difficulty level or allowable response time, and to provide a game format, to name some of the possibilities.

Individualization.   A computer program can provide multiple instructional paths, tailored to individualized needs. Game formats can add motivation and fantasy and maintain learners' attention (Malone, 1981). Concepts can be presented with the aid of illustrative animation or by dynamically creating an illustration and interspersing verbal explanations as it is created. Simulations can provide new insights into relationships, or experiences that would otherwise not be possible or would be dangerous for novices.

INCORPORATING CURRENT THEORIES OF LEARNING

Two very different theories of learning have dominated psychology during this century. Behavioral theory was dominant during the first fifty years and cognitive psychology is the major force today (Glaser, 1978). Behavioral theories have been applied to instruction in all modes including CAI. The application of cognitive theories has lagged behind. Research in cognitive psychology has much to offer to make instruction more effective. CAI can benefit by incorporating this knowledge.

Processes of Learning and Instruction

Current research in cognitive psychology suggests that learners construct understanding rather than reproduce instruction (Resnick, 1981). They do not simply add the information presented to the knowledge they have previously stored in memory. Rather, they try to link new knowledge to old, selecting, reorganizing, and restructuring it in the process.

Learning is influenced by many factors in addition to the knowledge that is specifically prerequisite to a task. General knowledge of the world and knowledge of learning strategies play significant roles. Thus, "instruction involves stimulating the learners' information-processing strategies, aptitudes, and stores of relevant specific memories in relation to the information to be learned "(Wittrock, 1979, p. 10).

Reading, for example, involves not only understanding individual words but also applying one's general knowledge and experience to interpret the text. A person understands the complete meaning of the sentence, "Amanda takes her lunch to work to save calories," not only by sounding out the words and understanding their individual meanings but also by drawing on her knowledge of the relationships between food, calories, diet control, and restaurants.

Decoding (sounding out) skills also influence comprehension. Good readers can devote most of their attention to comprehension because they decode almost automatically. Readers who expend considerable effort on decoding have few resources left for understanding. Some research even suggests that slow decoding is a cause of poor comprehension (Lesgold, 1983).

Although it is not clear that fluency in decoding is sufficient for comprehension, fluency is apparently necessary (Beck & McKeown, 1986). To provide the practice needed to speed up word recognition, one group of researchers developed a series of microcomputer lessons that provide intensive and motivating practice in the subskills associated with decoding, such as identifying a specific syllable within a word or collecting syllables to form a word (Beck, Roth, & McKeown, 1984).

A person's beliefs and expectations also influence learning. One group of children who were playing an arithmetic game, for instance, were unwilling to play against the computer because they thought the computer was cheating (B. A. Seiler, personal communication, 1976). In another situation, children studied a CAI lesson that presented subject matter they had not previously studied in their classroom. Although the CAI lesson presented simple directions, the children did not read them. Instead they turned around and asked, "What do I do?" Their failure to read was not due to inability to read or to follow written directions. When they were told to read the directions aloud they did so, said "Oh," and proceeded to study. They had simply expected someone to read the directions for them, just as teachers do in the classroom (Rothbart & Steinberg, 1971).

Psychological and Logical Task Analysis

A critical component in the instructional design process is an analysis of the task to be accomplished. Traditional instructional design includes analyses of the logical structure of content and of the skills needed to perform a task (Gagné, 1977; Tiemann & Markle, 1985). Analyses that address qualitative aspects of students' knowledge, such as their problem-solving strategies, are also important (Richardson, 1981). Analyses of learners processes provide a comprehensive representation of their current knowledge state (Hartley & Lovell, 1984), and thus a richer form of dialogue between computer and learner can take place. A tutor who understands why a student makes an error can do a better job of remediating than one who knows only the error itself.

SUMMARY

To summarize, CAI is a special kind of instruction. There are both differences and similarities between traditional modes of instruction and CAI. We should neither ignore relevant experience nor be bound by it. Wherever possible, CAI should build on available knowledge. Where this knowledge is inappropriate for CAI, it should be modified. Where knowledge is lacking because of the unique features of CAI, new information must be sought. Current developments in cognitive psychology and technology can also add significantly to generating effective CAI.

Because CAI draws on so many fields and is substantially different from other modes of instruction, it is helpful to have a structure for understanding it. Chapter 2 presents such a structure.

Chapter 2

A FRAMEWORK FOR CAI

Children enter kindergarten today with considerably more knowledge than they did twenty or even fifteen years ago. They know the colors and can identify simple shapes. Many can identify the letters of the alphabet. Substantial credit for this phenomenon is given to television programs such as Sesame Street. Although television programs are not interactive, they are able to engage children in learning because the programs combine knowledge about learning and child development with knowledge about how to exploit the medium of television. By merging educators' knowledge that make-believe appeals to children with television experts' knowledge of how to create and present fantasy characters, developers create programs that are motivating as well as educational.

A Six-Component Framework

Similarly, CAI draws on learning theories, instructional models, practical experience, and technology. To provide a mechanism for understanding how these domains contribute to CAI, a six-component framework for CAI is presented (see Figure 2.1). Four components are derived from learning theories and instructional models. They are: Target Population, Goals, Task, and Instruction. Two components, Computer Application and Environmental Implementation, reflect research and experience with CAI.

The rationale for the CAI framework is the next topic of discussion. It begins with an introduction to two learning theories. A synthesis of these theories follows and leads to the identification of four components of the framework. Each component is then discussed in some detail in the light of

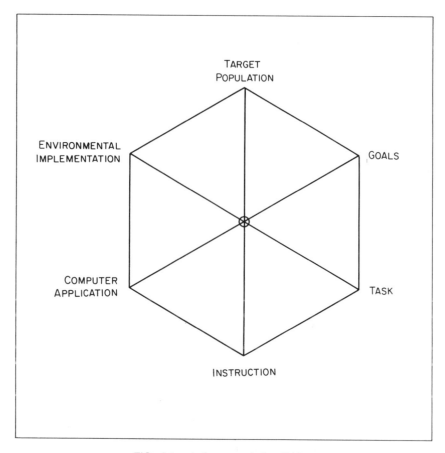

FIG. 2.1.   A framework for CAI.

research in learning and instructional models. Application and implementation issues in CAI are presented next and demonstrate the need to add two more components to the framework. Finally, the relationship among the six components and the significance of their interaction on learning is discussed.

TWO THEORIES OF LEARNING

To serve as underpinnings for a CAI framework, we need a learning theory that is general enough to encompass many categories of learning (e.g., verbal learning, learning strategies) and a theory that translates reasonably well to procedures for designing instruction. These criteria can be fulfilled by a synthesis of the theories of Bransford (1979) and Gagné (1977). Bransford's perspective is that of a cognitive psychologist, Gagné's that of an educational psychologist. Although different in perspective, their theories have much in common. An overview of the aspects of their theories relevant to a CAI framework is presented next.

Gagné's Theory

Gagné (1977) conceptualizes learning in terms of categories of skills and capabilities and the conditions under which they are learned. He notes that there are many different kinds of learning outcomes, such as knowing rules and concepts, saying the Pledge of Allegiance, monitoring your progress toward solving a problem, typing at a rate of 50 words per minute, and knowing how to deal civilly with an irate customer. Gagné groups these diverse outcomes of learning into five categories: intellectual skills, verbal information, cognitive strategies, motor skills, and attitudes.

Elements both within each person (internal) and in the surrounding environment (external) affect learning. Each type of learning outcome occurs under its own set of internal and external conditions.

Internal conditions are the knowledge and skills that are unique to each individual and prerequisite to the given learning outcome. For example, to learn an intellectual skill, such as how to punctuate a sentence, a learner must have previously learned concepts such as the meanings of commas and periods and the rules for using them. To acquire a motor skill, such as typing at 50 words a minute, a learner must have previously learned the positions of the letters on the keyboard, have gained a specific level of finger dexterity, and so on.

The external conditions of learning are events that occur through interaction with one's environment, either incidentally or through formal training or instruction. For example, one individual may learn to type at a given speed through formal instruction. Another person, say a computer programmer, might acquire this speed as a consequence of the extensive typing experience he has gained entering his programs into the computer.

The important ideas, then, in Gagné's theory are that (1) both attributes of the learner and events in the environment contribute to learning, and (2) each type of learning outcome has its own set of internal and external conditions.

Intellectual skills. Gagné defines intellectual skills as the rules and concepts that constitute a considerable proportion of school learning. These skills are a sequentially ordered hierarchy of capabilities. For learning to occur, each capability must be mastered as a prerequisite to learning skills at the next higher level. The most complex level of intellectual skills is learning higher order rules, which are a combination of other rules. This requires as a prerequisite learning other rules. A rule, in turn, is a relationship of two or more concepts, which must be learned in order to learn the rule. A rule, for example, is that blue and yellow combine to make green. But the concepts, blue, yellow, and green, must be learned before the rule is learned. The concepts can be analyzed into component skills, called discriminations, which enable a person to determine whether an item is a member of a conceptual category, such as whether a color is blue or green. Discriminations in turn require, as prerequisites, skills in basic associations and chains of associations such as associating certain colors with the word blue.

The internal conditions for learning an intellectual skill include knowledge of the component skills, the ability to recall the prerequisite skills, and knowledge of how to put the components together in new form. The external conditions for intellectual skills consist of events that help a learner combine simple skills into increasingly complex ones. They include stimulating recall of the subordinate skills, stating the performance objective, guiding learning by presenting information or asking questions, and providing practice. For instance, the internal conditions for multiplying two-digit numbers are the knowledge of addition and multiplication facts. The external conditions are the rules for multiplying two-digit numbers, examples, and practice exercises.

There may be some overlap between internal and external conditions. External conditions for multiplying two-digit numbers, for example, may include a review of addition and multiplication facts.

Verbal Information. Verbal information is the capability of verbalizing information, such as stating facts or presenting information in the form of sentences. Summarizing a body of text and paraphrasing a rule are examples. To learn verbal information, a person needs to comprehend verbal text and to have previously stored in memory well structured knowledge that is meaningfully related to the to-be-learned information. The external conditions for learning verbal information are events that help a student relate the information to be learned to the previously learned knowledge. If the task is to plan a vegetarian breakfast, the external event might be a suggestion to think about the foods in the student's own typical breakfast that are acceptable in a vegetarian diet.

Cognitive strategies. Cognitive strategies are those employed by learners to control their learning. They include activities such as handling the flow of information and selecting and activating various learning strategies. Cognitive strategies are sometimes called executive control processes. Some are largely independent of content and can be applied in various domains. For example, important strategies in problem solving include formulating alternative plans, selecting one, implementing it, and monitoring your progress to determine whether your plan is leading toward a solution. This strategy is applicable to many areas, ranging from physical science to medical diagnosis to troubleshooting an engine. Other cognitive strategies such as underlining the main ideas in a verbal message are domain-specific.

Internal conditions include prior relevant knowledge and some simple strategies, such as underlining the main idea. External conditions influence cognitive strategies indirectly rather than directly. This is because cognitive strategies are acquired over time through opportunities to develop and practice them. External conditions that promote cognitive strategies include verbal statements, demonstrations, and opportunities to learn by discovery.

Gagné's two other learned capabilities are motor skills and attitudes. They, too, have their own sets of conditions for learning.

Bransford's Theory

Bransford (1979) explores learning, remembering, and understanding from a process perspective. He presents a framework of four components: learner characteristics, criterial task, nature of materials to be learned, and nature of learning activities. Bransford emphasizes that the most significant idea underlying this framework is the **interaction** among components.

Learner characteristics. Learner characteristics are attributes that are intrinsic to each individual. They include a person's prior knowledge, the structure of that knowledge in memory, beliefs and expectations, knowledge about one's own knowledge, developmental maturity, and experience. To comprehend the following Japanese poem (*New Directions in English*, 1973, p. 95), a reader needs to know more than the meanings of the words.

> Fireflies in the gloom
> Among the water weeds, are like
> The water weeds in bloom.

The reader draws on her prior knowledge to make inferences about the implicit meaning of the text. It is possible for her to understand the poem without ever having seen a firefly, but it would be difficult. Furthermore the understanding would probably be different from that of a person who had seen fireflies.

Investigations of students' understanding of physics demonstrate how a person's beliefs affect learning. Students' beliefs about physical phenomena are often intuitive and ascientific. Although they learn to apply formulae and carry out calculations, they find it difficult to overcome their fundamental misunderstandings (Fuller, 1982; McDermott, 1984). Striley (1988) describes one group of high school seniors, most of whom had done well in a physics course. "On the final exam, the vast majority of the students calculated speed and position of moving objects in a variety of situations. When they were asked to draw the path of a ball kicked over a cliff, however, many of them showed the ball going straight out from the cliff parallel to the ground for some distance and then falling straight down — an event not uncommon in Road Runner cartoons, but one that violates the laws of motion the students had just used in their calculations" (p. 7).

Criterial tasks.   Criterial tasks are used to test learning outcomes. A student's task may be to memorize (e.g., foreign language vocabulary), to acquire a concept (e.g., acceleration) or to solve a problem (e.g., simultaneous equations). For effective learning, different activities are needed for different criterial tasks.

Nature of materials.   The nature of the materials to be learned varies along many dimensions. They may be visual or verbal, written or aural, difficult or complex, hierarchical in nature or not. Gathering information from maps, for instance, involves different skills than learning from verbal discourse.

Interaction of components.   Each of Bransford's components interacts with the others to affect learning. Even for a single criterial task, such as a memory task, the learning activities differ according to the nature of the materials and characteristics of the learners. If the task involves memorizing a long password or computer code, mature learners employ a chunking strategy, reformulating a 10-digit number (9925405982) into fewer, 2- and 3-digit numbers (992, 540, 59, 82). If the task is to memorize verbal information such as the bones in the body, a good learner might divide the list into categories (e.g. legs, hands), or invent some mnemonic device. Immature learners, unlike mature learners, are apt to use a single memory strategy for every task, repetition. Appropriate or not, they try to remember by repeating the material to be learned again and again.

The task of condensing a body of text requires different activities than memorization. The activities in which learners spontaneously engage vary with characteristics of the learners. Mature learners reorganize text and state the gist of it in their own words. Children from ages 11 to 15 years, however, do not manipulate text. They tend to delete relatively unimportant information, and then copy the rest almost verbatim from the text (Brown, Bransford, Ferrara, & Campione, 1982).

Implications for a CAI Framework

It is clear from the work of both Gagné and Bransford that four components are central to learning, regardless of the theoretical perspective or the labels used to identify them. They are: the Target population (who is learning), Goals (what they are supposed to learn), Task (the materials and skills involved), and Instruction (the externally planned activities).

Target population. Characteristics of the intended learners play an important role in learning. Gagné calls them internal conditions and refers primarily to the skills and knowledge that learners need to perform a specific task. Bransford's learner characteristics incorporate additional factors such as prior knowledge, knowledge about their own knowledge, motivations, beliefs, and expectations. In the CAI framework, the component Target population includes all of these characteristics.

Goals. The outcomes of learning are important in any theory of learning. Gagné describes the outcomes in terms of general categories such as intellectual, verbal, cognitive, motor, and attitudinal. Bransford calls the desired outcomes the criterial tasks and describes them in terms of the psychological processes required to accomplish them, such as memorizing or problem solving. However they are described, the implication for instructional designers is that they specify what the intended learners are supposed to accomplish. Thus, Goals is another component in the CAI framework.

Task. A synthesis of Bransford's criterial tasks and nature of materials and Gagné's classification of learning outcomes supports the need for a Task component in the framework. Task in the framework embraces both the nature of the materials to be learned and the skills and processes required to learn them.

Instruction. Individuals engage in various externally arranged activities that are supposed to help them learn. Gagné includes them as the external conditions of learning while Bransford calls them the learning activities. In the CAI framework, the preplanned external arrangement of activities is called Instruction.

The results of extensive research in learning and instruction attest to the centrality of these four components to CAI. The next section is an overview of some major findings of this research.

FRAMEWORK COMPONENTS FROM LEARNING AND INSTRUCTION

Target Population

Individuals as well as groups of individuals (e.g., third graders) are different in characteristics that impact learning. Maturational and educational development, knowledge prerequisite to a specific task, general knowledge, beliefs, attitudes, and experience vary widely.

However, all people share one trait that influences learning. It is a limited capacity for keeping a number of things in mind simultaneously.

Memory limitations. Miller (1956) states in his now famous paper, "The magical number seven, plus or minus two: Some limits on our capacity for information processing," that there are "severe limitations on the amount of information that we are able to receive, process, and remember" (p. 95). In immediate memory, that span is seven, plus or minus two. Anyone who has ever tried to operate a new camera by simply reading straight through all of the directions is undoubtedly aware that by the time you get finished you can't remember everything you are supposed to do. One of the reasons for this difficulty is the limited information processing capacity described by Miller.

The implication of this limitation for instruction is that the amount of information presented at one time should be limited to that which a person can reasonably process. A person learning to use a word processor, for example, is not likely to remember a long list of key functions if he does not have an opportunity to try using a few of them at a time.

It is, however, possible to get around this memory limitation by reorganizing incoming information into fewer chunks, with more information in each. Miller gives the example of a beginning radio operator learning Morse code. At first he hears each dot and dash as a series of separate sounds. Then he begins to organize groups of sounds into letters, so the letters are the recoded chunks. Subsequently, the operator organizes groups of letters into words. As the chunks get larger, from dots and dashes, to letters, and then to words, the operator can remember a correspondingly longer message.

Developmental limitations. Developmental limitations impact what a person or a particular group of individuals can be expected to learn. It is unreasonable to expect an infant to learn how to walk until he has the muscular coordination to do so. Similarly, we cannot expect children to succeed in cognitive tasks for which they are not developmentally ready. As they grow older, children get better at using cognitive strategies, such as chunking in memory tasks. This is due to an increase in cognitive capacity, experience and a greater ability to handle these skills.

Two critical cognitive skills accompany maturation (Case, 1975; Case, 1978). One is an increased capacity to coordinate several items simultaneously. Children have an even more limited memory capacity than adults for attending simultaneously to numerous items in a task. Case demonstrated this in the following experiment. A set of cards with a series of numbers, such as 2, 11, 15, 19, and 4 was presented to each child. The task was to place the last number in its "correct" position. Each child was given practice until he or she could do the task correctly. Then the task was changed and the numbers were presented sequentially rather than simultaneously. After a number was presented it disappeared before the next one was shown. This task required that the child hold more items in memory than in the previous task, and now the task had a strong age effect. Five- and six-year-olds could do the task for only two numbers, seven- and eight-year-olds could only handle three, and nine- and ten-year-olds, four numbers.

A second cognitive skill that comes with maturation is the ability to apply strategies correctly or appropriately. Some experimental tasks are presented in such a way that young children are easily misled, so they oversimplify and apply inappropriate strategies. An example from CAI illustrates this point. A lesson was produced on the PLATO system to provide practice in letter discrimination (Obertino, Fillman, Gilfillan, Silver, & Yeager, 1977). In the lesson, a covered letter was displayed that was identical to one of two letters presented above it (Figure 2.2). The covered letter was divided into six areas. The challenge was to identify the covered letter by uncovering (by touching the screen) a minimum number of the six areas. The mature strategy, of course, is to uncover the area that discriminates between the two given letters. Five- and six-year-olds simplified the task to one of letter identification rather than discrimination. They uncovered all of the areas before deciding which letter was hiding.

Prerequisite knowledge and skills.   All but the simplest tasks require some previously acquired component skills and knowledge (cf. Gagné). For any given goal an instructor or designer makes assumptions that learners have previously acquired the prerequisite subskills and knowledge. A lesson about the causes of revolutions is based on the assumption that the learners can read and that they have acquired a particular body of historical, economic, social, and political knowledge.

Prior knowledge.   Prior knowledge is different from prerequisite knowledge in that it is general knowledge of the world and not merely task-specific. We invoke prior knowledge to comprehend verbal information or to solve problems.

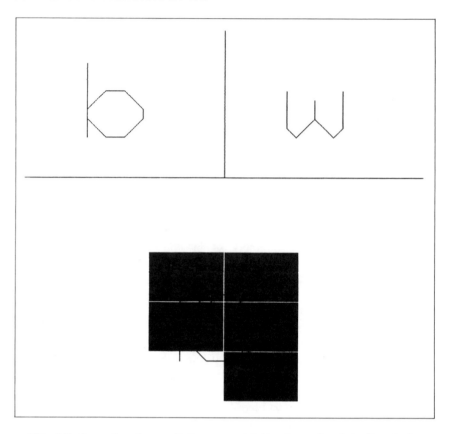

FIG. 2.2. Example of a partially covered letter in a discrimination task. (From CAI lesson, the Hiding Letter. Copyright 1978 by Control Data Corporation. Reprinted by permission.)

Prior knowledge is essential to understanding verbal discourse and to making inferences. It is the kind of knowledge that enables a person to read a paragraph and answer questions about it when the answers are not explicitly stated in the paragraph. To help you understand the significance of this statement read the next paragraph and then answer the questions that follow it (Schank, 1982, p. 100).

John was hungry. He went into Goldstein's and ordered a pastrami sandwich. It was served to him quickly. He left the waitress a large tip.

What is Goldstein's?

What did John eat?

Who took John's order?

Who served the sandwich?

Why did John leave a large tip?

You were undoubtedly able to answer all of the questions, yet you will notice that not one of the answers is explicitly stated in the text. It is your prior knowledge about restaurants and delicatessens that enabled you to do so. A person from a different culture would be unlikely to do as well.

Problem solving, like comprehension of verbal discourse, involves prior knowledge in addition to problem-solving strategies and other skills. To better understand this statement, stop for a moment and try to solve the following puzzle. Keep a record of the steps you take. When you have finished, go back and analyze the knowledge and strategies you employed.

The following is a quotation by a famous person, followed by his or her name. Each letter represents some other letter, the same one throughout. Your goal is to decipher the code.

GMI OKDDMP PTKOY K FKD KDGPYLDV: GMI OKD MDRG YTRQ
YLF PM ZLDH LP NLPYLD YLFETRZ. - VKRLRTM

(The solution to the puzzle is given at the end of the chapter.)

If you tried to solve the puzzle, you probably used your knowledge of the English language, both vocabulary and syntax, as clues for decoding the message. For example, knowing that there are just two one-letter words, tells you that K in the code must represent either the letter, A or the letter, I. To decide which it is, you scan the other words and notice that the next word has a K as the middle letter. Three-letter words with a middle letter A are more frequent than with I. Several words come to mind with a middle letter A: MAN, RAN, CAN, PAN. Select A as the substitute for K. You invoke rules of English grammar to decide that if K stands for A, then FKD cannot be a verb. Knowledge of quotations leads you to predict that MAN is a more likely candidate than PAN. Next you might test the most common three-letter word, THE, as a substitute for GMI. You test your hypothesis by substituting H for M in the word PM. You don't know any two-letter words that end in H, so you reject your hypothesis.

Of course each individual applies his own strategies, which are undoubtedly different from those proposed here. The intention here is not to demonstrate how to solve this problem but rather to illustrate the role of prior knowledge in problem solving.

Structure of knowledge.   The organization or structure of knowledge in memory, and the processes by which it is received, stored, and retrieved also play significant roles in learning and comprehending verbal information.

Anderson and his colleagues (1977) demonstrated the powerful effect of the structures of knowledge in memory in the following way. They asked physical education and music education students to read two deliberately vague passages. One passage could be interpreted as either a prison break or a wrestling match; the other could be understood as a rehearsal of a musical quartet or as an evening of cards. Students' backgrounds strongly influenced their scores on subsequent tests. Not only did they interpret the passages according to their backgrounds, but many of them said they were not even aware of alternative explanations.

The organization of knowledge in memory also influences problem solving. Simon and Chase (1973) asked novices and expert chess players to look at an arrangement of chess pieces and then to reproduce the arrangement from memory. Some of the arrangements were taken from real chess games; others were random arrangements of the same pieces. Experts were superior to novices in their ability to reproduce the arrangements taken from real games, but no better at reproducing board positions of the random arrangements. Thus, the difference between experts and novices was not in the number of positions they could remember but in the fact that experts organized the task in terms of the meaningfulness of the relative positions.

Metacognition.   Metacognition is knowledge about your own knowledge and cognitive processes. In contrast to comprehension, which is understanding a passage, metacognition is knowing whether you understand it. Metacognition is knowing your capacity limitations, knowing some learning strategies and when to apply them. Metacognition involves actively monitoring and regulating your learning activities (Brown, 1977).

Good learners monitor their own comprehension. They know when they understand a text and when they don't. Brown (1977, p. 244) notes that "Mature problem solvers not only have a reasonable estimate of accessibility of their known facts, they are also cognizant of which facts cannot be known and which can be deduced on the basis of what they already know. Adults realize immediately that they cannot know Charles Dickens' phone number (Norman, 1973)."

Control over one's own learning strategies is another metacognitive skill. Mature learners are more likely to plan than immature learners. Good readers allocate reading time according to their purpose. If the goal is to get the gist of an article, they spend less time than than if the goal is to analyze for ideas (Sternberg, 1986). Poor readers spend the same amount of time regardless of the purpose of reading.

Good learners analyze their errors (Bransford, 1982). They identify potential sources of error. If they get a wrong phone number they try to decide whether they dialed wrong or had the wrong number. They figure out what they already know that's applicable. If it's a memory task they ask, "What strategies do I know that are appropriate?" They actively intend to learn and they activate relevant knowledge.

Not all of these metacognitive strategies are available to young children, but rather accompany development (Brown, 1978; Flavell, Friedrichs, & Hoyt, 1970). For example, young children may know a learning strategy but simply not use it spontaneously. In one experiment, four- and five-year-olds were shown a set of pictures and told they would be asked to recall them. They were unable to do so. However, when the researchers told them to say the name of each picture as it was shown, they were later successful in the recall task (Flavell, Beach, & Chinsky, 1966).

Summary. Many characteristics of learners affect their ability to learn and to acquire new knowledge. An individual's subject-specific knowledge and general knowledge both affect comprehension. Other factors that influence learning include availability of learning strategies and skills for applying them, knowledge about one's own knowledge, and developmental level.

A general characteristic of all human beings is that they have a limited capacity to process information. This suggests that too much information presented simultaneously is not likely to be learned and remembered.

Goals

Instructional lessons are designed for a purpose, and that is to help a learner achieve a given set of outcomes. We most often think of goals in terms of performance, of behavior that can be demonstrated by taking a test. Goals may take other forms, particularly in CAI.

Performance. Sometimes goals are stated in terms of the behavior to be demonstrated upon the completion of learning. For example, the goal in a police training lesson might be to place in correct order a list of emergency procedures at an accident scene. In a music lesson it might be to name the notes on the musical scales.

Experience. In other cases goals are stated in terms of experiences or processes in which the learner is expected to engage. In a CAI simulation, the goal might be to step through emergency procedures at an accident. Experiences may be affective. In one CAI lesson, nurses take the role of a patient who has a terminal illness and is faced with making various decisions (Lambrecht, 1986). One decision is whether to undergo radiation therapy (Figure 2.3). The goal is for the nurses to become aware of their feelings about death in general and their own death in particular.

FIG. 2.3. Display from a lesson with an experiential goal. (From CAI lesson, Death: A personal encounter by M. Lambrecht. Copyright 1986 by University of Delaware. Reprinted by permission.)

Learning to learn.   The goal of some lessons is to help people learn how to learn a particular task. It may be to learn how to use context to infer the meanings of words you don't know. It may be to learn how to memorize a long list of words.

Attitudes.   Another goal of instruction is to influence attitudes. For example, the goal of one computer lesson is to influence a person's views about birth control and poverty (Gray, 1987).

Learner determined.   It is possible to allow learners to set their own goals. A CAI lesson can serve as a review mechanism for medical students preparing for board certification. As such it lets the student decide which topics to review and what level of proficiency to attain. A company that manufactures computer parts may want to give factory workers the opportunity to learn about how those parts are used, but let each worker decide how much he wants to learn.

Summary.   Goals are the expected outcomes of instruction. Goals in CAI may be lesson- or computer-determined. Many types of computer-determined goals are possible in CAI. These include demonstrating knowledge or skills, engaging in a simulated experience such as decision making, learning how to learn, or influencing attitudes.

Task

The skills and processes involved in a task vary with the subject matter and the nature of the materials. Each subject matter domain obviously has its own subject-specific skills but it also has some skills in common with other domains. The ability to read a textbook is a skill needed in both physics and history. However, reading a physics textbook also requires the ability to interpret formulas and equations, while reading about the Roman Empire does not. On the other hand, reading about the Roman Empire requires historical background, which physics does not.

Learning verbal material involves different skills than visual. To read and understand the rules for placing electric outlets in a house involves different processes and skills than to read the floor plan to locate the outlets in the house. Nor are all visual materials alike in their demands on the learner. The knowledge and abilities needed to interpret a graph, for instance, are different from those for reading a floor plan.

A single set of materials may be more or less complex, and require different skills depending on the task. Memorizing the Gettysburg Address and understanding it both involve reading it. However, memory skills are quite different from comprehension. It is possible to memorize information without understanding it. It is possible to understand verbal material without memorizing it.

Instruction

Instruction is the set of activities arranged by the instructional designer to facilitate learning. Sometimes artistry or intuition guides instructional development. Often models are invoked to guide instructional design.

Some instructional models evolve from common wisdom and experience successfully teaching a given subject — "this is the way we teach it." Other models are based on psychological theories of learning or on a combination of experience and theory.

Computers are excellent vehicles for implementing well established models of instruction. In addition, CAI can support some models of instruction that are not possible in other modes, such as mathematical/ statistical models and information-processing based automaticity.

Behavioral model. The behavioral model of instruction is an application of Skinner's principles of operant conditioning (Skinner, 1953). For

Skinner, behavior is contingent on the relationship between a response and its consequence, which is called reinforcement. A positive reinforcement, which is a desirable consequence, increases the probability of the occurrence of a given behavior; a negative reinforcement, that is an unpleasantness, decreases the probability. The laughter of your friend every time you tell a joke increases the probability of your telling him jokes. Failure to get your friend to laugh at your jokes decreases the probability that you will continue to tell them to him. Reinforcement must be immediate. Its effect can be negated if there is a lapse of even a few seconds between response and reinforcement. Behavior is "shaped" by reinforcing successively closer approximations to the desired behavior.

As Skinner (1986) puts it, "we learn when what we do has reinforcing consequences" (p. 107). Learning is controlled by careful manipulation of reinforcement. For Skinner, the steps should be small so that learning is errorless. Furthermore, a single errorless response does not constitute learning. Learning requires practice. The key ideas in this model then, are active responding, immediate feedback, errorless learning, and practice.

Applied to instruction, the model involves "priming," "prompting," and "fading" (Anderson & Faust, 1973; Gropper, 1983; Tiemann & Markle, 1985). You can't expect a person to give a correct response out of the blue. He must be prepared or "primed" for learning so that he behaves in a given way the first time. The instructor or computer can then reinforce the learner and thus increase the probability of a correct response the next time. As he continues to practice, the learner may need some help, or prompting. Gradually, however, prompts are withdrawn so that the learner can make the appropriate responses without help. Skinner (1986) gives the example of teaching his daughter to memorize 15 lines of a poem. First he wrote the lines of the poem on a chalkboard and had his daughter read them. The words were the primes. They enabled her to read the lines correctly on her first attempt to memorize the poem. Skinner then erased a few words and asked her to read the lines again, which she was able to do. The remaining words served as prompts for the ones that had been erased. Gradually Skinner erased more and more of the prompts until they were all gone but his daughter was still able to "read" the poem.

The computer is a good tool for implementing behavioral principles. However, some interpretation and modifications are necessary (and made by instructional designers) when Skinner's principles are applied to instruction in general and to CAI in particular. Active learning must be interpreted to mean overt, meaningful learning. A student who simply presses keys, or copies responses that appear elsewhere on a display is not necessarily engaging in learning.

The value of feedback probably lies in the information or motivation it provides rather than the stamping in of stimulus-response connections

(McKeachie, 1974). If a learner knows that the answer he gives is correct, feedback about the correctness (e.g., OK) won't increase the probability of his giving that response to the same stimulus again. A learner knows his answer is correct when the correct answer appears in a textual presentation on the same display as the question or when the correct answer is already known to him from previous study.

Negative reinforcement, information that a response is incorrect, may decrease the probability that a learner will repeat an incorrect response, but it does not necessarily help him learn the correct one. Moreover, reinforcement need not necessarily be immediate. Several studies (Kulhavy & Anderson, 1972; Sassenrath & Yonge, 1969; Sturgis, 1969, 1972) showed that feedback immediately following a test may not be as instructionally effective as delayed feedback.

The concept of errorless learning and small steps has been abandoned by instructional designers for several reasons. One is that small steps lead to fragmented learning. Another disadvantage of the concept of errorless learning is that it leads some lesson designers to put far more instruction into a lesson than is needed by the intended users (Markle, 1978). To avoid wasting designers' effort as well as students' time, first drafts of CAI lessons are designed with a minimum amount of instruction (Steinberg, 1984). If during trials of the lessons students' errors reveal that they need more instruction, the lesson designer can revise it at that time.

Defining an error is difficult, particularly in CAI. "Errors" may not be errors in understanding but rather errors in spelling or differences between the format the program expects and the one a student enters. A student might enter the correct word in responding to a question but spell it wrong. Is it an error? A student might give a numerical response without the units, such as 30 rather than 30 miles. Is it an error?

To summarize, a behavioral model is appropriate for CAI. Care must be taken, however, to adapt behavioral principles so that instruction is in harmony with the computer as instructional medium.

Information-processing models. Some models of instruction are based on an information-processing model of learning. They are concerned with architectural structures and how information is received, how it flows between structures, and how it is returned. The purpose is not to model the physical system but rather the processes in information flow. In this model, information flows from the environment very briefly (less than a second) into a sensory register, or buffer. Information in the sensory buffer is ignored or selectively perceived and then sent on to temporary storage in short-term memory, which lasts about 20 to 30 seconds. Some of this information is transformed and stored in long-term memory for later retrieval.

Information that is currently being used is held in short-term memory, sometimes called working memory. Processing information "consists of controlling the flow of information into and out of working memory by processes such as retrieving information from long term memory (LTM) and receiving information from the sensory buffer; by recognizing, comparing, and manipulating symbols in working memory; and by storing information in LTM" (Shiffrin, 1975).

A critical feature of information-processing theories is that information is stored (encoded) in meaningful conceptual nodes and not as an exact copy of information that is presented. A person selects and/or transforms information for retention and storage in long-term memory. A second critical idea is that learning involves retrieving appropriate information from stored memory and using it in conjunction with information in working or short-term memory (STM).

Gagné's model.   Gagné's (1977, 1985) events of instruction are based on his events of learning, which derive directly from information-processing theories of learning. The first event in learning is to selectively attend to incoming information. Therefore, the first event of instruction is to gain the learner's attention. Once attention is gained a learner must attend to relevant aspects of incoming information, so Gagné's next event in instruction is to inform the learner of the objective. Learning requires retrieval of information from long-term memory, hence stimulating recall of prerequisites is the next event. Succeeding steps in instruction are derived from the information-processing model in similar fashion. The steps are: presenting the stimulus material, providing learning guidance, eliciting the performance, providing feedback, assessing performance, and enhancing retention and transfer.

Gagné's model is generic. Every event does not necessarily occur in every instructional situation. In some instances a learner may spontaneously recall prerequisite knowledge, while in other situations an instructor may need to stimulate recall. Some of the proposed events of instruction, such as eliciting performance and providing feedback are specific to single interactions between student and instructor. Others, such as retention, relate to instruction that occurs over a longer period of time.

Automaticity.   Given the limitations of human information-processing capacity in working memory, how is it possible for a person to accomplish two tasks simultaneously? For example, a person can drive a car while carrying on a conversation or while monitoring the speedometer and other gauges and dials. One answer is that it is not impossible to do two things at once; it is impossible to handle more than a criterial amount of information at once (Broadbent, 1958). Schneider and Shiffrin (1977) and Shiffrin and

Schneider (1977) propose that there are two processes in information-processing, automatic and controlled. An automatic process is a sequence of elements stored in long-term memory that is so well learned that at appropriate times a person can retrieve and implement it with little or no attention (control). Automatic processing scarcely taxes the limitations of the information-processing system. Controlled processing, on the other hand, does require attention and control by the individual and is affected by the limits of information-processing capacity.

For an experienced driver, the subtask of steering a car while driving is almost automatic, so almost full attention can be given to a conversation. However, if the driver has to stop suddenly or swerve to avoid another car, his activities are no longer as fully automatized and he must take some attention away from the conversation and devote it to driving. At that time his conversation will slow down, or even stop if full attention must be given to driving.

According to the two-process model, then, automatization of subtasks enables a person to attend to those aspects of a complex task that require attention and control. An implication for instruction is that in order to teach people complex tasks, instruction should bring some subtasks to automatization so that learners can devote most of their attention to the cognitively demanding aspects of the task.

Automatization involves extensive practice, and computers are well suited for delivering it. CAI lessons have been produced to develop automaticity in subtasks in subjects as different as reading (Beck, Roth, & McKeown, 1984; Frederiksen, Warren, & Roseberry, 1985a, 1985b) and air traffic control (Schneider, 1985). One of the shortcomings of automaticity in CAI is that it requires so much practice (thousands of trials) that it gets boring. To alleviate this problem and to motivate students to persist, Schneider (1985) allows students to achieve a high success rate while others (Beck, Roth, & McKeown, 1984; Frederiksen, Warren, & Roseberry, 1985a, 1985b) employ a game format. Another troubling aspect of automaticity is the implicit assumption that instruction can be effective when divided into component skills. We do not know whether training component skills is accompanied by integration of those skills.

Information processing models of instruction lend themselves well to CAI. In fact, one model, automaticity, can be implemented only if the computer is the instructional medium. The most effective application of the automaticity model is to train subskills, but instruction must be consonant with learner characteristics such as motivation.

Mathematical models. Mathematical learning theories use mathematical equations as theoretical descriptions of the learning process. Their goal is to predict quantitative changes in learning. We can think of a mathematical model as a framework for describing data as analogous to a teacher using a normal curve as a framework for describing students (Snelbecker, 1974).

Mathematical models of learning are specific to subject matter, such as elementary mathematics. Given the quantitative nature of the models, they can be tested and revised to gain closer approximations of learning. Mathematical and statistical models of learning are discussed further in Chapter 8.

Subject-specific models. Research and instructional experience in specific subject matter areas leads to subject-specific models of instruction. The phonics method, for example, has been shown to be a successful method of teaching word recognition, which is one essential component of reading instruction.

Direct and indirect instruction. Instruction in CAI can be direct or indirect. In direct instruction the computer program controls the flow of instruction. In indirect instruction the student participates in directing the learning activities.

Tutorials are an example of direct instruction. Simply defined, a tutorial presents information, poses questions, waits for a student's response, and then provides feedback to the response. Remediation is provided as needed. Techniques for direct instruction in some tasks, such as concept and rule learning, have been extensively researched and reported (Tennyson, 1981; Tiemann & Markle, 1985). An advantage of direct instruction is that learning is efficient when proven instructional techniques are applied.

Indirect instruction is exploratory. Rather than being told a rule or a principle, a learner explores relationships between relevant components and hopefully infers the rule as a consequence of her findings. An example is a CAI chemistry lesson about the relationships between volume and pressure in a cylinder. The learner changes the volume and observes the resulting changes in pressure readings (Figure 2.4). The computer lesson records the data that the student collects and displays it in both tabular and graphic form. If the student does not try a broad enough range of values to adequately illustrate the relationship, the lesson suggests additional values to try. After the student finishes the investigation, the lesson asks her to draw conclusions from the data she has collected (Smith, Chabay, & Kean, 1980).

Practicing a procedure or stepping through a decision-making process is another form of indirect instruction in CAI. In these lessons, the student can see from the consequences of his actions whether they were satisfactory. For example, if he prescribes a medicine for a simulated patient and the

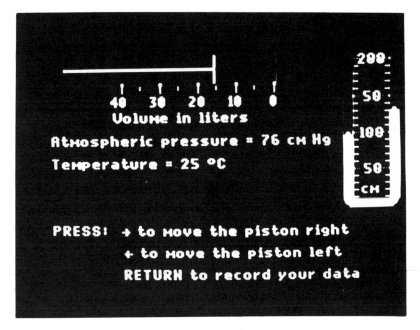

FIG. 2.4.   Example of an exploratory task. (From CAI lesson, Introduction to General Chemistry. Copyright 1980 by S. Smith, R. Chabay, & E. Kean. Reprinted by permission.)

patient's condition does not improve, he knows that it was the wrong medicine. However, he may not know why it was wrong. Therein lies one of the disadvantages of indirect instruction. A student may fail to learn what was intended or may even derive some incorrect conclusions.

An experiment designed by White (1984) illustrates this point. To help students learn some basic concepts about forces and motion, she designed a computer game in a spaceship format. One of the activities was to get the spaceship stopped inside its spaceport by controlling its direction and thrust. White hoped that by playing the game and trying to achieve the specified goals, students would make connections between their intuitive knowledge and principles of physics. However, students only noticed part of what they were "supposed to." They noticed the changes in the direction of motion of the spaceship but not the large changes in its speed. The explanation given by White is that unlike knowledgeable persons, novices do not know what relationships they are supposed to discover.

The difficulties encountered by White's students can be alleviated by the methods employed in the pressure-volume lesson cited above. One method is to guide the learner during the lesson. Another is to include some sort of evaluation measures at the end, such as to ask questions to assess the learning outcomes and then to provide remediation if it is necessary.

An advantage of indirect instruction is that the student uses different learning strategies than he does in direct instruction. Making a decision when confronted with a patient requires very different strategies and skills than the task of reading about the case and answering questions. Thus a learner gains different insights and understanding from direct and indirect instruction.

Summary. Many models of instruction can be implemented in CAI. Some, such as behavioral, information-processing, and mathematical models, are based on learning theories. Some are based on successful experience teaching a subject, while still others are based on a philosophy or perspective about learning. In many instances, a model (e.g., automaticity) is most appropriate for a specific task and goal. The relation between instructional models and other components of the CAI framework is discussed more fully in the section, Interaction of Components, later in this chapter.

APPLICATION AND IMPLEMENTATION COMPONENTS OF FRAMEWORK

Learning theories do not deal with factors that develop when theories are put into practice. A framework for CAI, however, must take them into account. Two critical issues are (1) the way computers are used as the vehicle of instruction, and (2) the way CAI lessons are implemented in instructional environments. Thus two components essential to the CAI framework are Computer Application and Environmental Implementation.

Computer Application

Appropriately utilized, the computer is a superb instructional tool. However, that is all it is, a tool. The computer is an appropriate instructional medium if the lesson it presents is effective, efficient, and acceptable to the intended learners (Steinberg, 1984).

Appropriate applications. Appropriate computer application means first and foremost the application of sound instructional principles. It should be self-evident that the subject matter content of instruction must be correct. Yet, CAI lessons that contain content errors are still being produced. Figure 2.5a is a paraphrased version of a commercially available lesson containing two content errors. First, the figure does not match the text. The figure is 12 feet long, but the text states that it is 8 feet. Second, there is an error in the feedback. It should read: $(4+8) \times 2 = 24$ feet. As presented, the display computes to 20; $4 + 8 (\times 2) = 4 + 16 = 20$!

The display in Figure 2.5a violates another instructional principle. It does not accept the student's response, which is correct but in a different format than the one that the author apparently expected. Unfortunately, the program did not specify that the answer must be computed. In addition, in this series of lessons, the program never tells the student that an answer is wrong. If the student's response is incorrect, the program simply provides corrective information. In Figure 2.5a the student might readily infer that his response is wrong even though it is correct. Figures 2.5b and 2.5c display reasonable feedback for a correct and for an incorrect response, respectively.

Appropriate use of computers also means appropriate application of the computer's capabilities when implementing instructional design principles. Consider as an example Gagne's first event of instruction, gaining the learner's attention. A prime way to gain attention in CAI is to design attractive displays by using graphics, color, and animation, sometimes accompanied by sound. Displays of this sort certainly do gain the learner's attention. Attractive, extended animations may be attention-getters the first time through the lesson. However, if they are excessively time-consuming, they lose attention after the first or second time a learner studies the lesson. It is more reasonable either to make the animation very short or else let the learner decide when to move past it.

Appropriate application of the computer includes techniques that are not feasible in other modes of instruction. An example is a simulated experience that might be harmful or that would otherwise not be possible, such as administering first aid or role-playing in history, respectively.

Not necessarily unique to CAI.   It is sometimes argued that CAI is appropriate only for instruction that cannot be presented via other media. This may lead to the erroneous conclusion that CAI is not an appropriate medium for commonly employed techniques, such as tutorials or drills. A good tutorial or drill is a perfectly acceptable computer application if it maintains attention and facilitates learning. Standard instruction such as drills can replace rather than duplicate classroom instruction, and thus free an instructor's time for other activities, such as discussions. In addition, a CAI drill can offer a different type of instruction than a drill presented in a group setting or in a workbook. A CAI drill can be individualized so that each student practices only what she needs to rather than a predesigned set of exercises that is the same for everybody. In this respect CAI does meet an instructional goal in a manner not otherwise possible.

What "appropriate" need not include.   Unfortunately, some people have the mistaken idea that a CAI lesson is unacceptable if "It does not make full use of the computer's capabilities." It is not full use but *appropriate* use that influences the effectiveness of CAI lessons. Every CAI lesson does not have

Solve the following:

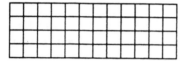

To decorate for Christmas, Mr. Smith has strung colored lights on a wire around his window.

How many feet of wire did he use if the window is 8 feet long and 4 feet wide?

Answer: 8+8+4+4   ← (Student's response)

4 + 8 (×2) ▪ 24 ft.   Mr. Smith would need 24 feet of wire.   ← (Computer's feedback.)

Fig. 2.5a Unacceptable display.

Solve the following:

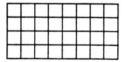

To decorate for Christmas, Mr. Smith has strung colored lights on a wire around his window.

How many feet of wire did he use if the window is 8 feet long and 4 feet wide?

Answer: 8+8+4+4   ← (Student's response)

Yes, 8+8+4+4 ft or 24 ft. ← (Computer's feedback)

Fig. 2.5b Acceptable version of Fig. 2.5a.

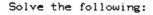

Solve the following:

To decorate for Christmas, Mr. Smith has strung
colored lights on a wire around his window.

How many feet of wire did he use if the window is
8 feet long and 4 feet wide?

Answer: 8+4   ← (Student's response)

No. The wire went all the way around the window.
The answer is 2×(8+4) ft. = 24 ft. ←(Computer's
feedback)

FIG. 2.5c.   Acceptable versions of Fig. 2.5a for incorrect response.

to include animation, graphics, color, and sound. The graphic capabilities
of computers are indeed wonderful, but should only be included if they are
necessary to promote learning or motivation.

Environmental Implementation

The sixth component in the framework relates to the environment in which
CAI is implemented. A match between the anticipated and the actual
conditions in which learning takes place is essential.

Physical conditions.   Whether in the classroom or in the workplace, a
lesson has to fit into the amount of time available to study the lesson. A
40-minute lesson is not appropriate for learners who have only 30-minute
time slots.

There are now many peripheral devices such as audio components, touch
devices, and videodiscs to enhance the capabilities of personal computer
systems. Obviously the equipment must be available on site if a CAI lesson
is to be successful. Where possible, experienced authors provide alternative
versions of their lesson for users who lack the necessary equipment. If a

lesson uses a touch device, authors might enable users who do not have one to move a cursor around the screen by keypresses.

Instructional conditions. Instructors need to know how the author expects a lesson to be used so it can be integrated with other instruction. Lessons that are meant to supplement lectures (e.g., that just review major concepts and then provide practice) will not be understood by students if used as initial instruction. Lessons intended as introductory practice will be ineffective if employed after students have already achieved the instructional goals in the classroom.

If teachers fail to perceive CAI materials as main line instruction, students get the impression that computer instruction doesn't really "count." In that case students do not take computer lessons seriously and perhaps fail to get the greatest benefit. One of the most significant findings in the evaluations of the PLATO Elementary Mathematics and Reading Demonstrations was that the impact of the courseware was influenced in part by the teachers' decisions about integrating the CAI lessons with ongoing instruction (Amarel, 1983). In the TICCIT demonstration project (cf. Chapter 3), differences in success between the English and mathematics courses were largely due to differences in the ways instructors implemented them (Jones, 1978).

INTERACTION OF COMPONENTS

Six components have been identified as essential in a CAI framework. They are: Target Population, Goals, Task, Instruction, Computer Application, and Environmental Implementation. Each is a necessary component, but the crucial aspect of the framework for CAI is that learning is significantly affected by the *interaction* of these components. For example, a computer can be used to implement many models of instruction. But, if the computer application is poor, or if the model is inappropriate for the target population, the goals, or the nature of the tasks, there will probably be little or no learning. One reason that so many CAI lessons are of poor quality is that the authors fail to attend to the interaction of all of the components of the framework. They fail to understand, for example, that lessons have to be appropriate to the developmental, educational, and physical characteristics of the intended learners. A lesson is not likely to be appropriate for a wide range of ages, "7 years and up," as some advertisements for CAI would have us believe.

Goals, Target Population, and Instruction

To illustrate the interaction of goals, target population and instruction, consider two lessons that have the same goal but involve different target populations. The goal is to discriminate between symbols. In one lesson, the symbols are the letters of the English alphabet; in the other, the Japanese hiragana. The letter discrimination task (described under *Developmental limitations* earlier in this chapter) is for the 5- and 6-year-old children and the hiragana for college or postsecondary students.

The task is visual for both sets of materials (see Figures 2.2 and 2.6). Doing the task requires knowledge of the discriminative characteristics of each symbol and knowledge of the strategy to uncover the discriminative part(s). To succeed a student has to know that he need only see discriminative parts of the symbol to identify it. This is knowledge that 5- and 6-year-olds do not ordinarily have, so the instructional technique proved to be inappropriate for them. On the other hand, this learning activity is both appropriate and successful for mature learners practicing discrimination between the Japanese hiragana.

The game just described is appropriate if the goal is to discriminate between Japanese hiragana, say between the symbols for "sa" and "su." However, if the goal of instruction is to recognize the Japanese hiragana, a different instructional technique is needed. In a clever application of computer features, Hatasa (1986) helps learners with the recognition task in a series of displays (Figures 2.7). In the first display, Hatasa draws a picture that has initial sounds similar to those of the hiragana. The picture of a cow reminds the learner that the sound to be learned is "mu" (Figures 2.7a,

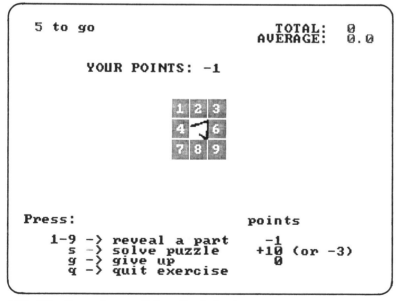

FIG. 2.6. Game for practicing discrimination among Japanese hiragana. (From CAI lesson, Japanese Hiragana, Part 2. Copyright 1986 by K. Hatasa. Reprinted by permission.)

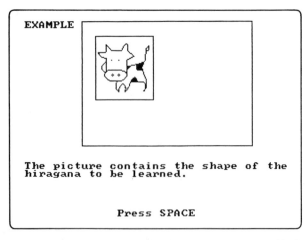

FIG. 2.7a. A picture to aid memorization of the hiragana. (All figures in this sequence are from CAI lesson, Japanese Hiragana, Part 1. Copyright 1986 by K. Hatasa. Reprinted by permission.)

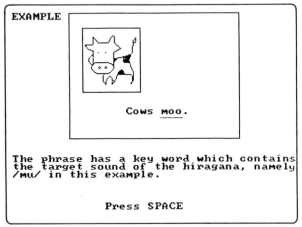

FIG. 2.7b. A reminder of the relation between the picture and the sound to be learned.

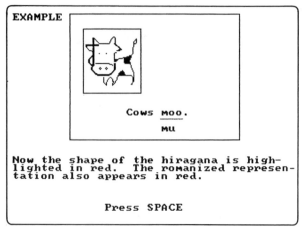

FIG. 2.7c. The shape of the hiragana is highlighted.

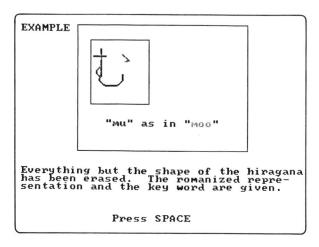

FIG. 2.7d. The picture is erased, leaving only the shape of the hiragana.

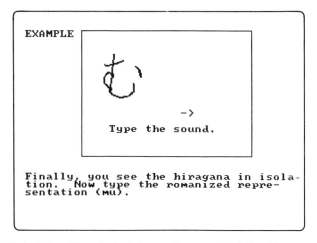

FIG. 2.7e. The student types the sound of the hiragana.

2.7b). Hatasa presents the picture in brown. In the next display, he overlays the picture with the hiragana in red, shown as the heavy lines in Figure 2.7c. In succeeding displays he fades out the picture leaving only the Japanese character.

Computer Application, Instruction, and Environment

CAI is different from classroom learning in that during the course of instruction, a teacher reviews topics at various time intervals, say on succeeding days or weeks. This is often not implemented in CAI. Time to learn is frequently shorter in CAI than in other instructional modes. All periodic reviews, even if included in a lesson, may occur within the 30–45 minute time period allotted. This time interval may not be long enough to promote long-term retention. Thus a single CAI lesson may be insufficient for retention. Developers of CAI lessons who have explicit ideas about the roles of their lessons in a curriculum can structure them so that learners can review selected sections at a later time. Alternatively, lesson developers can place reviews in successive CAI lessons. Of course, reviews can also be presented via nonCAI instruction.

Computers are generally not appropriate for instruction that involves lengthy verbal discussions. It is not as easy to read an extensive amount of text on a succession of computer displays as it is to read the same information in printed form. One reason is that only a limited amount of information can be presented on a single display. This makes it cumbersome to glance back or look ahead.

SUMMARY

Six major components are essential to a CAI framework. They are: Target Population (characteristics of the intended learners), Goals, Task (the nature of the materials and the skills needed to achieve the goals), Instruction, Computer Application (appropriate use of the computer as the instructional medium), and Environmental Implementation (consideration of the environment in which the CAI lesson will be used). The critical idea is that these components interact to affect learning. They do not act independently.

The implication for designing CAI is that each component must be addressed and internal consistency among these components sought. Procedures for designing such instruction are the concern of Chapter 3.

---

*Solution to word puzzle: You cannot teach a man anything: you can only help him to find it within himself. — Galileo

Chapter 3

PROCEDURES FOR DESIGNING CAI

Designing CAI, in some respects, is like planning for a trip. Each has its own basic constituents. For CAI they are the six components of the framework; for the trip they are the purpose of the trip, the budget, the time frame, and so on. Each component of the plan interacts with the others. The budget and time frame, for instance, impact the type and location of lodging accommodations. Drawing from your friends' past experiences (both good and bad) helps to shape plans for making a satisfactory trip. Similarly, experiences gained from pioneering projects provide useful information for planning and designing CAI. The success of a CAI lesson, like the degree of satisfaction with the trip, depends to a large extent on these planning procedures.

DIVERSITY AMONG PLANS AND PROCEDURES

Methods of planning a trip vary considerably. Some people plan every detail in advance. Others make partial arrangements, allowing for some changes in plans as the occasion arises. Some travelers prefer spontaneity. They let the events of each day determine the events of the next.

Spontaneity has some advantages. It frees the traveler from a tight time schedule and leaves her unencumbered with preplanned activities. On the other hand, without making arrangements in advance she may find that the only available lodging exceeds her budget or that tickets to a performance are all sold out. The success of a spontaneous trip is unpredictable.

51

Need For A Plan In CAI

Given the number of tools for developing CAI lessons, a person can produce a lesson without a preliminary plan. Like an unplanned trip, the quality of a lesson produced in this fashion is unpredictable. In fact, failure to follow a systematic procedure may result in trial and error production of lessons at an unacceptably high cost of time or simply in failure to produce completed lessons (Avner, 1975).

A systematic procedure fosters attention to the critical components of instruction and provides a structure for assessing the internal consistency among them. A systematic plan increases the probability that a lesson designer will write instruction that is appropriate for the specified goals, instruction that enables the intended learners to achieve those goals.

Three Design Procedures

Three procedures for designing CAI are (1) a systems, (2) an evolutionary, and (3) a mathematical/statistical approach. The best known and most frequently implemented system in instructional design is a systems approach. It is a step-by-step procedure for solving a problem, educational or otherwise. An evolutionary approach is also systematic, but not entirely predetermined. It enables a person to plan for what he would like to achieve, regardless of whether it is feasible at present, while the currently available system is being implemented (Nadler, 1981). Mathematical and statistical models of learning are the basis for a third type of design procedure in CAI.

Each of these approaches is exemplified by a large scale pioneering project in CAI. A systems approach is represented by the TICCIT system (Faust, 1974), an evolutionary approach by the PLATO® system (Alpert & Bitzer, 1970) and mathematical by the Stanford Drill and Practice programs (Suppes, Jerman, & Brian, 1968; Suppes & Morningstar, 1972). In the early sixties, microcomputer systems had not yet been invented. Extensive research in cognition and instruction had not yet accumulated. Tools to facilitate lesson production, such as text and graphics editors were not available. Nevertheless, some of the lessons learned from those early projects are applicable today for designing lessons delivered on microcomputer as well as on larger computer systems.

The systems and evolutionary approaches are discussed in this chapter, followed by overviews of the early TICCIT and PLATO projects and the lessons learned from them. Mathematical and statistical approaches involve sophisticated mathematical procedures that are beyond the scope of this text. They are of interest here as examples of sophisticated, quantitative, individualized instruction and are therefore discussed in Chapter 8, which is devoted to that topic.

SYSTEMS APPROACHES TO INSTRUCTIONAL DESIGN

Systems approaches are step-by-step procedures to solve problems. They have been applied to educational problems at all levels, from education as a whole (Lehmann, 1968), to training for a specific population, such as military personnel, to the design of programmed instruction, and even to the design of small modules of instruction that teach a concept.

Components of Systems Approaches to Instructional Design

In instructional design, systems approaches are sometimes referred to as instructional development systems (IDS). The plural is used because there are numerous models of this approach (Anderson & Faust, 1973; Briggs, 1970; Briggs & Wager, 1981; Dick & Carey, 1985; Gagné, Briggs, & Wager, 1988). Although the models differ in detail, such as the number and sequence of steps or the way in which specific components are grouped, all of them embrace several major categories. These include a statement of goals, analysis, development of instruction, and evaluation and revision (Lamos, 1984; Trimby & Gentry, 1984). For the purposes of this text, the steps are grouped into the following six categories: (1) goals, objectives, and test items; (2) analysis; (3) prerequisite knowledge; (4) media selection; (5) development of instructional materials; and (6) evaluation.

Goals, Objectives, and Test Items

Goals, objectives, and test items are grouped together here because they are conceptually related. Procedurally, goals are stated before tasks are analyzed. Specific objectives and test items are generated following task analysis.

Goals. Lessons are designed to serve a purpose. Goals and objectives express that purpose. Goals state the purpose in general (but not obscure) terms. The goal of a lesson might be, for instance, to "Plan a vegetarian breakfast."

Objectives. The term, objectives, is sometimes used synonymously with goals. More often the term refers to the knowledge and skills that are involved in achieving a goal. An objective for planning a vegetarian breakfast, for instance, is to identify typical breakfast foods that fall within the definition of vegetarian. Only the term, behavioral objectives, has an explicit definition that is universally accepted.

Behavioral objectives. Behavioral objectives state what the learner is expected to do, the standard of performance she is expected to attain, and the conditions under which she will perform (Gagné & Briggs, 1974; Mager, 1975). For example, "Without the aid of the manual, the applicant for a driver's license will match shapes of highway signs to the type of information they present with 100% accuracy."

Worthwhile behavioral objectives are not easy to generate. It may seem fairly straightforward to prepare behavioral objectives for skills training, memory tasks (e.g., arithmetic facts), or other routine tasks. However, even for such well defined tasks, it is all too easy to state the act to be performed rather than the intent of the performance (Mager, 1975). For example, one might generate the following behavioral objective: "Complete page 12 in the workbook with 100% accuracy." "Complete" is indeed a statement of performance, but the intent is not to complete a page in the workbook, but to accomplish some intellectual task. Nor is the statement "Circle the matching beginning letter sounds" any better. The real objective is not to circle the answers but to discriminate between letters.

A major criticism of behavioral objectives is that they are not suitable for more complex cognitive tasks such as nonroutine problem solving or medical diagnosis. Because it is difficult to state performance in a way that captures the intellectual intent of complex tasks, there is a tendency to trivialize statements of objectives. Understanding a concept, for example, reduces to rote memorization of a definition.

Another criticism of behavioral objectives is that stating achievement in terms of the number or percent of items correct does not necessarily provide sufficient information about a student's understanding. Two students may get the same score on an achievement test but for entirely different reasons. Consider two different incorrect rules for adding numbers with opposite signs, such as $-5+6$ and $5-6$. One student's incorrect rule is to add the two numbers and attach the sign of the one with the larger absolute value. She writes $-5+6=11$ and $5-6=-11$. Another student's incorrect rule is to get the difference between the numbers and attach the sign of the first number. He writes $-5+6=-1$ and $5-6=1$. The scores on their achievement tests might be the same, yet reveal nothing about their misconceptions.

Alternatives to behavioral objectives. Bloom (1956) attempted to address some of the shortcomings of behavioral objectives by creating a taxonomy that encompasses cognitive skills. He proposed the following categories: knowledge, comprehension, application, analysis, synthesis, and evaluation. The meanings of the first three categories are clear. Most people would agree on how to classify tasks according to these categories. Knowledge refers to facts, rules, definitions, and classifications. Comprehension is the ability to interpret, that is, to summarize or paraphrase. Application is the ability to apply rules, such as to insert appropriate punctuation marks in a sentence or to solve simultaneous equations. The remaining categories (analysis, synthesis, and evaluation), however, are vague. It is difficult to find agreement on how to categorize skills according to these classifications. Another drawback to Bloom's taxonomy is that the categories are defined in terms of unobservable intellectual skills. Consequently, there is little guidance for generating items to test them.

Seeking a way to test the intellectual content of performance, Williams and Haladyna (1982) developed a generic method of generating objectives. Their method includes three factors: (1) the content to be learned; (2) the task or operations on that content; and (3) the performance mode (see Figure 3.1). They specify three content categories: facts, concepts (classes of objects or events), and principles (relationships among concepts or events). Another important content category, procedures, is considered to be a subset of the principles category, and includes applications of principles. Of particular interest here is that they propose six intellectual tasks, each of which is a different operation on the content. These operations are named reiteration, summarization, illustration, prediction, evaluation, and application.

Reiteration is what we commonly call verbatim memorizing. It is

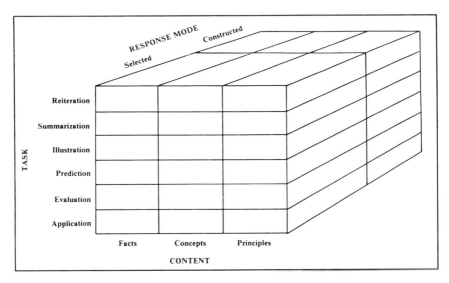

FIG. 3.1. Typology of educational objectives. *Note.* From "Logic operations for generating intended questions (LOGIQ)" by R. G. Williams and T. H. Haladyna in G. H. Roid & T. M. Haladyna (Eds.), *A technology for test-item writing* (p. 164), 1984, New York: Academic Press. Copyright 1984 by Academic Press. Reprinted by permission.

comparable to Bloom's category, knowledge. Reiteration is repetition or recognition of information exactly as presented. Summarization, like Bloom's comprehension and Gagné's verbal information, involves extracting the essence of some content. Summarization of a concept, for example, might be defining positive reinforcement in your own words. Illustration requires recognition or generation of a previously unseen example of a principle or concept. For instance, a learner might be asked to give an example of how positive reinforcement can be used to get a child to behave at the dinner table. In prediction, the task is to predict changes in a situation, given the circumstances surrounding it. An objective might be to predict the behavior of a child who gets a dollar for every "A" on his report card. Evaluation requires analysis of a problem situation and the factors involved in decision making. For example, a student might have to decide which of two medications to prescribe for a particular patient. Finally, application is just the opposite of prediction. A learner must select or recognize conditions that can bring about a particular outcome. The task might be to define conditions that would increase the probability of a child getting A's on his report card.

The two response modes in the Williams and Haladyna model are called selected and constructed. Selected responses require students to select the correct response from among several alternatives, as in multiple choice, true-false, and matching questions. Constructed responses require students to generate a response, as in solving a problem.

Not all of the intellectual tasks are applicable to all of the content categories. For example, the only task that is applicable to factual content is reiteration. By definition, it is not possible to summarize (parapahrase), illustrate, predict, or evaluate facts.

The important contribution of this "typology" is that it applies a performance-based analysis to complex skills as well as simple ones, prediction and evaluation as well as rote memorization. Furthermore, the meaning of each of the categories, including the complex skills, is clearly defined so there should be relatively little ambiguity for practitioners. Thus, the model provides a good operational guideline for writing objectives.

A disadvantage of the model is that writing questions for the complex processes requires a considerable amount of time and thought by the subject matter experts. However, this is not so much a criticism of the model as an acknowledgment that writing quality test items is a time-consuming process.

Test items.   Instruction is presented to help learners achieve specific goals. Test items are used to assess this achievement. Because test items should match the goals, they are generated after the task has been analyzed and detailed objectives specified.

Analysis

Task analysis begins at the curriculum level and is repeated at successively deeper levels down to analysis of lessons and individual topics of instruction (Romiszowski, 1981).

Purposes. The purposes of task analysis are: (1) to determine what needs to be taught; (2) to determine the sequence in which to do so; and (3) to identify the prerequisite knowledge and skills. A task analysis can also serve as a guide for generating assessment measures and for selecting an instructional strategy.

There are many kinds of analysis, such as content, performance, information processing, developmental, and cognitive. The systems approach typically includes only content and performance analyses.

Hierarchical analysis. A top-down hierarchical analysis is perhaps the best known and most extensively researched task analysis. Recall that a learner must master each of the lower level skills before she can master the ultimate task. The lower level tasks are not only easier to learn, but are also components of the complex ones (Resnick, 1976).

A hierarchical analysis of skills has several shortcomings for instruction. Resnick (1976) refers to it as an idealized performance because the analysis assumes that a person learns without error and without backtracking. The analysis also incorrectly assumes that there is a unique set of steps in every hierarchy.

Another serious deficiency is that there may be a discrepancy between a hierarchical task analysis and an analysis of the way students actually process information. When Resnick and her colleagues (1976) produced an arithmetic curriculum based on a hierarchical task analysis, they found that the sequence of steps in children's performance did not always match the sequence generated by the rational task analysis. The hierarchically ordered sequences were best for most of the students, but some learned the complex tasks simultaneously with intervening simpler ones. Thus the general sequence was valid, but the details of the analysis were not.

Achieving a goal sometimes requires more than learning the component skills. In mathematics, for example, experts apply some higher level strategies in addition to the skills determined by a rational task analysis (Schoenfeld, 1987).

Two additional shortcomings of the hierarchical approach are noted by Dansereau (1985). One is that students may develop processes that are effective with simplified materials at the beginning of training but that are not effective with more complex tasks. A second shortcoming is that a student may learn the individual components of a task but fail to understand how the entire task fits together. He may fail to learn the Gestalt of the task.

Behavioral analysis.   Instructional designers who employ a systems approach analyze content separately from operations (behavior) on that content. The Williams and Haladyna matrix (see Figure 3.1) is one example. Another is the work of Merrill and Boutwell (1973). They classify task content as paired associates (e.g., arithmetic facts), concepts, principles (rules), and problems (cf. Gagné, 1985; Tiemann & Markle, 1985). Their categories of behaviors are: discriminated recall, classification, rule using, and higher order rule using. Discriminated recall is the ability to recognize a definition of a concept and to recognize previously seen instances. Classification is the ability to identify an item as an example of a concept and, when given two items, to identify the one that belongs to the given classification. The rationale for this analysis is that more than one type of behavior may be needed to learn a particular kind of content. To learn a concept, for example, a person applies two behaviors, discriminated recall and classification.

Prerequisite Knowledge

When a task is analyzed into its components, the instructional designer decides what knowledge he will assume the target students have previously acquired. This is referred to as the prerequisite knowledge.

Media Selection

For the purposes of this text, the computer has been selected as the instructional medium. As with any instructional medium, it is important to select the computer for appropriate reasons.

Development of Instructional Materials

Development of instructional materials refers to generating the verbal messages (sometimes called the script), the questions to be asked during the lesson, and the graphic presentations. These topics require extensive discussion and are presented in Chapters 4, 5, and 7, respectively.

Evaluation

Evaluation is the last step listed in systems approaches to instructional design. The intention, however, is not that it be last but rather that evaluation be carried out during lesson development as well as after the lesson is completed. Evaluation is discussed in more detail in Chapter 10.

Critique of Procedures in Systems Approaches

Some of the benefits of a systems approach are characteristic of all systematic approaches. A systems approach serves as a management device and makes lesson production more efficient. Effective lessons are likely to result because a systems approach increases the probability that the lesson will match the goals (Roblyer, 1981) and not go off on a tangent. A precise statement of objectives serves as a basis for task analyses and evaluation measures. The approach is empirical and replicable. Instruction can be evaluated and improved through data collection and analysis (Dick & Carey, 1985).

Romiszowski (1981) criticizes the systems approach because it is frequently presented in a flowchart form, leaving the impression that it is both a mechanistic and a linear approach. However, analysis, design, and evaluation are on-going activities during all stages of lesson development. The process is not a mechanical, algorithmic, step-by-step procedure, but rather a general heuristic (rule of thumb) one.

It is this very heuristic aspect that has been criticized by others because it tells lesson designers what to do, but not HOW to do it (Montague, 1981). Statements such as "develop instructional prescription" or "develop first draft materials" are totally lacking in specific directions about how to generate a presentation. This argument is not entirely valid because there is a considerable body of instructional research that tells how to implement some of the steps in the systems approach. Mager (1975) provides some very specific guidelines for writing instructional objectives and others (Merrill & Tennyson, 1977; Tiemann & Markle, 1985) have done the same for teaching concepts.

One additional disadvantage of a systems approach is that it assumes that developers have adequate experience to predict the outcomes of instruction. Although valid in situations where instruction has been thoroughly evaluated, it is not a valid assumption when innovative techniques or new media are employed (Avner, 1975). An alternative approach for such situations is presented in the section, Evolutionary Approach To Instructional Design, later in this chapter.

Critique of Elements in Systems Approaches

There can be little argument about the importance of the elements of a systems approach. In fact, five of the elements have counterparts in the CAI framework. Goals and instructional materials tie directly to framework components Goals and Instruction, respectively. Media selection is a counterpart of Computer Application. Analysis relates to Task in the CAI framework and prerequisite knowledge to Target Population. However, the conceptualizations of analysis and of prerequisite knowledge in systems approaches are generally inadequate.

Beyond content and performance analysis. Typically, a systems approach includes only analyses of content and performance. These analyses are necessary but sometimes insufficient for instructional design. They do not include analyses of the processes involved in learning, information that can provide additional and useful insights to guide instructional design (cf. Gagné, Briggs, & Wager, 1988). Some examples of the potential benefits of information-processing, cognitive, and developmental analyses are presented next to exemplify this contention.

Information-processing analyses. An information-processing analysis can reveal critical cognitive steps that do not appear in hierarchical analysis (Dick & Carey, 1985) or in a behavioral analysis. Problem solving is a case in point. A hierarchical analysis lists the steps or skills in the process but not the decisions that are part of the process. It reveals the principles and rules that a person applies to solve a physics problem but not how the problem solver decides that those are the rules he should apply. For example, students usually know how to substitute numbers in a formula once the formula is given, but they do not know when it is appropriate to use the formula. It is precisely this kind of information that an information-processing analysis discloses.

An information-processing analysis may seem reasonable for heuristic problems, that is, problems for which there is no clearly defined set of steps to follow. But is it really necessary for algorithmic problems, for which the steps are precisely defined? The answer is, "Yes." There are many instances where an information-processing analysis can contribute significantly to the design of algorithmic instruction. In arithmetic problems, for example, the steps for adding, subtracting, multiplying, and dividing fractions are explicitly stated. Why is it, then, that students do not know which rules to apply when given a worksheet of mixed operations (multiplication, division, addition, and subtraction)? Why do they frequently ask, "Is this one where I tip the fraction over?" It is probably because only rational analyses guided instructional development. Rational analyses are sufficient for practice pages on which all problems are alike and on which a student does not have to make any decisions about which set of rules to follow. However, this analysis is inadequate for pages of mixed problems because the first step is not to apply a given set of rules but rather to determine which operation is called for. An information-processing analysis reveals this critical step.

An information-processing analysis can also assist in locating specific areas of students' misunderstandings (Romiszowski, 1981). The area of processing deficiency can be identified when performance is represented as a four-stage cycle: perceive incoming information, recall prerequisites, plan, and perform. A student's difficulty may be that he perceives a task inaccurately and attends to irrelevant information. He may not have the appropriate prerequisite knowledge or may have the necessary knowledge but not know that he should access it. He may fail because he does not formulate a plan or is unable to generate alternative plans or to select the best from among several alternatives. Finally, his failure in performance may be due to insufficient time, lack of motivation, or just lack of ability. If specific processing difficulties can be located, instruction can be tailored to overcome them.

Developmental analysis.   For Case and Bereiter (1984), instruction should recapitulate development. Because the developmental, naturally occurring sequence of steps in a task is sometimes not the same as the logical sequence, a developmental analysis is essential.

Developmental analysis involves presenting a particular task and observing how children at different levels of development respond to it. Siegler (1976) conducted such an analysis for balance beam problems (see Figure 3.2). The task is to decide which way the beam will tip when not artificially supported, given a particular configuration of weights on pegs equidistant from the fulcrum. From his own work and that of others, Siegler concluded that children's knowledge about balance scales can be represented in terms of a hierarchy of four rules. With development, children acquire more complex rules in the hierarchy. If the weights are on only one side of a

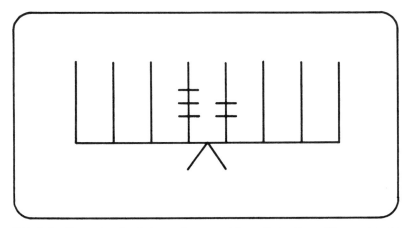

FIG. 3.2.   Example of a balance beam problem. *Note.* From "Three aspects of cognitive development" by R. S. Siegler, *Cognitive Psychology*, 1976, *8*, 481–520. Copyright 1976 by Academic Press. Adapted by permission.

fulcrum, three-year-olds can predict accurately which side of the beam will go down. However, if weights are placed on both sides and equidistant from the fulcrum, they do not make accurate predictions. Five-to seven-year-olds can make accurate predictions and are thus said to have Rule I. With increasing age, children apply more sophisticated rules until at about age 13 they attend to both weight and distance and apply all of the rules.

Siegler's developmental analysis showed that younger children's inability to predict accurately was due to their failure to encode both distance and the number of weights. Based on this information, he generated instruction that helped younger children encode both weight and distance dimensions.

A developmental analysis is most appropriate for specific kinds of tasks and students (Case & Bereiter, 1984). The tasks are those that are difficult for students when taught by current instructional methods, tasks that have specifiable objectives and methods of solution, and that can elicit consistent responses from those who fail them. A developmental analysis is particularly appropriate for retarded students, for adults for whom a task has the three characteristics noted above, for children who are handicapped or come from culturally different backgrounds, and for children who need remedial work.

Cognitive analyses. Cognitive analysis, as its name implies, is an analysis of cognitive skills such as the strategic or procedural knowledge required to learn some specific content. The cognitive skill most frequently required in arithmetic, for example, is to evaluate a symbolic expression, such as to compute $7 + 8$. A cognitive skill often applied in algebra is to transform a symbolic expression (Greeno, 1985). A student who is solving a linear equation such as $3 \times + 5 - 2 \times = 3 - 5 \times$, must transform it to the form $3 \times - 2 \times + 5 \times = 3 - 5$.

"Knowing that" is another cognitive skill. For example, knowing that if a letter appears in a rule such as A × B = B × A, then the letter is associated with the same number throughout the statement.

Cognitive analyses reveal aspects of tasks that affect their difficulty, hence instructional design. For example, the format in which a problem is presented affects the kinds of cognitive skills and operations that need to be implemented. Some formats involve operations that are easier and more natural to implement than others. Because students generally try to solve problems in the format in which they are presented, the presentation format makes the problems more or less difficult for them.

Cognitive, information-processing, and developmental analyses are not without disadvantages. The primary problem is that they are difficult to implement. A person can do the task himself and analyze his processes (Dick & Carey, 1985), get the protocols of an expert, or observe novice learners. However, there are two implicit assumptions underlying these proposals, neither of which can be substantiated in all situations. First is the idea that all experts employ the same processes. For complex tasks, such as problem solving, experts differ in their approaches. Second, the methods of process analysis are not necessarily reliable. It is not easy to elicit an expert's information processes. Asking her to think aloud is unsatisfactory because she may take some unobservable step (like making a decision) but not even be aware of it and therefore not report it. Subsequent probing or attempts to interpret her performance may be unreliable because she may not remember why she took a particular step but will devise a reason in retrospect. A person's analysis of her own information processes may also be incomplete or inaccurate.

Beyond prerequisites. In traditional systems approaches to instructional development, the term prerequisites refers to the specific knowledge needed for a given task. Current research, however, demonstrates that characteristics of learners beyond specific knowledge also influence learning (cf. Chapter 2). One such characteristic is a student's proficiency in knowing how to learn. Some people can learn concepts from definitions alone (Anderson & Kulhavy, 1972) whereas others require examples and additional instruction. Other learner characteristics that may be important in design include prior knowledge, developmental level, educational level, professional expertise, and deviation from the normal, such as deafness or mental retardation.

An example from Landa (1983) demonstrates how even a learner's native language affects instructional design. In the Russian language there are no articles. When native Russian speakers learn English they find the rules for using "a(n)" and "the" difficult and confusing. Therefore it is important to provide them with some simple procedures for using the rules. Landa suggests, for example, that instruction include the following. Ask yourself if you can put "this" or "that" before a countable Russian noun. If yes, use "the;" if no, ask if you can put a possessive pronoun before a Russian noun. If yes, use corresponding English pronoun; if no, use "a." The point is that instruction in such decision processes is necessary for students whose native languages do not have articles, but not for those whose native languages do.

Summary

A systems approach is an efficient and systematic procedure for designing instruction. A major advantage is that it specifies critical steps in the instructional design process. The procedure addresses five of the six components of the framework for CAI, and the sixth can easily be added. Some elements of systems approaches, such as analysis and prerequisites, are narrowly conceived and inadequate in scope, but these, too, can be elaborated. Despite the shortcomings of procedures for implementing systems approaches, they can be effective and efficient if appropriately implemented. An example of an application of a systems approach in CAI is the TICCIT system.

TICCIT: A CAI IMPLEMENTATION
OF A SYSTEMS APPROACH

TICCIT is a pioneer CAI system that, since its inception, has implemented the systems approach to instructional design. In 1971, the National Science Foundation funded the nonprofit MITRE Corporation to further the development of TICCIT in order to demonstrate the impact of CAI on education. The MITRE Corporation hired educational psychologists to develop an instructional design for the system and to produce TICCIT courseware (Wilson, 1984). Thus, TICCIT was designed to support a single instructional strategy. The TICCIT system has since been sold to for-profit corporations. It has undergone extensive expansion and change in response to advances in technology and to the lessons learned from the demonstration project and succeeding experience. Relevant aspects of the initial project are discussed next, followed by lessons learned and pertinent information about the current system.

The NSF-funded project.   Lessons in the NSF-funded TICCIT project were designed for community college students and were intended to be the primary source of instruction. Instructors were expected to be managers and advisors rather than lecturers. The courseware covered the concepts and rules that are taught in freshman level English and mathematics courses in community colleges. Instruction addressed two kinds of objectives. They were: (1) using a rule, such as calculating the area of a rectangle, and (2) applying a concept, such as, given a figure, determine whether it is a rectangle.

A systems approach was employed to design the overall project— objectives, courseware content (concepts and rules to be included), instructional strategy, and management system. The developers decided to implement a single instructional strategy, Rules-Examples-Practice. They were aware of many other instructional strategies, but selected this one because it is based solidly in learning theory. The developers were also aware that this strategy would not be instructionally effective for every single objective and topic. However, they chose it because it had the broadest application for their goals (Fine, personal communication, 1988).

In the instructional model, rules were available at alternative levels of difficulty, as were example and practice items. Students were free to choose both the presentation format and the order in which they saw the components. They could, for instance, see some examples before learning a concept and then practice, or choose to see a rule, then practice and ask to see the rule again. They could see as many examples as they chose. In some cases, students could also select the difficulty level of exercises: easy, medium, or hard.

Learner control and mastery were the primary elements of the instructional strategy. The philosophy was that "Students must be given a chance to use learning strategies they develop themselves and must be free to accept or reject any strategy advice" (Faust, 1974, p.95). The developers hoped that the lessons would be acceptable to learners, and that students would learn how to learn as a consequence of studying under this self-management system.

Lessons learned from initial project. Many lessons were learned from this pilot project. Only those relevant to instructional design and procedures are presented here.

1. A consequence of the decision to employ a single instructional model was that lesson authors did not have to generate a new design for every lesson. Because the components of the instructional design template were built into the system, authors and instructional designers merely had to supply the subject matter content.

2. The Rule-Example-Practice model proved to be viable for the given objectives and the intended students.

3. In the early seventies, CAI was new, and developers had yet to learn how to work with it effectively. Instructors who tested the courses were subject to the "not invented here" syndrome, and preferred to select their own content rather than that provided by the lesson designers (Sasscer, 1984).

4. Templates were efficient but authors needed (and have since been given) greater flexibility to meet a broad range of instructional needs. Thus, without adequate experience with CAI, an a priori commitment to a large scale project makes it difficult to make necessary changes before an extensive amount of time and effort is invested.

5. The attitudes and roles of the instructors dramatically affected achievement, even for these CAI lessons that were intended to be self-contained primary instruction. The percentage of students who completed the courses was heavily dependent on the way the courses were implemented. In the English courses, instructors took an active role and helped students overcome common problems. Completion rates were about the same in TICCIT sections as in straight lecture sections (Jones, 1978). The same was true of mathematics classes managed by instructors who were

familiar with the system. However, in mathematics classes managed by unfamiliar instructors, the completion rate was 16% compared to an average of 50% for lecture sections (Alderman, Appel, & Murphy, 1978). In order for full course instruction to be successful, instructors have to understand the system and be willing to serve as nurturants, advisors, and moderators between machine and student (Wyles, 1984).

6. In CAI, as in other modes, instruction interacts with learner characteristics. In English courses, TICCIT students performed significantly better than lecture students on objective tests of writing skills and on essay tests (Jones, 1978). Mathematics students also showed a significant positive effect in five of six cases (Alderman, Appel, & Murphy, 1978). However, the effectiveness of the mathematics lessons varied with initial entry ability. Students who needed a considerable amount of remedial help did not perform well. The design of the course apparently favored students of high rather than low mathematics ability.

7. Self-paced instruction is no different when presented by computer than by other methods. Learner control is not appropriate for all students for all courseware. Not all students are capable of, or even interested in, managing their own learning.

MicroTICCIT, the current TICCIT. Lessons learned from these early experiences, together with an awareness of the potential of the many technological advances (e.g., color, sound, videodisc) for CAI have resulted in MicroTICCIT, a tremendously expanded system. The present system continues to support the Rule-Example-Practice model but makes other instructional models available as well. A five-phase instructional design process (analyze, design, develop, implement, control/evaluate) is taught and used. "However, TICCIT is merely a tool to be used in accomplishing some of the phases in this process. An author can design and develop material for TICCIT without using these steps" (Fine, personal communication, 1988).

TICCIT is still intended for full course instruction and it is still a mastery learning system. The Rule-Example-Practice model continues to be used extensively, but authors have much more flexibility, such as control over management of students' routes through a course. TICCIT supports efficient authoring for both experienced and inexperienced authors. The system provides built in instructional models as well as three editing levels to adapt to authors at different levels of expertise. The system allows experienced authors the full range of power to create the most sophisticated simulations. TICCIT provides instructional management systems. Students can see a record of their work; instructors can see records of an entire class as well as of individual students. The TICCIT system can be used with many different configurations of "off-the shelf" equipment. Still used in academic settings and even in those that participated in the NSF pilot project, TICCIT is employed extensively for training by industry, the military, and other governmental units.

EVOLUTIONARY APPROACH TO INSTRUCTIONAL DESIGN

In CAI it is not necessary, and frequently not feasible, to implement both the overall plans and the entire first draft of the instructional materials before testing them with students. Although major overall planning should precede implementation, some aspects of instructional modules, such as responses and feedback and human factors and management cannot be readily anticipated. In CAI, they can be generated, tested, and revised before the entire first draft is completed. This approach to developing CAI may be characterized as an evolutionary approach.

Characteristics

According to Dunn (cited in Avner, 1975), an evolutionary approach includes both deterministic and incremental systems, in contrast to the systems approach to design, which is entirely deterministic. This means that in an evolutionary approach, planning can be predetermined for those elements of the process for which the user has confidence and adequate experience (e.g., goal specification). However, for other components in the process, tentative or short-term goals may be specified. For example, an instructional designer may want to employ a novel instructional technique for one objective, but may lack experience for deciding a priori whether it will be effective. In an evolutionary approach, this step can be implemented on a tentative basis. It can then be subjected to trials and evaluation before a decision is made to incorporate it in the overall lesson.

The evolutionary process is particularly appropriate for situations where there is limited past experience from which to draw guidance. An example of the value of an evolutionary approach is the following segment of CAI instruction written as a class project by a neurosurgeon. The goal was to help students relate their theoretical knowledge about the seventh cranial nerve to actual cases. The lesson asked students to engage in some physical activities (see Figures 3.3). Because the computer cannot monitor these activities, Drake did not know whether students would actually touch their faces before they responded to questions. It certainly would have been a waste of time to generate a large segment of a lesson on the assumption that this would be a viable approach, only to find out subsequently that it did not work. (Preliminary testing suggested that this is a viable option for mature students.)

Facial weakness always has a specific PATTERN.

The pattern varies widely, depending on the

anatomical level at which the lesion is located.

Touch your right eyebrow with your fingertips (in order

to feel for any muscle contractions), and at the same

try to raise the left eyebrow BY ITSELF.

Press RETURN to CONTINUE

Not many people can wrinkle one side of the forehead by itself.
This is because the frontalis muscle is innervated by lower motor
neurons in the facial nucleus which receive cortico-bulbar axons
from BOTH cerebral hemispheres.

If a person has a right hemiplegia as a result of a left

hemisphere cerebro-vascular accident, would you expect the

right frontalis muscle to be paralyzed?   y or n >

Press RETURN to CONTINUE

FIG. 3.3.   Request for a response that the computer cannot monitor, and the subsequent one that can be monitored. (From CAI lesson, The Seventh Cranial Nerve. Copyright 1985 by A. Drake. Reprinted by permission.)

Advantages.   A major benefit of the evolutionary approach is that it enables a user to test new ideas without making a long-term commitment. An additional advantage, and one particularly important for CAI, is that it enables a user to assess the interactions of subcomponents of a process (Avner, 1975), such as the interaction of computer feedback with learner characteristics.

Disadvantages.   Unlike a systems approach, an evolutionary approach lacks a predefined set of steps. Another disadvantage is that it is difficult to specify in advance the amount of time that will be needed to complete significant events in the design process (Avner, 1975). Avner (1975) cites Popper's observation that it is logically impossible to specify the outcome of an evolutionary process.

Comment.   Despite its disadvantages, an evolutionary approach can be successfully applied to developing CAI. The PLATO system represents a good example.

PLATO: A CAI IMPLEMENTATION OF AN EVOLUTIONARY APPROACH

The PLATO system for CAI was first developed in the 1960's as a joint venture of the University of Illinois, the United States government, and some private foundations. The systems approach to instruction was implemented at that time. It was assumed that instructional techniques were known and that CAI would simply be a technology for automating them. This proved to be an incorrect assumption. Thus, by 1972, when the National Science Foundation (NSF) funded the University of Illinois to implement the fourth version of the system and to develop courseware for elementary school and community college students, an evolutionary approach was implemented.

At present the University of Illinois has its own system, which is being succeeded by a new computer configuration and NovaNET communications systems. Numerous versions of PLATO were sold commercially by Control Data Corporation. The NSF-funded PLATO projects and lessons learned are discussed next in light of the issues relevant to instructional design and procedures. A brief review of the current computer system follows.

NSF-funded projects.   Under NSF funding, PLATO courseware was produced for elementary school arithmetic and reading and for community college mathematics, English, biology, chemistry, and accounting.

The evolutionary approach was apparent in all facets of the PLATO system (Avner, 1975; Steinberg, 1975; Stifle, 1975). Authors were free to pursue any instructional design procedure and instructional strategy they chose. Given such a flexible system and the fact that in the early seventies the computer was an untested medium for instruction, it is not surprising that PLATO courseware development groups implemented diverse instructional design procedures. The elementary reading group took a systems approach for the entire set of lessons. Other groups began with a systems approach but revised some of the predetermined aspects when student trials revealed shortcomings in the lessons. Some lesson designers spent considerable time exploring the potential of the PLATO system for enriching instruction in their subject areas before authoring an extensive number of lessons. Some authors transferred classroom techniques to computer lessons while still others had no apparent instructional design procedure. A few individuals just sat at the computer terminal and composed a lesson without any prior planning.

Authors could employ inquiry techniques or direct instruction. They could (and did) generate drills, games, simulations, and tutorial instruction. Lesson developers could design a template (a format) for all or some of their lessons, or generate as many different instructional strategies as they chose. PLATO lessons were not restricted to full course instruction nor to a prespecified role in a curriculum. Lesson designers were free to decide how their lessons would fit into a course, as introductory, supplementary or primary instruction.

The evolutionary approach to system and software design supported an evolutionary approach to instructional design procedures. One important feature, not widely available on other systems at that time, was that authors could generate a module of instruction and immediately view it as it would be seen by students. They could test the module with colleagues or students, evaluate it, and revise as needed. This feature enabled novice authors to gain experience and experienced authors to experiment with new ideas before making commitments to specific designs. As authors developed materials, they found they would like the system to provide additional features, such as alternative sizes of type, more flexible answer judging commands, and student management systems. They reported these needs to the systems staff, and the system was modified as warranted.

Lessons learned from the initial PLATO experience

1. A systematic approach to lesson production is essential even in an evolutionary environment. Some authors who produced substantive quantities of materials, explored the system and experimented with it before beginning full scale lesson production. Then, based on this knowledge, they produced tools such as instructional templates, which enabled them to generate new lessons rapidly and efficiently (Avner, 1979). In particular, when time for production was very limited, quality lessons could not be produced without a systematic procedure (Steinberg, Avner, Call-Himwich, Francis, Himwich, Klecka, & Misselt, 1977). Authors who had no plan, or who composed at the terminal, failed to complete lessons or else produced lessons that made full use of graphics and other computer features but were instructionally ineffective.

2. Effective CAI is not a function of the instructional design procedure alone. Many different procedures can result in useful lessons. The elemen-

tary school arithmetic lessons were developed as three separate strands, (whole numbers, fractions, and graphs) and each by a different group of authors using a different design procedure (evolutionary, systems, and transfer from classroom, respectively). Yet all strands were clearly successful (Swinton, Amarel, & Morgan, 1978).

3. When implementing the evolutionary approach in developing a CAI system, a large community of users in direct and instantaneous communication with systems developers is vital to identify problems, correct deficiencies, and expand capabilities to meet unforeseen needs (Avner, 1987). Consider, for example, the addition of extensive answer judging capabilities to Tutor, PLATO's programming language.

When multiple choice was the only kind of questions authors could ask, they could write feedback a priori for each of the choices or simply say yes or no. However, once it was possible for authors to ask open-ended questions, they needed different tools for giving students adequate feedback to their responses. Authors asked for programming commands that would enable them to accept or reject misspelled words, accept synonyms, ignore extra words, comment on word order, and so on. The systems staff implemented these features and also marked up students' responses with symbols to indicate the nature of their errors (e.g., an arrow to indicate incorrect word order).

4. Instructional techniques that are successful in a classroom do not necessarily transfer directly, or transfer at all, to CAI, regardless of the design procedure. If the underlying conditions of classroom instruction are essential to a technique but not available in CAI, chances of successful transfer are slim. For example, discovery learning techniques in a classroom depend on inter-learner interaction for success. If inter-learner interaction is not present in a CAI lesson, it is not likely to be effective.

5. A computer per se does not teach. No matter how delightful and attractive the graphics and animation may be, learning does not occur automatically. It is not full use of the computer's capabilities but appropriate use that determines instructional effectiveness.

6. There is no "best way" to present CAI instruction, even in a single discipline. Discovery as well as structured instructional strategies were implemented in the three arithmetic strands, and all were generally effective.

7. CAI is not impervious to situational influences (Amarel, 1983; Slottow, 1977). The most significant factor in the elementary reading and arithmetic programs was the powerful effect that elementary school teachers have on the outcome of implementation (Swinton, Amarel, & Morgan, 1978). Factors that influenced the way teachers implemented the PLATO lessons included their willingness to deal with logistics such as scheduling, their attitude toward pedagogical matters such as the compat-

ibility of the lesson design with their values, and their degree of flexibility in adapting to innovative techniques. Use of PLATO lessons at community colleges was also strongly influenced by the nature of instructors' implementation.

8. A good authoring environment is important. Authors need appropriate tools to design good instruction. For example, because there may be many correct answers to one question, all of the answers need to be judged and accepted as correct by the computer lesson. An author needs computer commands that enable her to transmit this information to the computer without writing a long or complicated computer program.

9. CAI is a viable instructional vehicle in many different settings. Lessons can be designed for diverse subjects and to serve diverse roles in a curriculum.

Current computer system and NovaNET. This centrally controlled computer system currently provides instruction to numerous academic, governmental, industrial, and private users as well as to the University of Illinois. The current system still operates under the original philosophy of permitting authors to pursue any design procedure and any instructional strategy they choose. The system provides many new tools to assist authors, such as text editors, graphics editors, record keeping, and management systems. Users are no longer limited to using PLATO terminals but may access the system through phone line connections to microcomputer systems. PLATO's successors, the computer system and NovaNet communications systems, support new features such as color, and at a much reduced cost, especially to distance users. This is accomplished through updated technology and through satellite communication from the system to the users.

DESIGN PROCEDURES FOR MICROCOMPUTER SYSTEMS

It would be interesting to review the design procedures employed by developers of CAI materials for microcomputer systems, and from systems other than PLATO/Nova and TICCIT. It is not possible to do so in this text. Theoreticians publish articles about design procedures, but practitioners do not. Attempts to gather this information (by phone and by correspondence) from several developers were unsuccessful. One large-scale developer, for example, wrote that their development process is confidential. A publisher of microcomputer lessons explained that they do not know what procedures individual authors employ.

A PLAN FOR DESIGNING CAI

A systematic plan for instructional design is essential for CAI as well as for other media. Because there is a considerable amount of research about instructional design procedures in general, it might seem reasonable to simply select the most appropriate one and apply it to CAI. Unfortunately it is not reasonable to do so. Known procedures provide valuable information, but none of them can be applied directly to CAI.

A plan for designing CAI should integrate applicable aspects of known instructional design procedures and add features unique to CAI. Components of known procedures can be modified to meet the unique aspects of computer-presented instruction and to apply current research findings in the psychology of learning. In addition, the plan should attend to all components of the CAI framework and their interaction. This suggests that the design process should be flexible so that when a change is made in one component, a change can be made in others that interact with it.

Features of Systems Procedures and Modifications Needed

Goals. A statement of goals is just as important in CAI as in other instruction, but the initial statement need not be cast in concrete. Flexibility is particularly important for designers who wish to set innovative goals. They may find, after a task analysis, that some of the component skills are outside the capability of the target population, or not feasible for computer presentation.

When an author evaluates instruction he may find that he had unintentionally omitted some important subgoals. The addition of instruction for these goals may necessitate a change in the emphasis or perspective of the initial statement. Thus the option of modifying initial goal statements is important in CAI.

Goals for the learner are an application of the component, Goals, in the CAI framework. Two additional kinds of goals require consideration and are direct applications of two other components in the framework. They are goals for the computer and goals for the curriculum. Goals for the computer are the reasons for selecting the computer as the instructional medium. These goals are an application of the component, Computer Application, in the CAI framework. Goals for the CAI lesson(s) in the larger course or curriculum are also essential for integrating the lessons with other instructional modes. These goals are an application of the component, Environmental Implementation, in the framework.

Evaluation measures.   The only way to know if a lesson has achieved its goals is to evaluate students' achievement. A systems approach is usually associated with performance, so assessment measures are test items. In CAI, not all goals can be or should be evaluated by test items. In a simulation, the goal might be to diagnose an illness while keeping the cost of laboratory tests below a preset amount of money. For other lessons the goal might be to maintain a minimum performance level throughout the lesson.

Task analyses.   Task analyses are an essential step and are related to the component, Task, in the CAI framework. The use of the plural, analyses, is deliberate, to emphasize that there are many kinds of analyses. They include not only content structure and skills but also the processes involved and the nature of the materials to be learned.

Prerequisites/target population.   It is essential to define a beginning point in instruction, a specific knowledge base, expected to be known by the intended learners. Beyond that, however, research in both cognitive and developmental psychology show how important it is for a designer to describe all characteristics that might influence learning. These include such characteristics as age, educational level, ability level, cultural background, and deviation from the norm. This step in the procedure is an application of the component, Target Population, in the CAI framework.

Additional Considerations for CAI

Traditional systems approaches do not include four elements that are essential to the development of CAI instruction. They do not address interaction, human factors, management decisions, or environmental factors.

Interactive sequences.   A unique feature of CAI is that computer and learner can carry on two-way communication. A computer program not only asks questions, as in other instructional media, but also judges responses. The computer has to be programmed to provide appropriate feedback to different responses, those that are correct, those that are incorrect but anticipated, and those that are incorrect but unanticipated. For lessons in which students gather information, the author makes decisions about how to guide the learner. A CAI design procedure includes a step for addressing all types of interactive sequences.

Human factors.   Another critical component in the development of CAI is the interaction of a person with a machine. Learners do not automatically know how to get around in a lesson, to go forward, to review, or to skip sections. They do not automatically know when they have reached the last display, or what options are available to them at that time. Therefore another important step in CAI design, which is not present in the systems approach, is to assess human factors requirements and to accommodate them.

Management. An additional step in CAI design not present in the systems approach is a decision about locus of control of the flow of instruction. It is not present in traditional programmed instruction because the sequence of instruction is automatically fixed by the lesson designers and the pace automatically controlled by the learners. Every learner goes through the same instructional materials in the same sequence. In CAI, both sequence and pace can be controlled by designer, learner, or some combination. Instruction can follow multiple paths, contingent on a student's performance. It can be individualized according to cognitive level, difficulty of exercises, standard of performance, and even instructional technique. Thus management decisions also constitute an important step in CAI development.

Environmental factors. Computer systems for CAI vary widely in physical equipment. Display screens may be monochrome or color, low or high resolution. Pointing capabilities and digitized sound may or may not be available. Lessons may be intended for use in quiet or noisy places, in the work place, in regular or in CAI-specific classrooms. Authors need some assessment of these environmental factors before making design decisions.

Production procedures. Producing a CAI lesson involves generating a computer program as well as designing it. When technology was less sophisticated, some lesson designers did their own programming, but many turned the task over to a person with programming expertise. The lesson was planned and designed by one or more individuals and then programmed by others. Today there are so many convenient tools for lesson production that a lesson designer can produce an entire lesson without becoming a programming expert. Computer programs, called authoring systems, take care of the programming. Tools, such as authoring languages and graphics editors, are available for more experienced CAI developers who want to design lessons that are beyond the capability of authoring systems. Consequently, it is feasible to produce small segments of a lesson and evaluate and revise them before producing the entire lesson. This is particularly helpful when an author lacks experience with the computer as an instructional medium.

It should not be necessary to develop a lesson in the order in which it will finally be shown to the learners. In CAI, it does not make sense to generate directions before you are certain of the lesson content and what a learner needs to be told. It is not reasonable to try to anticipate every type of error students might make and write feedback for every one if you don't know whether they're going to make those errors.

An adequate procedure for CAI allows an author to modify a lesson as it is being developed if student trials indicate that revisions are needed. It should be possible to test and revise, or even discard modules of instruction before a lesson is completed. It should also be possible to generate and test the core of a lesson before the introductory materials are developed. Simply stated, the procedure should be flexible enough to allow for ongoing additions and modifications.

PROPOSAL OF A MODEL FOR CAI: THE THREE-PHASE PLAN

Steinberg (1984) proposes an instructional design procedure for CAI that, with one exception, attempts to accommodate the above specifications, for a broad range of goals, learners, subject matter domains, tasks, and instructional techniques. She proposes a two-level, three-phase procedure; hence the name, the Three-Phase Plan. With the addition of the step, assess environmental factors, the plan meets all the desired criteria (see Figure 3.4).

Three phases, two levels.   Lesson design occurs in three phases. In the first phase, before production begins, initial plans are made for the lesson as a whole. In the second phase, units of instruction are designed, produced, evaluated, and revised using the Ripple Plan. The purpose of the third phase is to complete the lesson. Preliminary decisions made during Phase I are evaluated and completed during Phase III. Needed displays are added (e.g., introductory displays), the individual units are integrated, and the lesson as a whole is evaluated and revised.

The steps in Phase I and Phase III address the lesson as a whole and occur at the Lesson Level. The procedures in Phase II relate to designing and producing individual modules or units of instruction and occur at the Unit Level of design. Thus, lesson design occurs in three phases and at two levels.

First phase.   The first phase is devoted to initial planning. It includes many of the components of the systems approach but expands on their meanings as noted previously. The components are: a characterization of the target population, formulation of overall goals, task analyses, designa-

THE THREE – PHASE PLAN

I. Initial Planning: Lesson Level

    Characterize the target population.

    Formulate the overall goals.

    Analyze the task.

    Designate the prerequisite skills.

    Generate initial set of evaluation measures.

    Assess environmental factors

II. Ripple Plan: Unit Level

    Generate the presentation: program and evaluate.

    Expand response judging and feedback; program and evaluate.

    Make human factors and management decisions; program and evaluate.

III. Completing The Lesson: Lesson Level

    Complete management and human factors decisions.

    Generate introductory displays.

    Generate concluding displays.

    Complete initial set of evaluation measures.

    Evaluate and revise.

    Document.

    Plan maintenance.

FIG. 3.4.   The Three-Phase Plan. *Note.* From *Teaching Computers to Teach* (p. 21) by E. R. Steinberg, 1984, Hillsdale, NJ: Lawrence Erlbaum Associates. Copyright 1984 by Lawrence Erlbaum Associates. Adapted by permission.

tion of prerequisite skills, development of an initial set of evaluation measures, and assessment of environmental factors.

Second phase.   Design and production of the instruction per se occur in the second phase. Design begins at the heart of instruction, by generating the presentation. It includes not only the text, but visuals, question-response-feedback sequences and human factors information. According to the Ripple Plan, units (modules) of instruction are designed and pro-grammed and also tested with students. Based on the results of such early trials, a designer evaluates and modifies the presentation, adds informative feedback for commonly occurring errors, and designs supplementary instruction if needed. Management decisions about advancing the student through the lesson are also made.

The size of the instructional units and the frequency of the evaluate-and-revise cycles vary with the experience of the designers. A designer need not be limited to a single instructional technique nor to a single management plan for all units.

Third phase.   After all of the modules are completed, several loose ends remain to be tied at the Lesson Level. The instructional modules have to fit together to make a comprehensive whole. Steps in the third phase include final decisions about the flow of instruction (management and human factors decisions), production of introductory and concluding displays, completion or revision of evaluation measures, and evaluation and revision of the lesson as a whole. Two additional steps are documentation of the lesson and plans for maintaining it. Sometimes programming errors do not occur until after hundreds of users have studied a lesson. In addition, if the content of a lesson is subject to change (e.g., census data), plans must be made for updating it.

Benefits

Major benefits of following the Three-Phase Plan are its flexibility and its adaptability to the unique features of CAI. It addresses all six components of the CAI framework and fosters attention to their interaction. The plan enables authors to modify lessons as needed and thus helps them maintain internal consistency among the components of the framework. The Three-Phase Plan is applicable to a broad range of subject matter domains, target populations, and instructional techniques. It builds on the best features of known instructional design procedures.

SUMMARY

A systematic procedure is essential for producing CAI. It helps authors produce an effective lesson within a limited time frame. A CAI-specific procedure synthesizes applicable features of known development systems and the special needs of CAI lesson development. The Three-Phase Plan is such a procedure.

The next topic to be discussed is the instructional presentation itself. Presentations include verbal information, interactions, human factors, and display considerations. These are the subjects of discussion in the following four chapters.

NOTES

PLATO® and NovaNET® were developed by the University of Illinois. PLATO® is a service mark of Control Data Corporation. NovaNET® is a service mark of University Communications, Inc.

Chapter 4

INSTRUCTIONAL PRESENTATIONS

Presenting instruction is more than merely presenting information. Instruction also helps students learn and remember. Figure 4.1a, for example, presents information but Figure 4.1b presents instruction. While it is apparent that there is more information in Figure 4.1b, the significant difference between the displays is the content rather than the amount of information. Figure 4.1b prepares readers to better understand the message by activating relevant knowledge. The message encourages them to recall their own past experience in order to make the new information more meaningful. It is this assistance to learning that distinguishes Figure 4.1b from Figure 4.1a and makes it instruction rather than just a presentation.

Instruction includes visual as well as verbal aids to learning. Figures 4.2a and 4.2b, for example, present the identical information. But two visual techniques, the layout of the display and the use of capitalization, in Figure 4.2b draw attention to the critical concepts.

Verbal aids to instruction are discussed in this chapter. Visual aids are the topic of Chapter 7.

SIMILARITIES AND DIFFERENCES BETWEEN INSTRUCTION AND PRESENTATIONS

In many ways instruction is like a presentation. In other ways it is different. Let us first consider the similarities.

When a man or woman is admitted to a jail, all the outward symbols of personal identity have been taken away from that person. A set of loosely fitting jail clothes is given to that person in place of his or her street clothing. A watch and other jewelry are locked up and familiar items such as a belt, shoe laces, and cigarette lighter are often taken away.

Often a new prisoner is questioned and booked in full view of other people including other prisoners and jail personnel. The search procedure is usually very thorough and embarrassing to the prisoner. Chances are that this is conducted under semi-private conditions.

The new prisoner quickly finds that he or she can no longer direct his or her own life.

FIG. 4.1a. A presentation of information. (From CAI lesson, Jail Climate. Copyright 1988 by R. O. Walker and C. J. Flammang. Reprinted by permission.)

If you have ever been a hospital patient, you probably remember your feelings of helplessness and depression. Your surroundings were new, unfamiliar, and made you feel uncomfortable. You were forced to adjust to a new routine. You were totally at the mercy of others for your well-being and for daily care. Even for obtaining the most routine things such as food and water, you were obliged to depend on someone else.

Or perhaps you have experienced the difficult transition from a private civilian to a military man or woman. You might remember the experience as being confusing, embarrassing and unpleasant.

Undoubtedly you were questioned about personal matters in front of other people, given a semi-private physical examination, issued new, perhaps ill-fitting uniforms, and told to follow the orders of complete strangers.

Now, try to imagine what it feels like to be arrested and admitted to a jail.

When a man or woman is admitted to a jail, all the outward symbols of personal identity have been taken away from that person. A set of loosely fitting jail clothes is given to that person in place of his or her street clothing. A watch and other jewelry are locked up and familiar items such as a belt, shoe laces, and cigarette lighter are often taken away.

Often a new prisoner is questioned and booked in full view of other people including other prisoners and jail personnel. The search procedure is usually very thorough and embarrassing to the prisoner. Chances are that this is conducted under semi-private conditions.

The new prisoner quickly finds that he or she can no longer direct his or her own life.

FIG. 4.1b. An instructional version of Figure 4.1a. (From CAI lesson, Jail Climate. Copyright 1988 by R. O. Walker and C. J. Flammang. Reprinted by permission.)

```
  The basic tools for creating and controlling the jail
climate are (1) the attitudes of the correctional officers
and (2) the interactions of officers and inmates.


  Press - F10 - to continue, or press - F6 - to review.
```

FIG. 4.2a. A verbal message without visual aids. (From CAI lesson, Jail Climate. Copyright 1988 by R. O. Walker and C. J. Flammang. Reprinted by permission.)

```
                                      creating
  The BASIC TOOLS for                    &
                                      controlling

                  the jail climate are:

                  1.   ATTITUDES of correctional officers

                  2.   INTERACTIONS of officers and inmates


         Press - F10 - to continue, or press - F6 - to review.
```

FIG. 4.2b. The message in Figure 4.2a with visual aids. (From CAI lesson, Jail Climate. Copyright 1988 by R. O. Walker and C. J. Flammang. Reprinted by permission.)

Similarities

Good writing is a hallmark of both presentations and instruction. The text is understandable. Illustrations add interest and provide supplementary information.

While there are no specific guidelines for writing text that apply to all subject matter and diverse student populations (Thomas, Stahl, & Swanson, 1984), a few general recommendations exist. Active voice is easier to understand than passive and short sentences are easier than long ones. Vocabulary and syntax should be appropriate for the intended learners. A good presentation makes it possible for a reader to devote full attention to understanding the content rather than to deciphering convoluted sentence structure (see Figures 4.3).

Good presentations make accurate assumptions about the background knowledge of viewers or listeners. Consider a presentation about the Iditarod, the 1,000 mile dog-sled race from Anchorage to Nome. Children know that there are different kinds of dogs and that they must be cared for by someone. They are therefore able to understand a text that discusses the

```
In this lesson you will learn to solve problems
dealing with solving simple quadrilateral shapes
for their area.  It is not the purpose of this
lesson to teach trigonometric functions, so the
necessary dimensions will be given to you.
```

FIG. 4.3a.   Example of a confusing message.

```
In this lesson you will learn to compute the
areas of simple quadrilaterals.
```

FIG. 4.3b.   An understandable and simplified version of Figure 4.3a.

selection and care of dogs for the race. However, a discussion of the special problems of women participants will not be as meaningful to them. The same is true of good instruction, for as Anderson (1977) so aptly puts it, "Text is gobbledygook unless the learner possesses an interpretive framework to breathe meaning into it" (p. 423).

Understandable presentations are well organized and are displayed in accordance with good design techniques. The same is true of acceptable instruction.

Myths About Presentations

Perhaps because of the similarities between presentations and instruction, some people think that presenting is equivalent to teaching. Tell the students what they need to know and they will learn. Anybody who has ever taught, whatever the subject matter and whatever the educational level, knows that it doesn't work that way. While it is undoubtedly true that "there is no viable substitute for well written, clearly organized prose as far as maximizing the facilitative effects of written discourse" (Thomas et al., 1984, p. 205), well written presentations are not necessarily sufficient for learning. If that were true, people could learn everything they needed to know by reading and reading would be the only subject we would have to teach.

There is a also a myth about computer-presented instruction (Call-Himwich & Steinberg, 1977). Just present the information on the computer; students will be so highly motivated by the computer that they will learn. Students may be highly motivated, particularly by game formats, but they will not necessarily learn all that is intended. They certainly will not be motivated if the material is boring or hard to understand. Boring text is no more interesting on the computer screen than it is on paper.

Simply put, presenting is not equivalent to instructing. What students "can learn" from well organized, well written presentations or exciting computer simulations is not equivalent to what they actually learn.

Differences

One difference between instruction and presentation is that instruction prepares students for learning. Instruction helps them select the information to which they should attend when there is simply too much for them to hold in temporary memory. Instruction also prepares students by reminding them about what they already know that will help them learn the new material.

Unlike presentation, instruction incorporates aids that help students understand. Diagrams and headings serve as organizational aids to comprehension. Typographical cues such as different fonts or sizes of type clarify relationships between elements of the text. Questions inserted in text help students engage in meaningful processing and provide informational feedback to correct misconceptions.

Understanding is only one aspect of learning. Remembering is also essential. A person may listen to a well organized, clearly presented lecture or read a well-written textbook and understand it well. However, he will not remember very much of what he heard or read if he fails to apply some strategies for remembering. Not all students know how to learn every kind of subject matter. They may be very good in psychology but need some help with strategies for learning and remembering physics. Instruction provides this kind of assistance.

CAI-Specific Issues

The basic techniques for instructional presentations are also relevant to CAI. In addition, CAI requires special strategies to accommodate its unique characteristics.

Passage length.   The length of a passage is of special concern in CAI. When talking, the number of words used in an explanation is not restricted by space. In the classroom, an instructor may discuss a subject at some length, constrained only by time and his ability to maintain students' attention. Textbook writers may also present extensive discussions, limited only by publishers' page restrictions. In CAI, it is not feasible to present a great deal of verbal discourse. For some unexplained reason people read more slowly when text is presented on a display screen. Furthermore, students do not tolerate a computer program that is essentially an electronic page-turner. Perhaps this is because they are still unaccustomed to using a computer program for extended reading. It may be due to the expectation that a computer program should be highly interactive.

Control of display.   An additional presentation issue in CAI is control of the text. Text can be displayed on the computer screen one line, one sentence, or one group of sentences at a time, under either the learner's or the computer's control. Each of these features can enhance learning or interfere with it.

Computer presentation of text can facilitate learning by providing focus. This occurs when the computer lesson presents limited amounts of text on the screen and then waits for the learner to press a key to continue reading. This arrangement simulates a pause during oral communication, which indicates the end of a single thought.

Total computer control of the pacing of text presentation can interfere with learning. Slow readers may be unable to finish. Learners who are ready to continue reading before the computer presents the next section of text will be easily distracted and lose continuity.

Researchers have studied the efficacy of controlling the rate of presenting text to increase one's reading rate. Results suggest that this is not a useful approach (Gillingham, 1988).

Interdisplay continuity.   In CAI, students sense a lack of continuity when proceeding from one display to another. Therefore, concepts, or at least paragraphs, should not be split up and presented on two displays.

Other issues.   Other special issues in CAI presentations include interactions between computers and humans, the potential for dynamically creating figures and diagrams, and the opportunity to individualize instructional presentations. Interactions, displays, and adaptive instruction are discussed at some length in Chapters 5, 7, and 8, respectively.

INSTRUCTIONAL AIDS TO LEARNING AND REMEMBERING

Theories of learning identify numerous factors that promote learning. Among those cited in earlier chapters are prior knowledge, experience solving problems in a given domain, knowledge about when and how to draw on knowledge and/or experience, and the use of learning strategies such as making inferences or keeping track of one's progress toward a goal. Theories of instruction suggest ways to apply this information to instruction. Among the suggestions noted earlier are the following: gain a learner's attention, activate relevant knowledge already in memory, draw attention to salient features, induce meaningful processing, provide a context for learning, provide feedback, adapt instruction to developmental level, include strategies for learning, and avoid information overload.

Applicability to CAI.   Much of the research reported here comes from studies of verbal learning. Much of it is based on laboratory studies that may or may not be entirely applicable to real world classroom instruction. Moreover, the generalizability of the results to CAI and other technology-driven instruction has not been tested (Hannafin & Hughes, 1986). The question, then, is why bother with it? There are three reasons. First, there is very little CAI-specific research, so results of research in other media provide a reasonable starting point. Second, it helps CAI authors avoid inappropriate application of research results from other disciplines. Developers of CAI who seek a theoretical basis for their presentations tend to generalize results beyond the degree warranted. For example, lesson authors may automatically state behavioral objectives at the beginning of every lesson even though research indicates that behavioral objectives offer no advantage for certain kinds of students and tasks. Authors who are aware of the limitations of research results are more likely to apply them where they will be instructionally effective. Finally, CAI authors often consider only one instructional factor, such as activating relevant knowledge, without considering other components in the CAI framework, such as appropriate computer implementation. In the name of preparing students for instruction, they sometimes present such an extensive amount of review or background information before beginning the lesson that they lose students' attention. Thus they negate the potential value of their introduction.

Preinstruction

Instruction in new material is not the first step in the instructional process. Attention-gaining and orienting activities precede instruction per se.

Gaining attention.   Preinstruction begins with getting learners' attention. In many CAI lessons, authors attract attention with attractive graphics or animations. Some lessons play a content-related tune, such as Home On The Range for a lesson about the old West. Graphics and sound are not the only means of gaining attention in CAI. Verbal messages can also be effective attention getters, particularly if they pique a learner's curiosity as in the "Introduction to Jail Climate" in Figure 4.4.

Preparing for learning.   The next step after gaining attention is to prepare students for learning. The purposes of preparatory activities are to

```
┌─────────────────────────────────────────────────────────────┐
│                       INTRODUCTION                          │
│                                                             │
│  This program is about something which cannot be purchased or│
│  installed in the jail.  It can't even be seen although it is│
│  critical to the effective and efficient operation of a jail.│
│                                                             │
│      Press -F10- to continue, or press -F6- to review.      │
│                                                             │
└─────────────────────────────────────────────────────────────┘
```

FIG. 4.4.   A message that piques curiosity. (From CAI lesson, Jail Climate. Copyright 1988 by R. O. Walker and C. J. Flammang. Reprinted by permission.)

focus attention selectively, to activate relevant knowledge, to alert students to what is coming, to modify their perception of what is important, and to provide a framework for bridging the gap between old information and new. The techniques for implementing these activities include statements of objectives or goals, overviews, pretests, and organizers. Some of these techniques have theoretical underpinnings and others are intuitively appealing. Some orienting aids are facilitative, but under limited conditions. Some prestrategies are not facilitative, while still others may actually interfere with learning.

Orienting Aids and Activities

Although orienting activities are of limited value, they are discussed here in detail. CAI authors who are aware of the benefits and limitations of these techniques are more likely to use them to advantage rather than dismiss them entirely or apply them incorrectly.

Activating relevant knowledge.   As pointed out in Chapter 2, what a person already knows strongly affects what he learns. A person learns better if he can relate the new material to cognitive structures previously stored in long-term memory. However, that knowledge must be activated if it is to be useful in the acquisition of new knowledge (Bransford, 1979). A review of relevant formulas from trigonometry helps students understand the solutions to physics problems. A reminder of Skinner's principles of operant conditioning helps students understand principles of programmed instruction.

Advance organizers.   Advance organizers were proposed by Ausubel (1968) as a way of helping students relate new knowledge to old. An advance organizer is general, abstract, inclusive information into which students can integrate new knowledge. The concept is based on the theory that new knowledge is subsumed under broader, more inclusive knowledge in memory. The purpose of an advance organizer is to foster this process. As such it provides a structure to which new and detailed, easily forgotten information can be anchored.

An effective advance organizer indicates how the new knowledge is relevant to existing knowledge. If there are similarities between the known and to-be-learned knowledge, the advance organizer compares and contrasts them. Although usually verbal, graphic organizers also fit within the concept, provided they represent a truly inclusive framework and not merely a perceptual one (Ausubel, Novak, & Hanesian, 1978).

Consider the following task for elementary school children. Suppose that in their study of animals of Africa, they are expected to remember characteristics of a camel. A written description might include the following:

> The camel has special eyelids that cover its eyes but still allow some light to enter. The camel can close its nasal passages. It has very strong teeth. It has a lot of hair around its ears and even has hairy pads on its chest and knees.

A child might find it difficult to remember these seemingly disconnected facts about a camel's face and body. A picture can help, but it cannot convey all of this information in a way that is easily observable. However, a reminder about desert conditions and the implications for survival might be a useful advance organizer. Deserts are known to have hot blowing sand and blinding sun. These conditions must affect the bodies of animals who live there. If pupils are reminded of this information, the unusual characteristics of camels make more sense and are more easily understood and remembered. Their eyelids must protect from the blinding sun. The hairy knee and chest pads protect from the hot sand when camels kneel down, and so on.

Do advance organizers really help learners? Yes and no. Barnes and Clawson (1975) examined 32 studies and found that in 20 of them advance organizers did not result in significantly better performance. These equivocal results can be partially explained by assimilation theory (cf. Mayer, 1975). The effectiveness of an advance organizer is a consequence of its role in (1) activating relevant knowledge, that is, bringing it into working memory, and (2) providing the necessary concepts that help a learner form a relationship (integrate) between old information and new. If a learner spontaneously activates relevant knowledge from long-term memory, or is able to use available knowledge directly without further integration, an advance organizer is not likely to provide any real facilitation (Mayer, 1979).

To summarize, advance organizers are helpful if implemented under appropriate conditions. A CAI simulation of a medical case provides empirical evidence that supports this contention.

Advance organizers and CAI.   Medical students frequently find it difficult to diagnose clinical problems. Although they have the knowledge that is needed, they do not apply what they know. Krahn and Blanchaer (1986) generated a computer simulation of a medical case to test the efficacy of an advance organizer to overcome this problem. They deliberately chose a relatively complex case so that a preliminary conceptual framework might be helpful. Participants were first year medical students. Half of them saw an advance organizer; half did not. Posttest results showed that students who saw the advance organizer did significantly better overall. However, on straightforward factual questions, which required no integration of knowledge, there was no significant difference between the two groups of students.

Overviews.   An overview is a condensation or summary of information that will soon be presented. Its purpose is to preview the main ideas. It differs from an advance organizer in that it does not attempt to relate the material to be learned to existing cognitive structures. Most of the available research about overviews was done in connection with one instructional medium, films (Hartley & Davies, 1976). That research indicates little evidence that overviews are effective.

We do not know whether overviews might be effective in CAI. We do know from experience that when students sit down to study a CAI lesson, they want to "do something" very soon. Lengthy introductions that require no meaningful interaction quickly lose students' attention. Students frequently just skip them. In some instances, students quit a lesson if the overview is too long.

Graphic organizers that serve as structured overviews in advance of verbal information have received "lukewarm support at best" (Hawk, McLeod, & Jonassen, 1985). Theoretically, graphic organizers should signal content structure and key concepts and should also serve as retrieval cues. There is no evidence to support this theory.

Goals and objectives.   The purpose of providing learners with goals and objectives is to alert them to what is expected of them by the end of instruction. The assumption is that students will use the information provided by goals and objectives to organize their learning activities.

For verbatim verbal information, general statements of goals significantly affect retention better than no statement at all. For these verbatim verbal tasks, there is no advantage to behavioral objectives over general statements of objectives or goals (Hamilton, 1985). For other complex tasks that require analysis, synthesis, and integration, behavioral objectives are more effective than general statements (Hartley & Davies, 1976).

Objectives are not universally facilitative. Their effectiveness varies with the instruction, the task, and learner characteristics (Hartley & Davies, 1976; Hamilton, 1985). Apparently, stating objectives fosters the process of selective attention. Objectives help students focus on critical information. Obviously, if this process is to occur, instruction has to be present that provides the information students are supposed to acquire. Students must have the skills to use the information provided by objectives. Not all students do. Behavioral objectives are more effective with average than with low ability students (Hartley & Davies, 1976) and with students who have experience using objectives (Hamilton, 1985). Finally, there is no benefit in stating objectives if the task is so simple that students do not require this type of assistance.

Goals, objectives, and CAI.   CAI is often used for technical training where performance or behavioral objectives can be precisely stated. For example, "An electrician must be able to correctly position all of the legally required outlets in a room," or "A student of automotive mechanics must be able, without reference to a manual, to name all of the parts of a cooling system." Lessons of this kind can have as many as 10 to 15 objectives. Inexperienced authors tend to list all of the objectives at the beginning of the lesson. That is more than a student is likely to remember. When presented with three successive displays with long lists of objectives, a student is likely to ignore them, and the potential benefits of stating objectives is lost. This problem can be avoided by presenting a few objectives at a time, followed by appropriate sections of instruction.

Pretests.   Pretests, like objectives, are employed to increase students' awareness of what is expected of them and to help them organize related material. Pretests are effective mainly for students with high ability or maturity, or students who have some subject matter knowledge (Hartley & Davies, 1976). A learner who knows little or nothing about a subject lacks the knowledge needed to understand the significance of the questions in the pretest for studying the lesson. In CAI, pretests are generally used to determine whether students have the necessary prerequisite knowledge. They are also used to select the appropriate starting point in a lesson.

Filters.   Human information processing systems have limited capacities. When overloaded with information, people store only part of what they perceive in long-term memory. Students have to selectively attend to instruction when the amount of incoming information is excessive. They have to decide what information is crucial. Some designers alleviate this problem by divesting instruction of all but the simplest line drawings or the briefest verbal descriptions so that the relevant information becomes obvious. However, minimal presentations are not always possible. When instruction must involve films or complex displays or verbal descriptions, preinstruction can serve as a filter by helping learners isolate critical information (Travers, 1984).

Summary.   Preinstructional strategies facilitate learning under specific conditions. They are most likely to benefit learners if the material to be learned interacts with existing knowledge rather than when it is arbitrarily imposed. Preinstruction is likely to be most effective for meaningful rather than for rote learning (Hartley & Davies, 1976). Students' knowledge of learning strategies and familiarity with the subject matter also influence the value of preinstructional activities. Students who spontaneously invoke these strategies are not likely to find any learning advantages when these strategies are included as preinstructional activities.

Aids External to Instructional Message

Instruction includes both internal and external aids to learning. Internal aids are techniques incorporated in the instructional message per se that make it easier to learn, such as organization and structure. External aids are outside of the verbal message itself. They are activities such as directing attention, facilitating information processing, and suggesting learning strategies.

Directing attention.   It is just as important to direct and maintain attention during instruction as to gain it initially. Attention can be directed visually and CAI is a wonderful medium for this purpose. Color, geometric figures (e.g., circles and boxes), lines, arrows, and animations can all be used to highlight critical information. However, it is not only a matter of getting learners to direct their attention to this information. Instruction also helps learners understand what they are supposed to learn from looking at the designated areas of the display.

Promoting meaningful processing.   Instruction can facilitate learning by promoting meaningful information processing. An effective way to do so is to present questions.

Adjunct questions have been extensively researched and reported in the prose learning literature. They are questions that are inserted before (prequestions) or after (postquestions) sections of text. The evidence is overwhelming that adjunct questions facilitate learning (Anderson &

Biddle, 1975). Both prequestions and postquestions affect performance on subsequent tests in which the items are repeats of those inserted. Postquestions, but not prequestions, also improve performance on new test items. These differences in effects can be attributed to the learning processes they promote (Hamilton, 1985). Prequestions lead students to selectively attend to the specific information needed to answer the questions. Postquestions, on the other hand, promote both specific review of questioned materials and general review processes. The general review includes "material in the same topico-spatial areas as the target area questioned" (Hamilton, 1985).

Computer managed adjunct questions.   In ordinary classroom instruction, particularly college lecture courses, it is not possible to insert questions and require all students to answer them. Furthermore, it is not possible to force students to answer questions that appear in textbooks. However, if questions are presented on computers, students can be required to answer them. Given the potential benefits of both adjunct questions and computer presentation of instruction, Anderson and his colleagues (1975) implemented an experimental computer-assisted study management system (CAISMS) for a college level economics course.

Each student signed on to a computer terminal and received an eight to ten page reading assignment in the textbook. After reading the assignment he returned to the terminal to take a short quiz. If the student answered 75% of the questions correctly, he was given the next assignment; otherwise he was told to review and then required to retake the quiz. Students were required to complete all of the quizzes before taking each full length examination. Grades on the quizzes did not count toward the final grade.

Students who participated in the CAISMS project scored significantly higher on achievement tests than students in a control group. The rationale for this program is that it would cause students to study more systematically and efficiently. Indeed, in answers to questionnaires, students reported that they benefited from CAISMS because they studied more regularly and the program helped them understand the important points.

Including strategies for learning.   If learners are not likely to know how to carry out a learning task, instruction should communicate in an unambiguous manner methods or procedures for accomplishing it (Landa, 1983). For example, instruction in cognitive processes is frequently ambiguous. Learners may understand what they are supposed to do but not how they are supposed to do it. They need a description of a process as well as a prescription for how to carry it out, whether the prescription is a method for general use or a task-specific procedure. To illustrate this point, Landa (p. 183) cites a textbook that had as one of its objectives teaching legal thinking to high school students. "To answer the question raised in a problem or case, first read it carefully. Be sure you understand the question. Then analyze the situation, determine the rule of law involved, and reach a decision (p. XI)." The directions do not tell students what it means to read carefully or how they know if they understand the question or how they can analyze the situation. Even if a student were to generate a flow chart of these directions, he would still not know how to implement the necessary cognitive processes.

One helpful strategy is to tell students what to do under some prespecified set of conditions by providing rules of the "if . . . then" variety. In situations where there is more than one way to accomplish a goal, instruction might suggest, "If condition X exists, you may use action A."

Others (Brown, Armbruster, & Baker, 1986; Dansereau, 1985) note the importance of teaching not only strategies themselves but also why they are effective. Instruction should also include information about where they are applicable.

It is also possible to teach students general techniques that facilitate learning, such as imaging, making inferences, and elaborating. Computer graphics can be employed to "image" for students, as the work of Hatasa (1986) does for Japanese hiragana (see Figure 2.7b).

One of the big differences between good and poor readers is the speed with which they make inferences and elaborations. There is indirect evidence that elaborations help retention and that instruction can influence the amount of elaboration (Reder, 1980). In CAI, it is possible to offer help with these learning strategies and make it available for students who want it or need it. We do not know if students would follow computer-suggested strategies. However, given that students are accustomed to following directions and answering questions presented by the computer, it is not an unreasonable proposal.

Including dictionaries and background.   Two aids, which are possible in CAI, but which have not yet been researched, are online dictionaries and background information. It should be possible to make definitions and some background information available, but it is not known if students would use them or whether it would significantly affect either learning or attitude.

Aids Internal to Instructional Message

There are many techniques for making instruction easier for students to understand. These include drawing on relationships to knowledge already in memory, being explicit, organizing and structuring text, avoiding information overload, and applying content- and subject matter-specific instructional strategies.

Focusing on relationships: Models and analogies. New concepts are sometimes clarified by the use of models or analogies. Physical or visual models are frequently employed, particularly in mathematics and science. Like other instructional presentations, models must be used with care. Students may be able to manipulate the model but not understand its meaning (Steinberg & Anderson, 1973). Learners may understand the model but not its relevance for applying the principles. A number line, for example, is frequently used to help students learn how to add and subtract signed numbers. In one computer-presented lesson students computed sums and differences satisfactorily when using the number line, but failed when the number line was unavailable. They did not understand the relationships between their manipulations on the number line and the computational procedures (Tatsuoka & Eddins, 1985). Those relationships had not been made explicit in instruction, and the students did not discover them.

Analogies are also employed to build a bridge between that which is known and that which is to be learned. Analogies can help learners understand a concept; they can also lead to misconceptions. A perfect analogy is one in which a person can reason easily in the source domain, and in which all and only all of the operations of the target domain are represented in the source domain (Rumelhart & Norman, 1981). Consider instruction in fractions. Students can reason very well about cutting a pie or a candy bar (source domain) into equal parts. It is therefore not hard for them to understand the concept of unit fractions (target domain) such as 1/5 in terms of dividing a pie into five equal parts. However, the analogy is not viable for multiplying fractions. Who ever heard of multiplying pieces of pie? The operation, multiplication, can be implemented in the target domain, fractions, but it is not represented in the source domain, pies.

If an operation is needed in the target domain but not in the source domain, misunderstandings can occur. For example, when students first encounter CAI, they frequently enter an answer to a question and then just wait for the computer program to judge the response. They don't realize that they have to communicate to the computer that they have completed their response. They are making an analogy to learning in a classroom, where they do not have to tell the instructor when they are done responding. The instructor knows they are finished when they stop talking.

Consider another example. The flow of water in a pipe is sometimes used as an analogy for the flow of electricity. The problem is that water can flow through valves that are partially open but there is no partial flow of electricity in electric circuits. Current is either on or off. If water flow is used as an analogy, learners may erroneously attribute all of the characteristics of the flow of water to the flow of electricity.

The text in Figure 4.1b is an example of a good analogy. The target learners for this lesson are participants in a police training institute. They are likely to be familiar with one of the source domains. Most of the men and women have been in either a hospital or the military or have been close to someone with these experiences. A large percentage of the elements in the target domain, that is being jailed, are present in the source domain, being hospitalized.

A perfect analogy is hard to find. If an analogy is used, it should be limited to those aspects that are applicable. Moreover, its limitations should be made explicit to learners.

Being explicit.   Explicitness in instruction has various meanings. To be explicit may mean to be unambiguous about the meaning of a passage, to make explicit that which is implicit. In other situations it means to be explicit about how to accomplish a task or about the relationships between components of a task, or about the relationships between a task or concept to be learned and one or more already known (Marshall & Glock, 1978). For some learners, explicit instruction is instruction that keeps learners informed of exactly what they are supposed to do.

Most students require explicit instruction to learn specific concepts, principles, or rules. It cannot be assumed that students will learn general principles or procedures by merely participating in some relevant learning situation. Linn & Dalbey (1985) found that explicit instruction strongly affected the outcomes in introductory computer programming classes at the middle school level. Students in classrooms with explicit instruction in design skills outperformed those in classrooms where instruction was not explicit. Even the most able students, who are sometimes thought of as likely to learn despite instruction, benefited from explicit instruction.

Another example of the effectiveness of explicit instruction is its successful application with mildly handicapped high school students and a computer simulation of health problems (Woodward, Carnine, & Gersten, 1988). Students studied a unit in health, in two parts, over a period of 12 days. During the first part, the 30 students were instructed by "effective teaching strategies." For the second part the students were divided into two groups. One group worked on traditional enrichment and applications activities, and the other group worked on a computer simulation. Before students were allowed to try solving the simulated health problems on their own computers, they were given two kinds of explicit instruction. The teachers modeled each component of problem solving, and also provided guided practice in a group setting with only one microcomputer. Test results showed significant superiority for the computer simulation group. Simulation students even showed superior performance over nonhandicapped students from regular health classes. This "suggests the extent to which explicit strategy instruction can be successful in teaching problem solving skills" (p. 82).

The arguments for nonexplicit instruction using the discovery method are that students will learn better and gain deeper insights by "doing." Claims for *unguided* discovery learning lack empirical support. It has been claimed, for example, that children who learn to program in the LOGO language in a Piagetian type of exploratory, natural environment will acquire various intellectual skills (e.g., problem solving) and will learn powerful ideas of mathematics (Papert, 1980). There is no empirical evidence to substantiate the claims that LOGO by itself can accomplish such goals without some explicit instructional or teacher-related components (Moursund, 1983-84).

Discovery learning need not be totally undirected. Appropriate explicit instruction can greatly enhance the benefits of discovery learning. Learning LOGO, for instance, need be neither totally spontaneous nor tightly controlled by explicit instruction. Leron (1985) notes that it is possible to provide guidance that helps children acquire the desired skills and ideas without sacrificing the personally meaningful and exploratory learning. Leron proposes that this can be accomplished by "partially directing activities and prompting students to reflect on their results." These ideas seem appropriate for discovery learning in other content areas as well.

Organizing and structuring text.   Sometimes an author must present a fair amount of verbal material in a CAI lesson. Gillingham's (1988) review of research suggests three aspects of structure and organization that affect learning and remembering. They are: (1) superordination; (2) topic relatedness; and (3) cohesion.

A superordinate sentence (usually the topic sentence) explicitly states the main idea of the accompanying text. Research indicates that adults learn the top-level or superordinate ideas of text first and filter out peripheral information. They are less likely to forget superordinate information (Meyer, 1977; 1985). Although Meyer's studies involve recall of factual information (Carter, 1977), research with technical prose also reveals the importance of stating the main idea, and stating it first (Kieras, 1982).

Topic relatedness refers to the idea that text is expected to be on a single topic. It is particularly important in technical prose.

Cohesion is the connectedness of prose. Prose is most readily learned and remembered if writers follow some sort of plan and signal this plan to readers (Meyer, 1977). Writers might, for instance, indicate that a problem-solution plan is being used by writing, "Two problems are evident. . . . " Readers expect these types of connective ties (Gillingham, 1988). The implication for CAI is that it is counterproductive to display text one sentence at a time because doing so may interfere with understanding the relatedness of the text.

Learners' characteristics interact with the structure of text. There is a positive relationship between a reader's ability to use top-level structures and the ease of comprehension of the prose as well as of retention (Hamilton, 1985). Further, if learners spontaneously search for main ideas, structural techniques are not necessarily facilitative (Carter, 1977).

Sequencing subject matter. Analysis of the structure of subject matter aids in determining the best ways to sequence instruction and to show the interrelationships among components (Reigeluth, Merrill, & Bunderson, 1978). The most common analysis of content structure is Gagné's hierarchical analysis, which deals with learning-prerequisite relationships. A student must be able to do "A" before he or she can do "B." A different way of structuring content is by showing superordinate/coordinate/subordinate relationships among the concepts. Elaboration theory (Reigeluth & Stein, 1983) proposes a pattern of instruction that moves from simple to complex, from concrete to abstract. Begin with a few general, simple, and fundamental ideas called an epitome. Follow with several levels of elaboration, as appropriate for the learner. Then summarize and synthesize to relate and integrate the individual ideas.

Avoiding information overload. Learning is difficult if not impossible when the amount of instruction is more than learners can process. In lectures it is not uncommon for instructors to talk without pausing to interact with learners. So much information is presented that students cannot possibly keep it all in short-term memory or assimilate it quickly enough to store it in long-term memory. Some students get very little out of lectures. Others cope with the problem of overload by taking notes without trying to assimilate the information at the time it is transmitted. Travers (1984) addresses the problem more forcefully:

> All information systems respond in some way to overload. A telephone system, when subjected to overload, handles some calls and gives a busy signal to others. The human system has several ways of handling overload. When the human is under pressure to take in more information than the system can handle, the common response is for there to be a total breakdown in the reception and use of information (p. 119).

The problem of information overload can be very serious in CAI. Some developers present one display of information after another in book-like fashion. In some instances they occasionally insert a single question, but it makes so little demand on processing the information it does little to help retention. Some authors simply present a display full of information (see Figure 4.5) and expect students to be prepared to answer questions about it. This is not instruction.

In CAI there are several ways of avoiding information overload. For the example in Figure 4.5, the vocabulary might be presented in groups of three. Questions can follow each group. For complex topics that include many concepts, the lesson might allow a learner to decide when to advance

Study the following list of Igbo names and their meanings so that you can do the activity that follows after you press NEXT.

NAME	MEANING of NAME
udene	vulture
unbaja	container used for certain type of sacrifice, usually thrown away after use
anyawu	one who is as beautiful as rising or setting sun
nkpakugha	dust bin
nwaba	father's pet
adaku	a child that is complete, child born in wealth
ezenma	queen of beauty
ugagbe	that which reflects beauty as a mirror
uli	a natural beauty spot such as a mole
ezenwa	most kingly among children
obiagelo	one who comes to enjoy life
ugo	eagle, kind of birds
unwala	tree reddish in color, tall, straight, stately, and outstanding in the forest
ejime	first in a pair of twins
agiliga	second in a pair of twins
apara	he who comes and goes
iweobi	anger of the heart

Press -NEXT-

FIG. 4.5.   Example of information overload. (From CAI lesson, Welcome to Africa. Copyright 1979 by Board of Trustees of the University of Illinois. Reprinted by permission.)

from one concept to another. Another way to avoid overload is to ask questions of varying cognitive complexity after each concept, or after several related ones are presented.

Of course, one of the necessary decisions is how to segment the information. If it is divided into informational units that are too small, the learner may get a fragmented picture of the overall content. On the other hand, if units of information are too large, learners are likely to remember very little.

Applying content-specific strategies.   Presentation techniques for some types of content have been extensively investigated. Summaries are available elsewhere and will not be repeated here. For example, Tennyson and Park (1980) review the extensive literature about teaching concepts. Frederiksen (1984) presents a lengthy review of instruction in problem solving.

In addition, there are techniques for teaching topics in specific subject matter, such as reading, mathematics, foreign languages, and science. CAI offers a medium for the application of some of the well known techniques and for the development of new ones where old strategies are not satisfactory.

SUMMARY

Characteristics that make good verbal presentations are also present in quality instruction. The difference between instruction and presentation is that instruction also includes aids to learning. Preinstruction gains attention and prepares students for learning. Instruction is explicit and sequenced and structured to aid remembering as well as learning. Analogies, models, and subject-specific techniques are applied where appropriate. Information processing is fostered. To be effective, these techniques should be appropriate for the tasks and the target population.

Additional implications of this research for CAI are the need to include frequent questions that require meaningful processing, to take care not to fragment the displays of related information, to be judicious in the use of visual techniques intended to direct and focus attention, and to avoid information overload.

Quality instructional presentations and accompanying questions are necessary but not usually sufficient for learning. Also needed are interactions between students and the CAI lessons, that is, question-response-feedback sequences. Interactive aspects of instruction are the topic of the next chapter.

Chapter 5

INTERACTIONS

Interaction is a key feature of CAI. Advertisements often tout their lessons by proclaiming them to be highly interactive. Indeed, interactions can be a real asset to learning in many ways. Question-response-feedback sequences help learners attain higher cognitive skills as well as factual information. Students' responses to questions provide a measure of learning, a basis for diagnosing errors, and data for selecting appropriate instructional paths. Interaction in exploratory lessons enriches students' understanding by affording different perspectives and insights than those gained in computer-controlled interactions.

Interaction, however, is not synonymous with learning. Answering questions by copying information from another part of the display is interaction, but is not likely to result in learning something new. Gathering information without a plan or without understanding is interaction, but it is not learning and may even result in erroneous learning. Pressing keys to make things happen on the screen is also interaction, but not necessarily learning.

FACETS OF INTERACTION

Constituents of Interaction

Effective interaction in direct instruction involves the manipulation of three constituents: questions, responses, and computer feedback. In indirect instruction such as exploratory or experiential lessons, effective interaction includes computer guidance and feedback to student-initiated activities.

Functions of Interactions

Interactions serve two main functions in CAI. One concerns the mechanics of interacting with the computer system. The other relates to the acquisition of knowledge and skills.

Mechanics. As in any instructional mode, students need some way of communicating with the computer system. They may want the computer to move on to the next display or to erase an answer. They may want to get help or indicate that they have finished entering a response to a question and are ready to have the response judged. Students communicate this information by pressing the appropriate key or by touching a specific area on the display screen. The computer responds accordingly. These are mechanical aspects of interaction and are discussed in the next chapter.

Learning. The second function of interaction, and the focus of this chapter, is to foster learning. Interactions can be initiated either by the student or the computer system. Typically, the computer program presents questions, the learner answers, and the computer provides feedback to the learner's response.

Interactions may also be initiated by learners. A student may ask for the information she needs to solve a problem or to discover a rule or principle. In one lesson, for example, a student designs experiments to explore the principles of heredity. She selects characteristics of fruitflies to be crossed and the computer produces a generation of offspring in response to each request (see Figure 5.1). In another lesson, a student initiates interaction by "tuning" a violin. After listening to both the violin and a correctly tuned string, the student decides whether the computer should tighten or loosen the string, and continues to do so until he is satisfied that the violin is tuned.

Modes of Interaction

At present computer programs usually communicate visually. Information, both verbal and graphic, is displayed on a screen. Learners communicate by typing, touching the display screen, or pointing with a device such as a mouse.

It is possible for computer systems to communicate by speech, using tapes, speech synthesizers, and digitized speech. The disadvantage of tapes is that messages cannot be randomly accessed. If there are 25 messages on tape, and the program specifies message number 25, the program has to

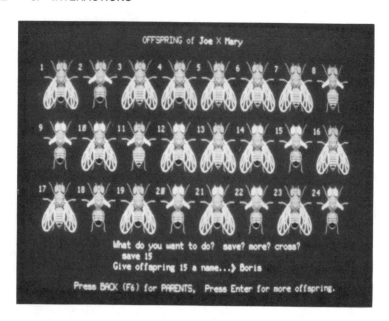

FIG. 5.1 Example of student initiated communication. (From computer-assisted lesson, Fruitflies. Courtesy Computer Teaching Corporation.)

wind past the first 24 messages. This causes an unacceptable delay for users. Speech synthesizers still do not faithfully reproduce human speech, although they have improved considerably. Voice communications adapters are now available that digitize human voice messages. Digitized speech overcomes the disadvantages of both taped messages and synthesized speech. It is normal speech and messages can be randomly accessed. These devices are so new that research into their uses is just beginning.

Question Response Feedback Sequences

In most CAI lessons interactions consist of a three-event sequence. The computer program initiates an interaction by asking a question. Students enter a response, and the lesson provides informational and/or motivational feedback. The following sections discuss each of the three elements in question response feedback interactions.

QUESTIONS

Questions are a powerful instructional tool. In one instructional technique, the Socratic dialogue, learning is guided entirely by means of a carefully planned questioning strategy, designed to lead students to "discover" the intended concepts or principle. Master teachers employ several questioning strategies. One is to ask questions that focus students' attention on relevant factors. Another strategy is to ask questions that force students to notice that their responses are irrelevant or incorrect. Still another is to get students to make predictions (Collins & Stevens, 1983).

Roles of Questions

Questions may be presented before instruction begins, during instruction, or after instruction has been completed. Questions serve different purposes at different points in the course of learning.

Before learning.   Instruction is not likely to be effective if learners are not adequately prepared. Questions presented before learning can determine whether they have the prerequisite knowledge. For example, a pretest can determine whether a student has the algebraic skills he will need to study a statistics lesson. If he does not, the lesson can either provide the needed instruction or suggest other lessons or resources.

Questions asked before learning can also serve as a placement device. If a pretest reveals that a student has previously learned some of the content of a lesson, the program can allow her to skip those sections. This saves time and avoids frustration and boredom. A pretest can also provide information for selecting an appropriate difficulty level in a set of practice exercises.

During learning.   Questions serve several purposes when employed during the course of instruction. They can be used to gain and maintain students' attention, to promote and monitor learning, and to foster remembering.

Questions can attract students' attention by piquing their curiosity. Using questions for this purpose is a little bit trickier in CAI than in a classroom. Suppose that in a driver education course an instructor gets students' attention by asking, "When you're driving, how do you manage to steer right down the middle of your lane?" In the classroom some students are apt to volunteer ideas. The instructor then uses these ideas as a starting point for the discussion.

It's not quite so simple in CAI. Some students might sit and stare at the terminal because they don't have any ideas or "haven't learned that yet." If students do attempt to answer, a lesson designer would find it difficult to anticipate what they would say, because supposedly they had not yet studied that material. That makes it difficult, if not impossible, for a lesson designer to prearrange a way of judging students' responses or of providing adequate feedback.

There are ways around this dilemma. One is to say, "Let's see if you're right," and then proceed with the lesson and let the student decide for himself if he was right. Another way of handling such a situation is to indicate that the question is rhetorical and the student is not expected to answer it.

Questions help students process information by focusing their attention on a critical feature of the material to be learned. For example, suppose that an author wants to emphasize that the shape of a highway sign tells you the kind of information it presents. Eight-sided signs always mean stop; triangles mean yield. To focus attention on these relationships an instructor might ask questions such as "What information is presented on triangle shaped signs?"

Questioning is not the only technique for focusing attention. Display techniques such as highlighting information with boxes or underlining also serve that purpose and involve less programming. One may well ask whether there is a significant advantage to asking questions over applying display techniques. The limited number of research studies suggest that there is. The superiority of questions over highlighting was demonstrated in a series of studies with college students who were studying special education (Schloss, Sindelar, Cartwright, & Schloss, 1986). On posttest questions taken from the computer modules, asking questions during instruction was significantly more effective than highlighting that information. This was true for both factual items and higher cognitive questions.

Questions help maintain students' attention. All of us have experienced "mind wandering" either when reading text or sitting in a classroom. When we are obliged to answer a question, our attention is quickly brought back to the task at hand. Questions keep students alert.

Mastering information is particularly important when the to-be learned knowledge is dependent on understanding preceding concepts, principles, or rules. Computers can monitor mastery by presenting questions and evaluating responses.

As in other instructional modes, questions are a valuable tool for determining whether students are "keeping up." While additional methods, such as observing students' facial expressions, are available to classroom instructors, questions are the only vehicle for monitoring learning in CAI. Computers do not see learners nor are they so advanced that they can interpret students' nonverbal behavior.

Good teachers base their selection of questions on their model of students' knowledge and misconceptions (Collins & Stevens, 1982). Students' responses to well chosen questions help instructors diagnose common errors. This enables them to correct misconceptions before they become ingrained. A student's responses to questions about lenses, for example, can help a teacher determine whether a student has confused the concepts of concave and convex.

In CAI, instruction is presented concisely and briefly so information tends to be densely packed. Learners may understand each concept as it is presented but be unable to retain all of it as they progress through the lesson. Questions can prevent this problem from occurring by giving students an opportunity to process information well enough to remember it. Consider the very simple goal of learning the nature of the messages on the shapes of highway signs. It would be very difficult, indeed, for a novice to remember all of them if they were presented in succession with no intervening questions, that is, with no opportunity to practice. Questions placed after every three to five shapes would make it easier to learn and remember them.

It was noted in Chapter 4 that questions inserted in text improve students' performance on repeated questions. Postquestions that require comprehension and not merely rote repetition of facts even result in improved performance on subsequent new questions. A word of caution is in order. If a learner spontaneously engages in good study habits, insertion of questions in text will not significantly influence learning (Rothkopf, 1966).

After learning.   Questions presented after instruction are useful in three ways. (1) They can assess each learner's knowledge and skills. (2) They provide information about performance of an entire group. (3) They can assess the effectiveness of the lesson.

Tests that measure achievement of each learner relative to other members of the group are called norm-referenced tests. They measure the differences between students. These tests present only questions that discriminate between individuals. Questions that all students can answer, or that none can answer are excluded.

Criterion-referenced tests, on the other hand, are constructed to measure each individual's specific knowledge and skills in a given domain (Glaser & Nitko, 1971). They measure what a student knows rather than how his knowledge compares to other students. For CAI lessons, criterion-referenced tests are most appropriate for measuring both individual and group achievement.

Performance of a class as a whole demonstrates the adequacy of a lesson and pinpoints its deficiencies. If an unacceptable proportion of a class responds incorrectly to a question or group of questions, it is evident that something is awry. It may be that the topic was inadequately presented. Alternatively, the questions may be ambiguous or misinterpreted by the students.

Generating Questions

Questions that foster learning display many of the characteristics of good verbal instruction. These include relatedness, clarity, appropriate vocabulary, brevity, and completeness.

Match to goals. Since questions are supposed to help a student learn some skill or acquire a specific body of knowledge, the questions inserted during instruction should be related to that goal. Questions that ask students about related, but tangential information simply interfere with learning. If the goal is to learn the duration of musical notes (e.g., half note), questions should ask for the duration, and not for the names of the notes, too. Questions inserted just to see if students remember some related information are merely disruptive. Of course, if the goal is to help learners integrate their knowledge, then it is appropriate to ask questions that draw on related information that is relevent to the goal.

Cover full range of skills. Questions should require students to perform the full range of skills needed to reach the goal. Unfortunately, it is too often the case that questions during instruction do not require students to perform all of the tasks needed but rather relate only to some of the subgoals (cf. Mager, 1975). If the goal is to be able to troubleshoot a loud speaker system, questions should not only ask for knowledge but should include problems that ask learners to troubleshoot. A knowledge question might be, "One of the capacitors in the loud speaker system has failed. What will the symptoms be?" A question that asks learners to troubleshoot might say, "You are getting a growling sound out of the speaker. Locate the faulty part or parts."

Apply good writing techniques. The principles recommended for writing good questions are parallel to those for writing good instruction. Questions, like instruction, should be explicit, understandable, as brief as possible, and simply stated (Gronlund, 1982; Roid & Haladyna, 1982). Good questions are not excessively wordy. They are stated so that they test learners' knowledge of the subject matter, not their ability to interpret the questions. The vocabulary is within the range of the intended users.

Like instruction, useful questions are unambiguous. One source of ambiguity in questions arises when they test more than one idea at a time. Gronlund (1982) gives the following example. "A worm cannot see because it has simple eyes. True or false?" A learner has no way of knowing what information the questioner is requesting. Is it whether a worm can see or whether a worm has simple eyes?

Require processing.   One of the most important lessons CAI designers can learn from the work in programmed instruction is that a user should have to process the information on a display to answer a question. If a learner can simply copy the answer from another part of the display, or answer a question from previous knowledge, the question does not contribute to learning.

Question Formats

The selection of question formats is guided by the behavior you want a student to display. In CAI, format selection is also guided by the ease of entering a response and the ability of the computer to judge the response adequately.

Recall and recognition.   In the concept and rule learning literature, questions were traditionally categorized as recognition or recall. In recognition questions, students select the correct response from among two or more alternatives. In a sense, all selection questions are versions of multiple choice. Matching is multiple choice with a single list of choices for many questions. True-false, or any two-valued choice, is multiple choice with two alternatives.

In recall questions, learners generate responses. These questions take forms such as fill-in-the-blank or list. The word, recall, implies exact recall of memorized information.

Beyond recall and recognition.   Of course, there are other types of questions that do not fit within the conceptualization of recall and recognition. Neither recall nor recognition captures complex processes or procedures such as making inferences from text or solving previously unseen problems. It is useful to describe question formats for these types of tasks as construction (cf. Williams & Haladyna, 1982).

About selection questions.   It is easier for students to select an answer than to generate one. Although selection questions may not match the ultimate goal of constructing a response, they can serve as good initial questions, to be followed later by constructed questions (Gropper, 1974).

In CAI, multiple choice questions have numerous advantages. It is easy for students to enter responses and it is easy to write computer programs to check them. However, multiple choice questions have some disadvantages as well.

Skinner (1961) proposes that seeing plausible incorrect alternatives might disrupt the learning you are trying to build up. Another disadvantage of multiple choice is that, if questions are poorly constructed, learners can guess the correct answer. This happens when the syntax of some of the alternatives does not match the stem or when learners can apply their general knowledge to guess the right answer by the process of elimination, as in the following example (Friend & Milojkovic, 1984):

Which of the following is the major export of Costa Rica?

1. Wheat
2. Automobiles
3. Coffee
4. Electric appliances

An additional disadvantage of multiple choice is that it is difficult to come up with enough alternative choices (called distractors) that are plausible but incorrect. If only one of the distractors is a reasonable though incorrect answer, the multiple choice question becomes effectively a two choice question. In that case the probability of guessing the correct answer goes up to an unacceptable 50%.

One additional disadvantage of multiple choice, particularly if it is the only format in a test, is the potential of getting "position effect." As previously noted, some individuals, particularly children, exhibit a preference for position in space or time. They may, for example always pick the first option offered. Damarin and Damarin (1983) give the MECC CAI program, Odell Lake, as an example. In this program about the effect of the environment on fish, a student can choose to have a fish do one of the following: Attack, Chase, Ignore, Escape Shallow, or Escape Deep. If a learner has a response set for one of these she may come to some erroneous conclusions. For example, if she consistently chooses "Ignore," she will totally misunderstand or neglect the effect of the environment on the fish.

New ways with old ideas.   Carlson (1985) presents several suggestions for circumventing some of the disadvantages of multiple choice questions. The keylist method employs a multiple choice format but avoids the need to generate false responses. The roles of the distractors and the questions are reversed. A master list of specific words or ideas is displayed and the learner matches them to more general concepts. Figure 5.2 is an example (Carlson, 1985) in which the goal for the learner is to identify the literary technique applied in each quotation.

Matching questions have limited value in the sense that they relate just two ideas. Sometimes an author wants students to integrate three related concepts. Double matching fulfills that purpose. For example, every highway sign has three specific features — color, shape, and message. Figure 5.3a is an example of double matching questions to help learners relate shape, color, and message.

Each quotation below contains an example of a literary technique or device. From the list below, choose the answer that best describes the techniques used. Letters (A–D) may be used more than once.

> A. use of comparison   C. use of slang
> B. use of exaggeration   D. understatement

____ 1. "His furious, bloodshot eyes flashed like wet marbles in a pool of blood."

____ 2. "I cried an ocean of tears when he left."

FIG. 5.2 Example of a keylist question. *Note.* From *Creative classroom testing* (p. 111) by S. B. Carlson, 1985, Princeton NJ: Educational Testing Service. Copyright 1985 by Educational Testing Service. Reprinted by permission.

After the correct responses have been entered, the display "1 OK ▼ c OK" is not very informative. In CAI, a designer can arrange to replace the numbers and letters with the actual words and colors. So, after a student types in the correct answers, "1" for red and "c" for yield, the computer erases the symbols and replaces them with the words, red and yield and then colors the sign red (Figure 5.3b).

Format selection in CAI. In CAI, an additional consideration in format selection is the ease with which a learner can enter a response. A student should be able to answer questions with minimum effort. Typing ability or skill in manipulating a tool such as a mouse or joystick should not interfere with demonstrating knowledge or skill. A second constraint in CAI is that the question has to be posed in such a way that a learner's response can be adequately judged by the computer program.

Frequency of questions. It was stated earlier that questions should be inserted throughout a lesson. There is no research that provides hard and fast rules about how frequently questions should be inserted. The frequency varies with the difficulty of the materials and task for the intended learners. If students need a considerable amount of structure and guidance, then a question should be asked on every display. On the other hand, a question after two or three displays might be adequate for college students. If a complex concept requires several displays, it is unreasonable to interrupt the flow of the presentation with a question on every display.

```
ROAD SIGNS
For each shape choose the correct
color and type its number.  Then
choose the letter for its message.

  1.   red        a.   stop
  2.   green      b.   motorist service
  3.   brown      c.   yield
  4.   yellow     d.   school zone
  5.   blue       e.   distance info

     COLOR     SHAPE      MESSAGE
     _1 ok_      ▽       ___c ok___

  _____     □      _____

  _____     ⌂      _____
```

FIG. 5.3a Example of a double matching question with a student's responses. (From CAI lesson, Questions and Answers. Copyright 1990 by E. R. Steinberg and D. Chirolas. Reprinted by permission.)

```
ROAD SIGNS
For each shape choose the correct
color and type its number.  Then
choose the letter for its message.

  1.   red        a.   stop
  2.   green      b.   motorist service
  3.   brown      c.   yield
  4.   yellow     d.   school zone
  5.   blue       e.   distance info

     COLOR     SHAPE      MESSAGE
     _red__      ▼       __yield___

 ▶ _____     □      _____

  _____     ⌂      _____
```

FIG. 5.3b Computer's feedback to student's response in Figure 5.3a. (From CAI lesson, Questions and Answers. Copyright 1990 by E. R. Steinberg and D. Chirolas. Reprinted by permission.)

110

RESPONSES

Computers are still a long way from being able to emulate human instructors. This is particularly evident with respect to judging and managing students' responses to questions. Furthermore, computers do not understand speech and cannot interpret handwriting. Consequently, many CAI-specific issues arise with respect to response modes, response management, and response judging.

Environment and Responses

As noted in Chapter 1, students have the physical skills to give responses to questions in traditional modes of instruction. They know how to speak, write, and point. They know from experience or at least can assume that their response was heard or seen by the instructor, and that it is clear to the instructor when they have finished responding. If responses are to be written, students know where to enter them. They know that a response will remain intact unless they themselves modify or remove it.

In CAI, not all students have the physical skills they need to respond. They find it difficult to enter responses if they are not good typists or if they must manipulate some object with which they are unfamiliar, such as a mouse. They cannot count on experience to anticipate where the response will appear on the visual display unless that information is visually obvious or explicitly stated. They do not know that they have to inform the computer when they have finished entering a response unless they are told to do so. If, as in some poorly written CAI lessons, the computer erases incorrect responses and simply says, "no," or if the computer does not respond at all, users have no way of knowing whether their response was received by the computer.

Response handling requires special consideration in CAI, even for multiple choice questions. Consider a discrimination task that asks the learner to tell which of two instances is an example of a given concept, the one on the left or the one on the right. In traditional instruction a user might be instructed to respond with "L" or " R." In CAI this would be confusing because R is on the left side of keyboard and L is on the right. Of course an author could letter the alternatives "A" and "B." That solution presents a different problem because finding the A and B on the keyboard is more cumbersome for nontypists than writing "A" or "B" on paper.

There are ways around this dilemma. If touch is available, a user could be asked to identify the answer by touching it on the display screen. Programs can be designed to use plastic overlays in which the user touches an area on the keyset. The point is that responding in computer programs is not merely a matter of direct translation from paper to computer (Damarin & Damarin, 1983; Steinberg, 1984).

Managing Responses

Classroom instructors make numerous decisions about managing students' responses, some based on a particular pedagogical philosophy; others made ad hoc. During the course of question-response interactions, an instructor decides whether to allow students more than one chance to give a correct response, whether to allow or to require students to correct themselves, whether to limit the time allowed for responding, and whether to allow students to respond covertly. In CAI, decisions like these are made a priori and programmed into the lesson.

Overt or covert responses. A time-honored decision in instructional design is whether to require learners to enter an overt response or simply allow them to think the answer. For most situations, research favors an overt response.

Anderson, Kulhavy, & Andre (1971) studied this issue using a computer-presented lesson on diagnosis of myocardial infarction from electrocardiograms. They found that students who were allowed to peek at the correct answer before they responded learned substantially less than students who were required to answer before they were given knowledge of the correct response. Students who were allowed to peek even learned less than students who were required to answer but received no knowledge of correct response. The researchers concluded that if students can see a response before they have to give it, they are likely to short-circuit instruction and not learn.

DeKlerk and DeKlerk (1978) tested the hypothesis that the requirement to make an overt response interrupts a student's concentration. The thinking was that covert responding enables a learner to better absorb the relevant information. The hypothesis was not supported. In a study with students in a secondary technical school, the researchers found that although performance on an immediate test was better under covert than overt conditions, it was not as good on the retention test.

Avner, Moore, and Smith (1980) found that the requirement to respond overtly in a CAI chemistry lesson subsequently resulted in better performance in the laboratory in those activities that required some decision making. Two versions of a CAI lesson for a set of laboratory tasks were designed. In the experimental versions learners were required to answer questions and were not allowed to proceed unless the answer was correct. In the control version students saw the same information and displays but just pressed a key to step through the information.

Students' errors in the subsequent laboratories were analyzed to assess the effects of response conditions. Results showed that if laboratory procedures involved simple instruction-following, most students made no observable errors and there were no significant differences between the response conditions. However, if a laboratory task required decisions based on understanding underlying principles, students who had been required to give responses performed better than those who merely stepped through the lesson.

The results of this study can be considered generalizable because it was done in a realistic learning situation and included more than 700 students in 30 sections over the course of two semesters. Apparently most students in a beginning chemistry course do not process information adequately if not required to do so.

The requirement to respond is also essential if the purpose of asking questions is to determine whether a learner understands. The learner must display the answer in order for the computer program to make that determination.

Number of attempts to allow.   How many chances should a learner be given to correct an error? Some CAI authors suggest allowing a fixed number of attempts to get the correct answer, say two chances (Friend & Milojkovic, 1984). However, once students become aware of that situation, they can just enter any response twice and wait for the correct one to appear. Poorly motivated or less mature learners are likely to engage in this practice.

On the other hand, there are times when all of us like to have a second chance, or even a third. It is not reasonable to force students to continue to enter responses until they answer correctly. If students really do not know the answer they will be trapped in the lesson and unable to proceed. The objective is to prevent students from guessing, and at the same time to allow them to reconsider their answers and possibly to learn from their mistakes.

In fact, there is no blanket rule for the number of attempts to allow. A good rule of thumb is to allow more than one attempt to answer a question if the intended students are likely to benefit from that opportunity. For memory questions such as arithmetic facts or names of parts of a machine, more than one chance to answer might become a guessing game—if one answer isn't right, try something else. For two-choice questions (Figure 5.4), if one response is incorrect the other must be the correct one. A student can infer the correct answer so there would seem to be no value in giving her a second chance. For constructed or complex responses, a second chance accompanied by some helpful feedback can aid learning.

Requirement to enter correct response.   Friend and Milojkovic (1984) state that when young children give an incorrect response they should be required to type the correct one because this will focus their attention on the

```
Type the number of the word that needs
an apostrophe.     >  1      No


Its motor is small, but its my very own car.
 1                              2
```

FIG. 5.4 Example of a two-choice question.

correct answer. Children are often eager to get on with a task and are likely to ignore a display of the correct answer unless they are required to attend to it. But, if the answer requires a considerable amount of typing, the student should not have to enter the correct one. There are several flaws in these proposals. First, young children or any unskilled typists should not be required to answer questions that require a lot of typing. Second, merely typing in a correct answer has little merit if the student does not pay attention to the question. The response in and of itself is meaningless. It is the combination of question and response and feedback that promotes learning.

Judging Responses

Adequate response judging is a major concern in CAI. There is nothing more frustrating to a student than to have a correct response judged wrong. And of course it does not benefit a student if the computer program accepts an incorrect response as correct. A classroom teacher knows when a response is correct, even if it is not expressed in the same way or in the same format as the teacher has in mind. A teacher understands when a response is conceptually correct but perhaps grammatically incorrect (e.g., present rather than past tense). A teacher knows the difference between a word that is incorrect and one that is misspelled or mispronounced.

Judging responses can be difficult in CAI lessons, particularly when the subject matter is mathematics or science. Computers will accept both $3 + 4$ and $4 + 3$ as the equivalent of 7, but they also need to accept algebraic equivalents such as $N + (d/a)NX$, and $(d/a)NX + N$. That engenders some programming challenges. An interesting solution to this problem is to display the elements of formulas that a student might want to enter and to let the student point to the ones he wants the computer to display (Lederman, 1975; Leibowitz, 1985; Nesbit, 1985). In Figure 5.5, for example, the student either touches a box or types its identifying letter. The computer displays the expression on the screen and also makes an internal representation of the character string. The computer then assigns a prime

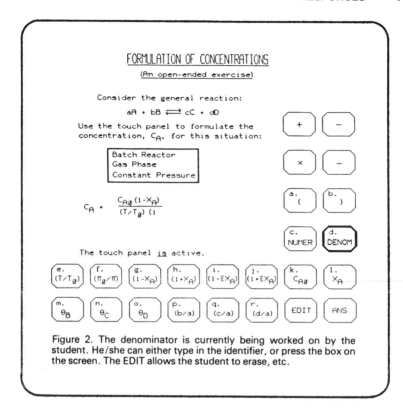

FORMULATION OF CONCENTRATIONS
(An open-ended exercise)

Consider the general reaction:

$$aA + bB \rightleftarrows cC + dD$$

Use the touch panel to formulate the concentration, C_A, for this situation:

Batch Reactor
Gas Phase
Constant Pressure

$$C_A = \frac{C_{A\vartheta}(1-X_A)}{(T/T_\vartheta)(1}$$

The touch panel is active.

Figure 2. The denominator is currently being worked on by the student. He/she can either type in the identifier, or press the box on the screen. The EDIT allows the student to erase, etc.

FIG. 5.5 Display for entering complex responses. (From CAI lesson by Leibowitz. Copyright 1985 by the Association for the Development of Computer-based Instructional Systems. Used by permission.)

number to each correct expression, and the same prime numbers to the student's expression. If both expressions have the same value, the student's expression is correct.

FEEDBACK

Feedback is a message that is presented to a learner after she gives a response. The mode of the message may be visual or aural, verbal or nonverbal. The content of the feedback may vary from simple to complex.

Feedback and Reinforcement

Recall that for behavioral psychologists the function of reinforcement is to increase the probability of a correct response and to decrease the probability of an incorrect one. In programmed instruction, immediate feedback in the form of knowledge of the correct response (KCR) was expected to facilitate learning because KCR was equated with reinforcement. However, numerous studies found that programs teach as well when the KCR after each frame is omitted (Anderson, Kulhavy, & Andre, 1971). There is considerable evidence that the function of KCR is to provide corrective feedback rather than to reinforce.

In a literature review of feedback after written instruction, Kulhavy (1977) found little evidence to support the idea the feedback acts as a reinforcer. Two examples are illustrative. Anderson, Kulhavy, and Andre (1971) compared several feedback treatments in a computer-presented lesson on diagnosis of myocardial infarction from electrocardiograms. Four of the feedback conditions are of interest here. They are: (1) no knowledge of correct results (no KCR); (2) 100% KCR; (3) KCR only after correct responses; and (4) KCR only after incorrect responses. Pencil and paper posttest results revealed that every group with at least some KCR performed better than those with no KCR. KCR after wrong response only was almost as effective as 100% KCR. That is, the information that a response was correct added very little to students' learning; it did not strengthen the probability of a correct response. However, feedback about correct responses after an error did improve learning.

Roper (1977) noticed that in most feedback studies students were taught subject matter that was not in their primary area of study. He hypothesized that this factor might have influenced the failure of KCR to benefit instruction. Therefore, he investigated the role of feedback when learning was in a subject familiar to the students who participated in the research study. The subject matter in Roper's experiment was statistics. His subjects were college students who had completed either one or two years of statistics. Students studied under one of three feedback conditions: (1) no feedback; (2) information that a response was correct or incorrect; or (3) information about the correctness of response plus the correct answer. There were significant differences between groups on the posttest, with the scores 38%, 46% and 60% correct for no feedback, correct or incorrect, or correctness plus correct answer, respectively. Again, the conclusion must be that the main function of feedback is to provide information rather than to strengthen or reinforce correct responses.

Functions of Feedback in CAI

Feedback serves two functions in CAI. They are (1) to inform and (2) to motivate (Steinberg, 1984).

Motivation.   Some, but not all, students are motivated by rewards for correct responses. Feedback has to be valued by the learners to be motivating. If students value a teacher's praise, it can be highly motivating. If they do not care what the teacher thinks, praise is not likely to be motivating.

Feedback can motivate students by encouraging them when learning is difficult for them. Lepper and Chabay (1985) report that tutors transmit noninstructional information that seems to have motivational goals. Of particular interest in CAI are two categories of feedback that they observed, and that are also found in CAI lessons. One category is commiseration, frequently accompanied by attributing the child's performance to external factors (e.g., "This is sure a hard one, isn't it?" or "That was really bad luck on that one."). A second category is encouragement (e.g., "You almost have it."). The effects of these kinds of motivational feedback are not known for CAI or any other instructional mode.

If students are internally motivated, rewards or external forms of encouragement are not likely to be motivating.

Information. The second function of feedback is to provide information. The task for an instructor or lesson designer is to decide how much and what kind of information to provide. The nature of the feedback can vary on a continuum from simple to complex. It may simply tell a learner that his response is correct or incorrect. It might include the correct response, a hint to help the learner generate the correct response himself, a detailed explanation of a correct response, and/or a statement about why the learner's response is wrong.

Effective Feedback

Effective feedback is response contingent and understood by students (Friend & Milojkovic, 1984; Hartley & Lovell, 1984; Steinberg, 1980b; Stevens, Collins, & Goldin, 1982). Response contingent refers to feedback that is specific to the nature of the response. The feedback to the incorrect response in Figure 5.6 tells the student why her response is wrong. If the error is a misspelling rather than content, feedback should address that problem. For example, suppose that a question asks a learner to name the psychologist who is most widely associated with behavioral psychology, and the learner responds, "Skiner." The response contingent feedback might say, "Correct name, but misspelled."

Explicit. Feedback, like a presentation, is most helpful when it is explicit. Feedback should say exactly what you mean. A vague response, as in Figure 5.7a, leaves a student wondering whether his answer is right or wrong. Although the student's response was wrong, the author meant to encourage him with a kind remark, "Nice try." The author might have

```
          Which of the five Right to Financial Privacy Act methods
     would be best used to  obtain Commissioner Green's records?

     Press F2 to review scenario.

              1.   Search warrant
              2.   Customer authorization
              3.   Formal written request
              4.   Judicial subpoena
              5.   Administrative subpoena

     >   1                          ←——— (STUDENT'S RESPONSE)


          Incorrect.  A search warrant cannot be used because the
     FBI has not developed probable cause to search Green's
     records.  Try again.   ←——— (COMPUTER'S FEEDBACK)
```

FIG. 5.6 Example of response-contingent feedback. (From CAI lesson, Right to Financial Privacy Act. Copyright 1988 by the FBI. Reprinted by permission.)

confused the student rather than helped him. The feedback in Figure 5.7b is explicit and not confusing.

Telling the student to "think harder" is an example of feedback that is neither explicit nor helpful. Feedback that tells the student how to think about the material at hand is considerably more useful.

Attuned to cause of error.   It is one thing to determine that a student has made an error; it is quite another to determine the underlying causes of that error. That is, feedback given at the surface level may correct the response but not the reason for it.

Ideally, feedback should respond at this deeper than surface level. This ideal has not yet been achieved even by developers of intelligent tutoring systems. For example, Anderson and his colleagues (Anderson, Boyle, Farrell, & Reiser, 1985) note that when students try to prove geometry theorems, they sometimes make inferences that are logically correct but that do not lead to problem solution. Unfortunately, in such cases Anderson's intelligent geometry tutor does not understand why the student does not solve the problem.

Developers of the WHY system (Stevens, Collins, & Goldin, 1982) encountered a similar experience. Their lesson about physical systems could tell if a student gave a wrong step in the process, but it didn't know why the student did so. It could not determine, for example, that the student failed to integrate two concepts. The system could provide feedback only at a superficial level, telling the learner what the process should be. Unlike an intelligent human tutor, it could not help the student overcome basic misconceptions.

How would you classify the potential
evidence value of fingerprints? Type "c"
for class or "i" for individual.

>> c   ←——— *(STUDENT'S RESPONSE)*

Nice try! Recall that the courts have
taken judicial notice that fingerprints
are a positive means of establishing a
person's identity.   ←——— *(COMPUTER'S FEEDBACK)*

How would you classify the potential
evidence value of fingerprints? Type "c"
for class or "i" for individual.

>> c   ←——— *(STUDENT'S RESPONSE)*

No. The potential value of this evidence
is individual because fingerprints are
uniqe to each person. Thus they are a
positive means of establishing a person's
identity.   ←——— *(COMPUTER'S FEEDBACK)*

FIG. 5.7   Examples of nonexplicit and explicit feedback. (From CAI lesson, Evidence Potential. Copyright 1988 by R. O. Walker. Adapted by permission.)

Commensurate with competence.   The nature of feedback should be commensurate with a learner's competence. In one study (Hartley & Lovell, 1984), 29 second-year undergraduates in chemistry saw one of three feedback treatments: (1) whether or not the response was correct; (2) whether the response was correct and if not, where the error was and information about how the correct answer could be obtained; or (3) correctness of response, source of the error, how to get the correct response, and in addition, the learner had to type in the correct answer. The first treatment took the least amount of time but showed the least satisfactory results overall on posttests. However, the better students (as measured by scores on traditional chemistry examinations) did equally well in all three treatments. They were apparently able to figure out how to get the correct answers without the additional feedback.

Role of response confidence.   The value of feedback may very well be related to a student's confidence in her response. If a student is quite sure that she has given a correct answer, she probably gives only cursory attention to the feedback (Kulhavy, 1977). On the other hand, if the student is quite confident that her response is wrong, she may take some time to try to understand the materials. At that point feedback may be most valuable as corrective information.

Commensurate with developmental level.   Steinberg (1980b) found that first grade students did not benefit from feedback because they did not know how to use it. In a computer-presented lesson, students were given a reasoning task in which the goal was to generate an appropriate problem-solving strategy. In addition to a yes or a no, the feedback included a record of the problems that the student had done earlier and the responses she had given. The idea was to enable the student to see which combinations of problems and responses were correct and which incorrect. The expectation was that students would use this information to make inferences about why some responses were right and others wrong, and consequently generate a correct strategy. The feedback was ineffective because six-year old children do not understand how to use this kind of information.

Should feedback be immediate?   A key principle in the behavioral approach to instruction is that feedback must be immediate. Immediate feedback is reasonable if feedback is equated with reinforcement, because you want to strengthen the probability of a correct response or diminish the probability of an incorrect one. If it is not the role of feedback to strengthen responses, then there is reason to ask whether feedback must be immediate, or under what conditions immediacy is essential.

There appears to be a paradox in recent literature. On the one hand, R. C. Anderson and his colleagues (who were once behaviorally oriented) demonstrated that not only is immediate feedback not essential but in some cases it might even be detrimental (Kulhavy & Anderson, 1972). On the other hand, J. R. Anderson, a cognitive psychologist, states that an important principle in his intelligent tutoring system is that on errors, feedback must be immediate (Anderson, Boyle, & Reiser, 1985)! The reason, however, is not negative reinforcement.

R. C. Anderson notes that a test strengthens response tendencies. After a delay, a student forgets the responses he gave on the initial test. Error tendencies interfere with his learning the correct answers when feedback is immediate. Consequently, there is more error perseveration in immediate feedback. Also, students who get delayed feedback take more time to study it than those who get it immediately.

J. R. Anderson provides immediate feedback in his geometry lesson. He quotes Skinner "that the importance of immediacy of feedback to skill acquisition is one of the best documented facts in psychology." Anderson contends that it is difficult for a student to find and correct her errors if she makes an error in her proof and then continues with a series of steps based on that error until she hits an impasse. She may be overwhelmed by information overload when trying to backtrack and recover from her errors. Further, she may not actually learn the correct procedure. Anderson does not deny that a student can learn how to find and correct errors, but sees that as a different goal that should be taught separately. Further, when feedback is delayed, students may learn incorrect procedures. In a complex problem-solving task students spend much more time trying to solve problems when feedback is delayed than when it is immediate. Another benefit of immediate feedback is that it avoids frustration. If feedback is delayed, some students get demoralized.

Why the differences in results between these researchers? The explanation lies in differences in the subject matter and differences in the nature of the tasks (Figure 5.8). One body of research involves mathematics (geometry), the other prose materials. The geometry is a tutoring situation involving skill learning; the prose materials, testing and overcoming previously acquired errors. The purpose of the feedback is different in the "conflicting" results. The geometry tutoring system expects students to learn to do geometry proofs in a preset way. That is, it becomes skill learning. Feedback in the geometry program keeps students from going awry. The intent is to prevent their getting lost, or taking too much time, or getting frustrated. Feedback for the prose materials is intended to help students overcome previously acquired errors.

CAI-Specific Issues

Not all questions have a "right" or "wrong" answer. There may be a "preferred" rather than a "correct" way of performing a complex task. Figure 5.9 is an example of a decision-making question used in conjunction with a workbook. The problem for the student is to select a style fororganizing a report. The feedback in Figure 5.9 does not state that the

	J.R. Anderson	R.C. Anderson
Subject Matter	High school geometry	Prose
Learning situation	Tutoring Skill learning	Testing Overcoming errors
Reasons for view	Prevent learning incorrect procedures Avoid students' frustration Takes less time to learn	Prevent error perservation Prevent interference with learning

FIG. 5.8 Comparison of two studies relating to immediate feedback.

```
Before answering the following question review the section in
your workbook entitled, "FD-71 Exercise.   Sequencing the flow
of the facts of the complaint."   If you need to review the
facts, press key F1.

    Which of the following is the preferred sequence for the
flow of facts contained in the Facts of Complaint section?

    A.   Sequence A
    B.   Sequence B
    C.   Sequence C

    >>  A                          ◄─────  (STUDENT'S RESPONSE)

    Not preferred.   You selected organization by time
sequence.   While this organization would not be incorrect, it
does not efficiently provide the Supervisor with the needed
information.   Try again.   ◄─────  (COMPUTER'S FEEDBACK)
```

FIG. 5.9 Example of feedback to a preferred response. (From CAI lesson, FD-71 Complaint Form. Copyright 1988 by the FBI. Adapted by permission.)

learner is wrong. Rather, it provides reasons for selecting the preferred method and rejecting the one selected by the learner.

Students' acceptance of feedback. If a student gives an incorrect response, one form of useful feedback is to tell him the correct response and why it is correct (cf. Markle, 1978). There is no guarantee, however, that the student will accept the information. In problem solving, for example, students' misconceptions are robust (Steinberg, 1980a; Case, 1978; Fuller, 1982) and not easily corrected. In one arithmetic game the computer coach gave students advice but they did not want to use the computer's suggestions about better strategies for winning (Burton & Brown, 1982).

Performance feedback. Feedback about their performance gives students information they can use when deciding how to manage their study. In Figure 5.10, for example, feedback informs the student that he repaired the faulty equipment, how much it cost, and how the costs were distributed. If the goal was to contain the cost at less than $500, he can see that he was very close. He can determine where he might be able to cut costs in the next task.

In some concept-learning lessons students can select the number of examples they want to see and the number of exercises they want to practice. Feedback about how well they are performing toward mastery and advice about how many examples they should look at can be very valuable in helping them achieve their goal (Tennyson, 1981).

Adaptive feedback. Students may use informative feedback to accomplish a given task, but be unable to do the task when the feedback is

```
┌─────────────────────────────────────────────────────┐
│                                                       │
│         IT WORKS!   IT WORKS!                          │
│                                                       │
│                                                       │
│     TROUBLE SHOOTING TIME            $    24          │
│                                                       │
│     MODULES REPLACED                 $   380          │
│                                                       │
│     CONSULTING HELP USED             $    58          │
│                                                       │
│     TIME WASTED ON IRRELEVANT        $    45          │
│     MODULES                        ─────────          │
│                        TOTAL COST    $   507          │
│                                                       │
│                                                       │
│                                                       │
│     Press MAP to try another failure,                 │
│     or EXIT to quit.                                  │
│                                                       │
└─────────────────────────────────────────────────────┘
```

FIG. 5.10 Example of performance feedback. (From a MicroTICCIT CAI lesson. Copyright by Ford Aerospace Communications Corporation. Adapted by permission.)

removed. Feedback may become a crutch for getting the correct answers rather than a tool for reaching the instructional goals. In one study (Steinberg, Baskin, & Matthews, 1985), the computer provided matrix charts as memory aids to help students keep track of inferred information while they were trying to solve a succession of problems called Pico-fomi. Students marked their inferences on the computer display. In one experimental condition students were required to mark on the chart all of the inferences that could be made after each step in the problem-solving process. The computer provided feedback on additional inferences that the student had not made. The expectation was that students would learn new strategies from this feedback and thus improve their problem-solving performance. Results showed that some students solved the problems as long as they received feedback from the computer, but did not succeed when feedback was removed.

Inappropriate feedback. Instructional designers can inadvertently create an unfriendly learning environment by providing feedback that is viewed as aversive or intimidating by the learners. Aversive computer feedback can take the form of an insulting verbal message, a graphic display (such as a flashing red X), or even an unpleasant sound. This kind of feedback can interfere with learning.

At the other end of the spectrum is feedback that is insincere, such as fake praise. It is a particular problem in CAI. All but the very slowest students are aware that comments such as, "fantastic," are a fake if they are given after students have tried three times before getting the right answer.

A third type of inappropriate feedback is irrelevant information. A historical comment about when fingerprints were invented, for instance, would seem to be irrelevant after a question that asks whether fingerprints can be classified as having individual or class characteristics. Although historical information is interesting, it could interfere with the momentum of learning the topic at hand.

Motivating feedback for errors.   An interesting phenomenon that is not reported in research journals, is the experience of many CAI developers with certain kinds of feedback for wrong answers. Sometimes students give wrong answers, just to see what will happen. If the feedback is particularly interesting or motivating, they continue to give wrong answers. The classic anecdote is that in one CAI lesson, the feedback for an incorrect response was a display of a child with tears running down its face. This so fascinated the students that they continually entered incorrect responses to see this display.

Useless feedback.   Feedback is not always essential in CAI. In some instances feedback is intrinsic to the lesson. Learners can see for themselves if an answer is correct. They don't need to be told what they already know. For example, in a CAI physics lesson that displays the path of a projectile, learners can see if they hit the target or not. They don't need to be told whether they have missed. Feedback, such as "You missed," does not provide additional useful information, and may seem abrasive. Additional corrective information can be useful. For example, in the physics lesson the feedback might be, "Try a higher angle of elevation."

SUMMARY

A considerable amount of learning takes place through question-response-feedback interactions, provided that appropriate questions are asked and relevant feedback is presented. The requirement to respond to questions helps students learn and remember. Feedback helps them overcome misconceptions. Feedback can also provide motivation.

Four elements are considered when questions are generated. They are: subject matter content,desired behavior, ease with which students can enter a response, and the flexibility with which the computer can judge it.

Learning is also affected by students' beliefs and expectations, by their learning styles, attitudes and motivation, as well as by their cognitive skills and mental abilities. These human factors are the concern of the next chapter.

Chapter 6

HUMAN FACTORS

No matter how good a system is, or how much memory it has, or how speedy it is, no matter how wonderful the graphic features or how elegant the software that runs the system, "users are attached" (Moran, 1981). A program will be successful only if users find interacting with it to be acceptable. Human factors are as critical in CAI as in other uses of computers such as word processing and spread sheets.

Three categories of human factors are discussed in this chapter. They are: (1) the learner's role in managing learning; (2) the roles of motivation in learning; and (3) the role of learners' expectations.

LEARNER CONTROL

Many of us have experienced classroom situations in which total control by the instructor led to anxiety, frustration, or boredom, and ultimately to lack of attention or failure to complete an assignment. We wanted to skip the parts of the lesson that we already knew or were perhaps totally unprepared to do. We might have wished to study a lesson in a different sequence than the one prescribed. It is therefore intuitively appealing to believe that giving learners control can improve motivation, reduce anxiety, and increase attention and consequently improve achievement. Research indicates that this intuition is only valid under certain conditions.

Locus of Control

The source of responsibility for managing the many aspects of instruction is called the locus of control. In traditional classrooms the locus of control

125

is primarily the instructor. In contrast, CAI affords alternatives in the locus of control.

Sources of control.   A CAI lesson can be designed to place all management decisions under computer control. These decisions include the amount of time a learner is allowed to view each display, the difficulty level of exercises, the number of exercises, the sequence of topics, and the conditions for advancing through a lesson.

In a different configuration, some aspects of instructional management are allocated to learners and others to the computer. For example, a learner may control the pace of instruction or the amount of practice, but the computer program can control other matters, such as the difficulty level or sequence of topics. Another plan turns over all management of learning to learners. This alternative is most often implemented in games and in simulations. Students make all of the decisions about how to proceed. Some CAI programs provide advice, such as a good strategy to invoke, but do not require students to accept it.

One additional alternative in CAI is to allow an instructor to adapt a general program to the needs of her students. For example, some CAI drills are written in such a way that an instructor can enter her own subject matter content (e.g., vocabulary) or select criteria for advancing through the lesson.

Some issues.   A review of the literature shows that learner control is neither "good" nor "bad." It is not a one-variable issue. Learner characteristics such as prior knowledge, motivation, and metacognitive and cognitive skills play an important role in influencing the effectiveness of learner control, as do the instructional goal and instructional variables. It is not realistic to expect students to know how to plan and direct their own learning, given that much of their previous learning took place in structured environments. Further, not all learners are interested in managing their own learning.

Review of Research

Early studies.   In a review of research, Steinberg (1977) found that learner control resulted in higher achievement but only under very limited conditions. Some students achieved as much under learner as under computer control, but students who were poor performers in the subject area learned the least. When allowed to control course flow, students demonstrated two major deficiencies. First, they failed to employ adequate review strategies. Second, they did not know how to manage their time and frequently did not complete a course during the allotted time. Essentially, only learners who were high performers in the subject matter of the lesson performed better under learner than under computer control.

Giving learners control of one or two instructional variables, such as the amount of practice or the difficulty level, yielded equivocal results. Neither elementary nor college students selected practice exercises at appropriate difficulty levels. For the most part, they learned less when they, rather than the computer, chose the instructional sequence. High performers were most likely to be skillful instructional managers. Data were equivocal with respect to control of the amount of practice.

The few studies of motivation and attitude in CAI revealed that learner control sometimes resulted in greater task engagement and better attitudes, but not necessarily in greater achievement. Performance under learner control was not better, and sometimes worse than under computer control. Aptitude and trait-treatment research yielded no definitive conclusions about learner control. Many students were motivated by learner control but others were indifferent to it. The motivational aspects of learner control were not accompanied by better performance.

Theoretical issues, 1977–1988.   These early studies concentrated mainly on instructional design variables: the amount of practice, the level of difficulty, and the sequence of topics. They did not take into account the psychological processes in learning. Nor did they consider how individual differences in students' learning skills and strategies might influence the effect of learner control. Learner control may have been unsuccessful for some subjects because they did not have clearly formed objectives (Romiszowski, 1981) or because they employed naive or erroneous learning strategies (Steinberg, 1977). They may have lacked metacognitive skills (Allen & Merrill, 1985; Rigney, 1978) or lacked the information they needed about their learning progress to make meaningful decisions about how to manage learning (Tennyson & Rothen, 1979).

During the last decade, attention has been devoted to processing aspects of learner control. Merrill (1984) proposes that most instruction automatically involves some amount of learner control. Some aspects of control, such as selection of topics to study and selection of instructional strategy, can be controlled externally either by the instructional system or by the learner (if a lesson is so designed). However, learners always exert some conscious-cognitive control over learning, and those aspects of learning are totally under their control. Each learner selects strategies for learning, such as paraphrasing or imaging; each has some kind of internal model of how to learn. It is this model that drives the student's use of whatever types of control are available in a lesson. Thus, the key issue for Merrill is not whether to provide learner control but how to maximize a student's ability to use the learner control that is available.

Allen and Merrill (1985) suggest three types of control, each of which reflects a different amount of reliance on a learner's skill at managing his own strategies. Some students have metacognitive skills that are relevant to a task. They not only know appropriate strategies but also know that those strategies should be applied to the task at hand. They should be allowed total freedom to control learning. Other students may have strategies or appropriate knowledge, but are not aware that they should apply them. In such cases the system should guide students in the selection of appropriate processing strategies. Finally, instruction should embed information-processing strategies for those students who are totally deficient in these skills. For example, to get students to process information, ask questions that will lead them to do so.

These theoretical suggestions sound reasonable but there is a major obstacle to implementation. The theory makes an implicit assumption that the instructional system has some means of making a cognitive model of each learner. This is a goal that many are pursuing but that still eludes success. A student may have a spontaneous strategy that, though not ideal, is adequate for the learning task. A system-assigned strategy could very well interfere with rather than aid learning. For students who have no learning strategies, care would have to be taken that they do not become so dependent on the system that they cannot function on their own when system assistance is withdrawn.

Motivation as well as cognition influences learner control. Motivational aspects are discussed in the section, Motivation later in this chapter. It will be shown that as with cognitive factors, individual differences influence the motivational impact of learner control.

Empirical studies, 1977–1988. Empirical studies of learner control during the last decade can be grouped into three broad categories. They are: (1) students' learning strategies (or lack thereof); (2) feedback; and (3) tools or aids to promote or support learners' spontaneous strategies.

Learner control and learning strategies. Students' learning strategies interact with learner control to influence its effect on learning. Gray (1987) compared two types of instructional sequence in a sociology lesson for college students. In each of ten exercises, students made decisions about social policy and received feedback about the consequences of their decisions on poverty and on the inflation rate. Under computer control the sequence of decision exercises was linear. Under learner control a student could control the sequence and could go forward or backward to any exercise and in any order.

Although learner control resulted in better performance on an immediate paper and pencil posttest, this difference disappeared on a retention test given a week later. While doing the lesson, students in the learner control condition scored better on reducing poverty but not on reducing inflation rate. Students under learner control had a more negative attitude toward the CAI lesson. Gray suggests that too much sequence control may have distracted students from the task at hand.

In a high school algebra course, Rubincam and Olivier (1985) found that the consistency of learning strategy influenced the effect of learner control of sequence. In this study, 105 students studied eight topics in a computer controlled sequence, but within each topic students controlled the sequence of objectives. In addition, students decided whether to take instruction before the test or to proceed immediately to the test. They had to pass a test on every objective in a topic before they were allowed to go on to the next topic.

Analysis of students' instructional decisions revealed that 54% of the students could be considered consistent in their strategies. They selected either tests first or instruction first most (81–100%) of the time. Students who adopted a consistent strategy, whether test first or instruction first, performed at a somewhat higher level than those whose strategy was inconsistent. It was not the strategy employed but rather the consistency of strategy that influenced performance. Interviews revealed that about half of the students were able to assess their own knowledge and select the instructional strategy that was most appropriate.

A study with college students (Gay, 1986) replicated the finding of studies conducted in the early seventies that prior knowledge interacts with sequencing and other strategy decisions. Students with high scores on a pretest did equally well under learner or computer control in a biology lesson that used a rule-example-practice paradigm. Students with low pretest scores made poor sequencing decisions. In addition they practiced too little, emphasized topics with which they were familiar,and avoided topics that were difficult for them.

Feedback. When given control of learning, students need feedback about how well they are performing to make decisions such as how much to practice (Tennyson & Rothen, 1979). Tennyson (1980) tested the hypothesis that learner control with adaptive advisement is more effective than either adaptive computer control or learner control without advisement. Working with college students, he compared three conditions for learning physics concepts. Under adaptive control all decisions about sequence and amount of instruction were made by the adaptive instructional program. Under learner control students selected sequence and number of examples and also received diagnostic and prescriptive information.

Results showed that performance was about the same in both adaptive control conditions and both were better than total learner control.

Tennyson concluded that advice that provides meaningful information is a highly significant variable. Students who did not receive this advice took less time to complete the lesson, indicating that they quit instruction before they had mastered the task.

Working with seventh graders enrolled in a remedial math class, Goetzfried and Hannafin (1985) compared three conditions in a rule learning task. Under adaptive control the program branched students to review instruction and/or more examples on the basis of their responses. Under learner control with advisement students were continuously advised of their progress but were allowed to make decisions about accessing reviews and additional examples. In linear control conditions students simply advanced through instruction and did not interact with the system. They were not able to review and they could not request additional examples.

There were no significant achievement differences resulting from the design conditions, but there was a significant difference for prior achievement. These results for remedial students replicated earlier findings for other target populations that (1) prior achievement affects learning, and (2) students with low pretest scores do not make effective learning decisions.

In a comparison of learner and computer control of review after incorrectly answered questions, Schloss, Wisniewski, and Cartwright (1988) found that learner control resulted in superior performance for students who were given feedback on their cumulative performance, compared to those who were not. Feedback about performance played a more significant role in performance than learner control alone.

Learning aids. Two studies of problem solving skills investigated learner control of the use of organizational/memory tools. The lessons provided tools that enable learners to improve their own strategies rather than impose the strategies of experts. The purpose of the studies was to determine whether students would use these tools if not required to do so, and how learner control would affect performance.

In one study (Steinberg, Baskin, & Matthews, 1985) the task was to generate strategies for solving a puzzle-like game called Pico-fomi. A chart was provided on the display screen to help learners keep track of all of their inferences. The chart served as an organizational as well as a memory aid. Students in one group were required to use the chart; students in the other group were given control over its use. In the initial task 80% of the students under computer control successfully solved the problems. However, only half of the students were successful on the maintenance task where computer control (and accompanying informative feedback) were withdrawn. Computer control helped the students solve the problems, but it did not necessarily help them develop their own strategies. On the other hand, learner control was not entirely successful either. Only 8 out of 26 students succeeded in the initial task, and 14 on the maintenance task. Thus, the presence of the charts alone, with no advice on how to use them, was not sufficient for all learners to develop a successful problem solving strategy.

In another study (Steinberg, Baskin, & Hofer, 1986) it was hypothesized that shared control of computer tools would be better than total control by either the learner or the computer alone. The mere presence of an aid is not useful if a learner does not understand how it can be beneficial. However, forcing a student to use the aid may interfere with her spontaneous strategies. In addition, a learner might find the aid beneficial only at early stages in the learning process, but a nuisance later on.

During the initial task in this study, students solved problems under one of four experimental conditions, learner or computer control of use of the tool with or without feedback. The tool was a marking capability for keeping a visual record on the screen of information gained during the course of problem solving. On the subsequent maintenance task no feedback was provided and use of the marker was optional for all students.

Analyses revealed that the tool was used and was helpful. During the initial task students under learner control did use the tool. All students, whether initially under learner or computer control, used the tool during the maintenance task.

It was not computer or learner control of the tool but rather the tool in conjunction with feedback that positively affected performance. Without feedback, many students failed to perceive the value of the tool. Students who were initially under learner control with feedback used the tool even more on the maintenance task than those under learner control without feedback. The learner control option enabled them to adjust uses of the tool to the dynamics of learning, using it only when they needed it. The feedback helped them understand the value of the tool. Unfortunately, some students used feedback as a crutch. When feedback was removed, their performance deteriorated.

There are several implications. One is that it is beneficial to allow learners to control use of a learning aid, but is also important to provide information about how the aid can help. Thus, feedback should be provided when tools are first made available. However, feedback should gradually be phased out, lest the student become dependent on it and fail to develop his own strategies.

Conclusions

Learner control of instruction is beneficial if students have appropriate learning strategies for the given subject and know where they should apply them. Students with prior knowledge about a subject are more likely to benefit from learner control than those with little or no knowledge.

Feedback about performance enhances the potential benefits of learner control. It can prevent too little or too much practice and aid in better allocation of time to topics of study. A promising technique is to give a learner control accompanied by diagnostic and prescriptive advice—advice based on the nature of a student's errors rather than on the number of errors. Of course,developing such a diagnostic and prescriptive program is no easy task. Furthermore, we do not know whether most students would accept this advice. This would undoubtedly be influenced by students' perceptions of its value and their motivation to succeed. Low achievers may be incapable of pursuing good learning strategies even with advice.

CAI can also be employed to gradually shift responsibility for learning from the computer program to the student. We should expect students to require a decreasing amount of assistance as learning progresses because learning is a dynamic process.

MOTIVATION

Every teacher knows that motivation is an important part of learning. That is why teachers give praise, gold stars, and good grades for good work. That is why some CAI authors include embellishments such as graphics, animations, color, and sound and others write lessons in game format. Lepper and Chabay (1985, p. 217) go so far as to assert that "Motivational factors may often exert as great an influence on children's achievement as do cognitive factors."

Theoretically, motivators enhance learning because they get students to attend more carefully and for longer periods of time. The more time spent studying, the better the learning, and perhaps even the greater the retention. Motivators can also promote a better attitude and sometimes help students feel better about themselves and about what they learn.

CAI can provide motivators that are not feasible in traditional environments as well as motivators similar to those used in traditional instruction. Computer lessons can allow learners to manage instruction and thus let them feel that they are in control. CAI can involve students in fantasy environments or present immediate and individualized feedback about how well they are progressing toward their goal.

The question is, are these features really motivating? For which learners? What are the processes by which motivators affect learning? Why are some CAI lessons motivating and others not? While the answers to all of these questions are not available, some insights and information can be gained from theories of intrinsic motivation as well as from empirical studies of motivation and CAI.

Theories of Intrinsic Motivation

Motivation is influenced by both internal and external factors. When motivation comes from within, without any obvious external rewards or punishments, we say that the student is intrinsically motivated. This is in contrast to extrinsic motivation, which comes from external factors such as money or praise..

Classes of intrinsic motivation.   In a taxonomy of intrinsic motivation, Malone and Lepper (1987) define two broad categories of motivators, personal and interpersonal. Within the category of personal motivators, three classes, challenge, curiosity, and control, are derived from traditional views of intrinsic motivation. A fourth category of personal motivation, fantasy, comes from studies of motivation and CAI (Malone, 1981).

Interpersonal motivation depends on other people. The three classes of interpersonal motivation in this taxonomy are cooperation, competition, and recognition.

Challenge.   One theory among psychologists is that the greatest intrinsic motivation comes from activities that provide some optimal level of difficulty and challenge. From this perspective, an individual is viewed as a problem solver. The challenge is in solving a problem by applying a skill that the person values. Challenge is thought to be motivating because it seems to give individuals a feeling of self-esteem. Of course, failure to meet a challenge can lower one's self-esteem.

If an activity is to provide challenge, it has to have one or more goals. These goals may be fixed or changing, externally set or set by the individuals themselves. If a person knows he will achieve a goal, the element of challenge does not exist. Therefore, some amount of uncertainty, such as variable difficulty levels or randomness, is also essential. A third important element in a challenging activity is feedback about performance. The role of feedback is to help a person evaluate his progress and decide whether to reformulate his goals.

This theory may very well explain why people are so motivated to play computer games such as Little Brick Out. In this game the goal is to knock as many bricks out of a wall as possible, by hitting a ball with a paddle. Since the player does not know which direction the ball will come from, there is an element of uncertainty. Feedback is self-evident in that the paddle either hits or misses the ball. The player gets five chances to knock out the bricks. The game can become more challenging if the player tries to knock out all of the bricks with fewer than five balls.

It would seem to be a good idea to apply these principles to educational lessons, but the application is not as easy as it sounds. Lepper (1985) gives a good example of a problem that arises with computer software that presents increasingly more challenging problems as a child masters each level in the sequence of instruction. If the program does not tell the child of this sequencing, the child begins to perceive herself as unable to succeed. Rather than motivating the student, the program undermines her self-esteem. Lepper quotes one child, "Every time I think I've got it, I just miss one of them." There is another aspect, too. The assumption is that the child values the skill in the lesson. If the challenge, for example, is speed in arithmetic facts, and the child doesn't care about giving the answers quickly, the lesson is not motivating for her. There is also the problem of how to give feedback to incorrect responses, feedback that won't destroy the motivation to continue.

Curiosity. A different view of motivation is that it derives from curiosity or novelty. Curiosity may be related to sensory variations, such as changes in light or sound, or to cognitive factors, such as a discrepancy between what we expect to find in a given situation and what we actually find. We may be motivated at some optimal level of surprise or incongruity.

This perspective of motivation explains why graphics and sound are so appealing in CAI. Students are surprised to see animated figures move around a screen. It's not what they are accustomed to in traditional instruction. However, finding an optimal level of surprise is not so easy in CAI. Many lessons show graphics, animations, or sound after every correct answer. Chances are that once the novelty wears off and the student is no longer surprised, the motivational value of the feedback is depleted and may interfere with learning. It is also possible that these kinds of motivators distract learners' attention from the task and thus interfere with learning.

There is cognitive as well as sensory curiosity. Cognitive curiosity is stimulated when students are interested in a topic and are confronted with a situation that is incomplete or apparently incongruous. It is cognitive curiosity that stimulates a reader to stay up late to finish a mystery. It is cognitive curiosity that stimulates a student to "see what happens" in a simulation if he enters out-of-range values.

Control. A third view is that intrinsic motivation comes from a sense of control, of self determination. In this view, a person is motivated in an empowering environment, one in which the outcomes depend on his own responses.

Proponents of simulations, games, and exploratory environments in CAI claim that one of the benefits of these instructional formats is that the learner-control aspects make them more motivating. Learner control is so motivating that it will increase a child's interest in the subject. Furthermore, the child's interest will be retained when he is no longer doing the computer lesson (cf. Lepper, 1985). It is also suggested that learning is more enjoyable when students have control. At this time there is no empirical support for this hypothesis. Only anecdotal evidence has been presented.

There are individual differences in the motivational value of learner control. Some students are motivated by total freedom in learning strategies; others want computer advice at early stages in the learning process; still others are motivated by a totally controlled system.

One aspect of control that is feasible in CAI is choice. A student can be allowed to make decisions that are either instructionally incidental or critical. An incidental choice might be whether to have sound or graphics or be called by a name of one's choice. Instructionally critical decisions deal with matters such as sequence and difficulty level. The relative motivational and learning effects of these two types of choice are not known.

Choices can be highly intrinsically motivating, but as with other motivational elements there are some potential dangers. Gray (1987) found that students had a negative attitude toward a CAI lesson because too many choices interfered with the flow of learning. In the initial TICCIT project the many instructionally critical choices did not prove to be motivating for students who were low achievers. They did not complete the course.

Fantasy.   The fourth category of intrinsic motivation is fantasy. Fantasy helps to satisfy emotional needs and enables students to vicariously experience power, success, fame, and fortune. It enables them to master situations that are unavailable in real life.

Interpersonal motivation.   Interpersonal elements can provide intrinsic motivation that is not present when working alone. Sometimes what seems like interpersonal motivation is effectively personal motivation (Malone & Lepper, 1987). For example, competition may be motivating because it provides an appropriate level of challenge. Interpersonal factors, such as recognition, may provide external motivation for learning. Some CAI lessons provide recognition by keeping a Hall of Fame that lists the names of individuals with the highest scores or the fastest times. A discussion of interpersonal motivation is outside the scope of this book. For an extensive discussion and references see Malone and Lepper (1987).

Comments.   The various models of personal motivation are not necessarily conflicting or mutually exclusive. For instance, some of the motivating elements of a feeling of control may overlap with elements of the feeling of power that comes from fantasy involvement. A single program such as Little Brick Out might pique one's curiosity as well as provide an element of challenge. Theories of motivation are a good starting point for instructional design, but as noted earlier they do not necessarily transfer to

CAI exactly as stated. Some motivators are possible in CAI that are not feasible in traditional instruction.

Motivators, like other aspects of instruction, interact with characteristics of the target population and the nature of computer application. Clearly, motivators that affect small children are not necessarily motivating for older children or adults. In CAI, motivators can even be adapted to individual differences within a target population. In fact, it should even be possible to vary motivation as learning progresses and as a student's need or desire for motivators diminishes.

A number of empirical studies have investigated both internal and external motivation in CAI. They are the next topic of discussion.

Empirical Studies

In his classic study, Malone (1981) employed an arithmetic game to find out what makes games intrinsically motivating. In the experiment, he varied potentially motivational features: arrows popping balloons, music, score-keeping, and several forms of verbal feedback. The main finding was that although these embellishments did help to create a motivating environment, there were considerable individual differences in the features students found appealing. There were also gender differences. Boys liked the fantasy of the arrow popping the balloons. While girls didn't much care for that, they did like the music.

In a second study, Malone compared identical instructional sequences with activities that differed in motivational appeal. One was a game format and the other a drill that had neither the music nor the balloons popping. Some students were allowed to choose between the game and the drill; others were given either the drill or the game format. As one might expect, the motivational appeal was greater for the game format. Students chose the game 50% more frequently than the drill. However, the game version did not produce more learning.

Extrinsic motivation. Self-paced instruction, which is feasible in CAI, results in considerable time savings for students who are high achievers and highly goal oriented (Kearsley & Hillelsohn, 1982). Nonetheless, some adults need some kind of motivation to keep them going. The Navy found that a record of one's progress led to a significant decrease in training time (Van Matre, 1980). However, Kearsley and Hillelsohn warn that access to progress records should be available on demand, when a student wants it and it should not be automatically forced on him.

Many CAI programs include extrinsic motivators such as graphic feedback "fireworks" or fantasy types of animations, color, and sound effects. Anecdotal evidence abounds concerning students' positive reactions. Unfortunately, there is little empirical evidence to support the learning advantages claimed by these anecdotes. Two studies, one with nine- and ten-year-olds (Surber & Leeder, 1988) and the other with high school students (Jaeger, 1988), showed that these types of feedback are neither particularly motivating nor educationally beneficial. In fact, they can interfere with learning.

Jaeger (1988) prepared four versions of a CAI mathematics lesson for high school students, each with identical content but a different level of feedback, from a simple "Correct" to color, sound, and animation feedback. With each additional correct response, the feedback became even more complex and more elaborate. In all conditions, the feedback to incorrect responses stated that the answer was wrong, and displayed the question along with the correct response. Students could watch any display as long as they wanted and could exit whenever they chose. For the first few exercises students spent considerably more time on the motivational than on the simple feedback. However, once the students knew what to expect, they lost interest and chose not to watch the motivational embellishments. In fact, students watched the displays that demonstrated the question and correct information longer than they watched the elaborate displays after correct answers. Jaeger states that after the first two exercises, particularly those with sound feedback, some students "frantically hit the spacebar to avoid what I had designed as pleasure."

Similar results with a spelling lesson for fourth and fifth graders are reported by Surber and Leeder (1988). Students were not more motivated, and did not perform better after cartoon-style feedback of verbal information (e.g., WOW!) than after the same feedback by standard characters.

Children's positive comments about graphic feedback sometimes conflict with their actions. They say they like the graphics but when given the opportunity to return to lessons, they display no greater rate of return to lessons with graphics than without (Surber & Leeder, 1988). Frequently there are discrepancies between students' ratings of lessons on questionnaires and their comments during interviews. They might make negative comments about lessons that they had previously rated as having high motivational appeal (Perez & White, 1985).

The graphic feedback in these studies was not an intrinsic part of the subject matter. They provided no corrective information but simply elaborated on the the correctness of the response. One might wonder whether graphic feedback would be motivating if it were intrinsic to the task.

In interviews with children, Perez and White found a motivator that has not been discussed in theories—the computer technology itself. Perhaps this can be explained as an example of curiosity as the motivating element. At this time there is no evidence that children get tired of computer lessons and turn away from them. The "novelty" does not seem to wear off.

Conclusions

Individual differences.   There are individual differences in motivation just as there are in cognition. Goal oriented high achievers are more likely to be motivated by learner control than low achievers. Individual differences in experience and knowledge determine whether an activity is surprising or curiosity-provoking and hence motivating.

Optimal level of motivators.   Both the theoretical and experimental literature stress that there is some optimal level of motivation. Challenge, for example, must be within a range that is achievable. The optimal level of challenge needs to adapt to the student as learning progresses. Curiosity or novelty is motivating only as long as it is not satisfied. Motivating embellishments, for example, may need to be phased out or else presented at random intervals in order to maintain their influence.

Selecting instructional technique.   An important decision for designers of CAI is selecting an instructional technique. Should a lesson, for example, be written as a drill or should it be presented in game format? Students, at least young ones, seem to be more motivated by games. Games take more time and are consequently less efficient than drill and practice. Games may be distracting and thus interfere with learning. Students may come to expect all learning to be game-like, and find routine classroom learning boring and dull. On the other hand the motivating aspects of games may increase students' attention and their active processing and thus result in superior learning. The concrete and visual aspects of a game might even promote retention of material learned. Students might get more interested in the subject or acquire a better attitude toward school.

Suppose that there are no significant differences in performance results between a highly motivating lesson and one that lacks extensive motivators. Is the extra effort involved in designing the motivating lessons worthwhile? The answer depends on whether there are important goals in addition to performance, such as students' attitudes. The answer to this question also depends on the cost in time for studying the lesson and also for developing it. There are no easy answers. The decisions depend on a cost/benefit analysis of time and effort to produce and study the lesson versus the achievement of the desired goals.

LEARNERS' EXPECTATIONS

The following message is printed on page 3-32 of the users' manual for the IBM proprinter:

"This page intentionally left blank."

Why did the editors insert this information? Why didn't they just leave the page blank? It is probably because they knew that people expect to find information on every page of a manual. If they encounter a blank page they think that their manual is defective. Their expectations are based on previous experience reading books.

Experiences in Traditional Instruction

Learners' expectations are based on past experience. These experiences affect learning behavior. Even though CAI is widely available in schools and computer-based training is widespread in military and industrial settings, most learning still occurs in traditional classrooms. Learners build their expectations of CAI on these classroom experiences.

In traditional environments students know what resources are available to assist them. For example, good learners characteristically plan learning strategies (cf. Chapter 2). If they are studying print materials they know how many pages and how much information there is to cover. If they have a limited amount of time, they can decide whether to read for details or to skim some sections and give more attention to others. If an assignment involves rules to follow or directions they have not previously encountered, good students know whether they should memorize this information, or depend on asking the teacher for it, or get it from other known resources. Students know that in the classroom the instructor will provide all of the information they need to do an assignment.

Students know about the nature of interactions in the classroom (cf. Chapter 1). Learners know what reactions they can expect from the instructor if they do well and what to expect if they make a mistake. They know how to communicate.

Experience With Other Computer Programs

Many students are gaining experiences with computer programs other than CAI, such as word processors and data bases. This experience affects their expectations in CAI. Although the situation is improving, many computer programs cause difficulties for users. In some instances users get trapped in an irreversible situation and can't get back to a previous location. When users ask for help, they cannot readily access the specific information they want. Rather, they have to read all the way through an extensive amount of text until they find what they want. Even though these difficulties are relatively infrequent, students are likely to have strong negative reactions to them (Shneiderman, 1982).

Implications for CAI

Designers of CAI need to include information that anticipates students' experiences in other instructional modes. One example is information that students depend on for learning. In a drill, a lesson can help learners by displaying progress toward their goal such as the number of exercises they have completed and the number they have left to do. A tutorial might include the display number and the total number of displays, such as Page 4/15. In a game or simulation that has a considerable number of rules to remember, the lesson might provide access to these rules at any time, and also inform learners that this aid is available. An explicit statement like "To see the rules, press key F1," can greatly expedite interaction with the lesson.

Some lessons employ many keys, each with a different function (e.g., back, index, help). Many students, particularly novices, are afraid that they won't remember all of them. They might forget how to get back to the index or how to review a section. These students frequently take the time to copy down all of the information about keys and their functions. A lesson can prevent students from wasting their time this way if information about these keys is displayed on the screen at all times (see Figure 6.1), and if students are told that this will be the case.

Unique features in CAI.   Some features exist in CAI that are not present in traditional instruction. Students need to be informed if these features are

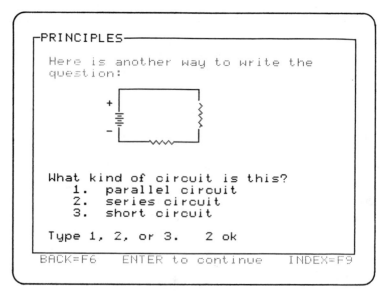

FIG. 6.1   Example of reminder of key functions on every display. (From CAI lesson, Questions and Answers. Copyright 1990 by E. R. Steinberg and D. Chirolas. Reprinted by permission.)

likely to cause them concern. If a screen will be blank while the computer is gathering data, the lesson should say so. It is a simple matter to display a message on the screen explaining the situation in language the student can understand. For instance, the message might read, "The system is gathering information. Please wait."

SUMMARY

Human factors, such as locus of control of instruction, motivation, and learners' expectations, play a significant role in learning. Learners' characteristics and the nature of the task interact with each of these factors to affect their influence on learning. Learner control is most likely to benefit students who have prior knowledge about a subject and appropriate learning strategies. Low achievers do not make good learning decisions and are unlikely to benefit from learner control. Feedback about performance increases the potential value of learner control.

Differences among target populations as well as among individuals influence the effectiveness of motivators. For any given task, a motivator functions at some optimal level. As with learner control and motivation, individual differences in experience affect learners' expectations and hence the design of CAI.

Human factors, presentations, and interactions are three of four factors that significantly affect instruction and learning. The fourth factor is the design of the instructional display. Display design is particularly crucial in CAI. Chapter 7 addresses visual displays and videodiscs.

Chapter 7

DISPLAYS AND INTERACTIVE VIDEOS

Graphic designers generate advertisements to attract our attention and convey a message that we readily understand and remember as well. They apply numerous techniques, such as typographical cues, nonverbal visuals, and screen layouts, to achieve this goal. Instructional designers can significantly aid learning by applying many of these techniques.

The interactive videodisc is an exciting new technology that makes available sophisticated visuals and the realism of films accompanied by sound. Thus it extends considerably the instructional potential of CAI.

ROLES OF VISUALS IN COMPREHENSION AND LEARNING

Nonverbal visual materials can increase learner motivation and concentration. Visual materials can prepare students for learning by grabbing their attention with pictures or animations related to the subject matter, such as a map of a country to be studied. In CAI, visuals can display inaccessible processes such as changes in the shape of sound waves that accompany changes in pitch, or changes that evolve over long periods of time, such as genetic changes in fruit flies. Visuals can illustrate, clarify, or supplement verbal information (Dwyer, 1985; Steinberg, 1984). Graphic displays can supplement understanding even when verbal text is straightforward, as in Figure 7.1.

Visuals also provide an alternative mode for learning. In many real world settings, visual displays are the major; if not the sole means of transmitting

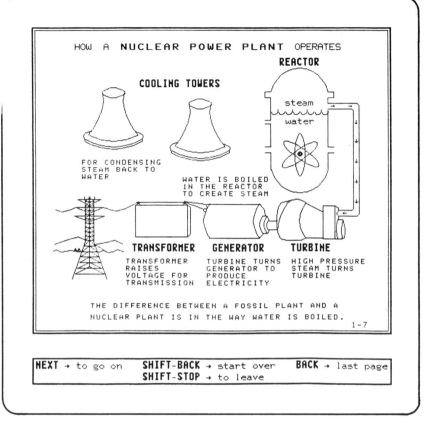

FIG. 7.1. Graphics that supplement verbal information. (From CAI lesson, Electrical Equipment and Terms. Copyright 1988 by Detroit Edison. Reprinted by permission.)

information. Airplane pilots, air traffic controllers, and operators of other complex systems are guided by extensive information presented in the form of dials and gauges. The dials on electric meters provide the only source of information about power usage in homes (see Figure 7.2) and power company employees need to interpret the readings. Instruction for these kinds of tasks must include graphic displays in conjunction with verbal information.

Although a considerable body of research demonstrates the effectiveness of visuals, the mere presence of graphics or specific display features, such as color, does not automatically guarantee better instruction. Color, for example, can serve as a coding cue in CAI to differentiate between several types of information being displayed simultaneously. Subject matter presentation might be colored yellow, directions white, and feedback to

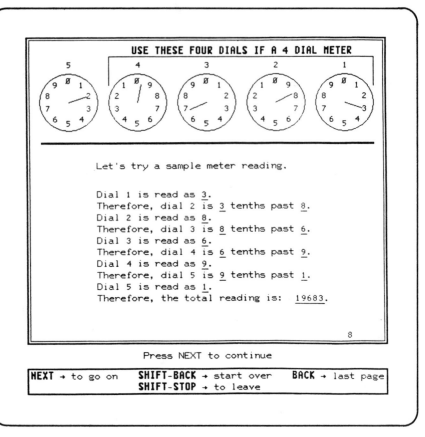

FIG. 7.2 Example of a visual display that is critical for learning. (From CAI lesson, Dial Post Cards. Copyright 1988 by Detroit Edison. Reprinted by permission.)

responses red. However, as the number of color-coded cues increases, the value of color coding decreases (Dwyer & Lamberski, 1982-83). Too many colors can simply cause confusion.

Appropriately designed, displays enhance learning. Designed without an understanding of how people derive meaning from them, displays can have no effect or can even interfere with learning. Display design synthesizes the techniques of graphic designers, instructional designers, and psychologists' understanding of how visual information is processed and how it facilitates learning.

How People Remember What They See

There are two opposing theories about how knowledge is represented in memory. One view states that all knowledge is stored according to its meaning in the form of logically complete statements, called propositions (Anderson & Bower, 1973; Anderson, 1980). Even pictures are stored in memory in terms of their meanings rather than as images. In contrast, dual coding theory (Paivio, 1974) proposes that a person's knowledge of the world is stored in two separate systems, one verbal and the other perceptual.

The imagery system (visual perception) is qualitatively different from the verbal. The imagery system organizes elementary units into higher order elements that are synchronous or spatial in character. For example, when we look at a face we see several features at one time and in certain spatial relationships to each other. The verbal system organizes linguistic units into higher order elements that are sequential structures. Thus, for instance, we organize sequences of letters into words and sequences of words into sentences.

The verbal and imagery systems are similar in that both are dynamic. Both systems reorganize, manipulate, or transform cognitive information. The imagery system transforms spatial characteristics; the verbal system, linguistic characteristics. We may remember a general impression of a face rather than each individual feature. Likewise, we are more apt to remember the meaning of a paragraph than the specific words and sentences.

The two systems are functionally independent but interconnected so that an activity in one system can initiate activity in the other. A picture (e.g., one's home) can initiate recall of verbal information (e.g., my home). Likewise, a verbal phrase, such as "my home" can initiate recall of images of one's home.

Studies of memory for pictures strongly suggest that there is a different kind of memory for pictorial material than linguistic. Haber (1970) reports an experiment in which subjects recognized as many as 600 pictures they had seen only for a short time. In another experiment subjects recognized 85% to 95% of 2500 slides they had seen over a series of two- or four-hour sessions. Although people might be able to recognize these pictures, they frequently are unable to recall details of a specific picture when asked to do so. This might be due to failure to notice the details in the first place; it might be due to forgetting. However, research revealed that neither of these hypotheses is correct. With probing, people were able to recall some information about fine details. Thus, there is strong evidence that picture recognition must be based on some kind of representation in memory that is maintained without verbal labels.

How Visuals Aid Comprehension

Haber and Wilkinson (1982) state that "The human visual system is designed to produce organized perception" (p. 25). We see a picture as an organized whole and not as separate lines or pieces. We do not have to add chunking procedures to unify it because every picture is a coherent chunk with its own organization. Most studies show that if material is organized, people perceive, understand, and remember it better than if it is not organized.

Because pictures have characteristics with which everyone is familiar, such as color and texture, it is possible for people to perceive and store information in a familiar, global schema. It is this capability that enables us to perceive and organize pictures presented in two dimensional space as if it were three-dimensional.

Graphics and complex information.   Diagrams and charts present information spatially. One of the advantages of diagrams is that they can, if used properly, reduce the complexity of relationships by allowing students to inspect related pieces of information at a glance (Tufte, 1983; Winn & Holliday, 1982). Like pictures, diagrams and charts organize and chunk information, making it easier to learn and remember.

Chernoff's (1973) cartoon faces dramatically demonstrate the power of visuals for comprehension and retention of complex information (see Figure 7.3). Chernoff used faces to represent multivariate data in such a way that viewers can readily grasp the relevant information. Each variable is represented by some feature of the face, such as the length of the nose or the size of the eyes. Chernoff stated that we can easily detect very small differences because we react to faces all of the time. Furthermore, we tend to filter out insignificant visual phenomena. In fact, we relate faces to emotional reactions and that seems to have a mnemonic advantage for remembering what we see.

The faces in Figure 7.3 represent an analysis of 12 characteristics of each of 53 equally spaced core samples drilled from a mountain. Notice how readily patterns emerge. The shapes of the faces of samples 223 through 231 are different from all of the others. In addition, the mouths change from noncommittal to happy.

Graphic representations of statistical information can do even more than organize and chunk information. They can "encourage the eye to compare different pieces of data" and even reveal the meaning of the data (Tufte, 1983). Each of the four sets of data in Figure 7.4a has the same mean and standard deviation yet each has an entirely different graphical distribution (see Figure 7.4b). The data of Table I are scattered. The graph of Table II is parabolic in shape while the graphs of Tables III and IV are straight lines with different slopes. These differences are not immediately apparent when the data are presented in tabular form.

Graphic analogies were found to help students learn complex electro-chemical concepts (Rigney & Lutz, 1976). Presented with one of two versions of a CAI lesson, students who saw graphical analogies performed

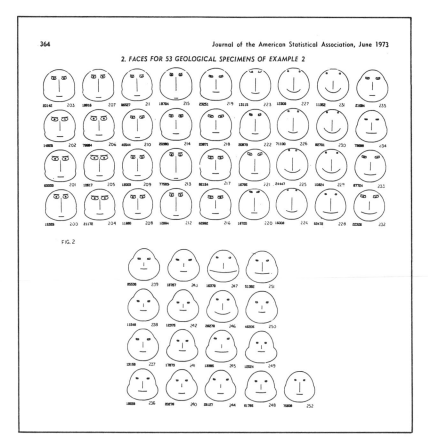

FIG 7.3   Chernoff's faces. *Note.* From "The use of faces to present points in k-dimensional space graphically" by H. Chernoff, *Journal of the American Statistical Association*, 1973, *68*, 361-368. Copyright 1973 by the American Statistical Association. Reprinted by permission.

better and had a better attitude than those who saw verbal descriptions alone.

Graphic representations can be misleading, as for example, when the sizes of the physical representation are not proportional to the numerical quantities they represent (Tufte, 1983). An example is a graphic that represents the differences in the average costs of homes in various cities. Pictures of different sized houses are displayed in order from the smallest house to the largest. However, the houses are not proportional in size to the costs. Order is maintained but magnitude is ignored.

Charts and diagrams.   Charts and diagrams are not equally effective for all students. Winn and Holliday (1982) hypothesized that the use of a chart

I		II		III		IV	
X	Y	X	Y	X	Y	X	Y
10.0	8.04	10.0	9.14	10.0	7.46	8.0	6.58
8.0	6.95	8.0	8.14	8.0	6.77	8.0	5.76
13.0	7.58	13.0	8.74	13.0	12.74	8.0	7.71
9.0	8.81	9.0	8.77	9.0	7.11	8.0	8.84
11.0	8.33	11.0	9.26	11.0	7.81	8.0	8.47
14.0	9.96	14.0	8.10	14.0	8.84	.8.0	7.04
6.0	7.24	6.0	6.13	6.0	6.08	8.0	5.25
4.0	4.26.	4.0	3.10	4.0	5.39	19.0	12.50
12.0	10.84	12.0	9.13	12.0	8.15	8.0	5.56
7.0	4.82	7.0	7.26	7.0	6.42	8.0	7.91
5.0	5.68	5.0	4.74	5.0	5.73	8.0	6.89

Mean of X's=9.0; standard deviation of X's=3.32
Mean of Y's=7.5; standard deviation of Y's=2.03

FIG. 7.4a. Data in tabular form.

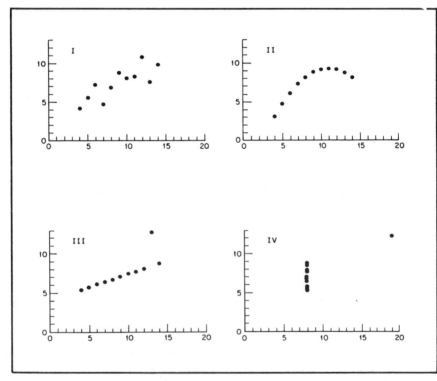

FIG. 7.4b. Data from Figure 7.4a in graphic form. *Note.* Both figures from "Graphs in statistical analysis" by F. J. Annscombe, *The American Statistician*, 1973, *18*, 17–21. Copyright 1973 by the American Statistical Association. Reprinted by permission.

or a diagram would be particularly helpful for students with either low verbal or high spatial ability. This is intuitively reasonable because it matches the way these students would be expected to process information. The hypothesis was not supported for either verbal or spatial ability. Diagrams did seem to help students with high verbal ability more than those with low verbal ability. The unexpected results were attributed to the tests that were used to measure ability. The tests of verbal ability may have measured general intellectual skills and not merely linguistic. That would explain why students who scored high on the verbal ability test were better able to process information than those with low verbal ability.

The implication of this work is that diagrams and charts are not automatically facilitative. Students have to know or be taught how to extract information from them.

Graphic organizers.   Graphic organizers are sometimes helpful, but they are not likely to be an additional aid to learning if the text itself is well organized. Further, if learners are sophisticated enough to enlist their own strategies, graphic organizers will not add value.

Illustrations and reading.   Some researchers find that pictures facilitate text comprehension, while others find that they either make no difference or that they interfere with reading (Schallert, 1980).

A study by Samuels (1970) reported that pictures were distracting stimuli when children were learning to read sight words. Samuels presented words under different training conditions: in sentences, with pictures, with both, or in isolation with neither sentences or pictures. When he tested the words in isolation, he found that pictures interfered with learning. Samuels attributed the results to the principle of least effort. The picture could elicit the word immediately while the printed word could not, so the children just "read" the word from the picture. Winn and Holliday (1982) report similar findings with college-age students.

In contrast, others have found that pictures that illustrate one or two previously unknown words in a sentence help students learn not only the illustrated but also the nonillustrated words (Schallert, 1980). These discrepancies in research results can be attributed in part to differences in experimental methodology. Emphasis in Samuels' work was on speed and efficiency. Words were read aloud to the children. Because they were told whether they were right or wrong, the information in the pictures was superfluous. Also, in contrast to other research, Samuels' pictures did not carry new information. They were essentially just adjuncts to the words.

In general, pictures help comprehension and retention when they are related to text in certain ways. These include situations "when they illustrate information central to the text, when they represent new content that is important to the overall message, and when they depict structural relation-ships mentioned in the text" (Schallert, 1980, p. 514).

HOW DISPLAY DESIGN AFFECTS PROCESSING AND LEARNING

Instructional designers can support learning by directing learners' scanning and processing strategies (Duchastel, 1982; Reilly & Roach, 1986; Waller, 1982). They do so by conforming to natural ways of scanning information and by incorporating design techniques.

How People Scan Displays

Some ways of scanning a display are natural (Tufte, 1983). People in "western societies" tend to scan from left to right and top to bottom. When people look at photographs they tend to look at the upper left hand corner or left side first (Heinich, Molenda, & Russell, 1985).

Implications for instruction.   Students are most likely to view informa-tion in the desired sequence if the designer presents it the way they will process it naturally. Unfortunately, some CAI designers overlook the importance of matching display design to natural ways of scanning. They erroneously present text at the top of a display after a learner has finished reading at the bottom. Chances are that the learner will not even notice the material added at the top.

Sometimes, an author finds it necessary to present information in a way that violates human tendency. In these situations it is possible to avoid potential difficulties by providing aids to direct the scanning process. This can be done with lines and arrows to direct the eye. Another technique is to show one segment of the display at a time and ask the learner to press a key to see the next segment.

Display Design and Text Processing

The design of text display can influence learning in two ways. It can (1) control processing and (2) facilitate learning (Gropper, 1988). Processing is controlled by directing a reader's attention to important ideas (Glynn, Britton, & Tillman, 1985). This is accomplished by using typographical cues such as bold face, inverse print, or "white" space around important ideas to separate more important information from the main body of text. Color or boxes can also be employed to provide emphasis or to focus attention on key ideas.

Organization and structure affect the ease with which students learn verbal information. The arrangement of text on the display screen can provide structure. For example, topic and paragraph headings signal the content and enable a learner to skim to get a quick overview of the material at hand (Waller, 1982). Information presented in lists or tables shows the organization and structure of information in a way that is not immediately apparent when the information is given in paragraph form. For example, compare the difference between reading the material in Figure 7.6 and the paragraphs of text in the next section entitled "Comparison of CAI Displays and Printed Pages."

Displays in CAI often present two kinds of textual information: subject matter and directions about the mechanics of interacting with the lesson, such as how to review or advance. Displaying the different kinds of information in separate areas by their functions can help learners avoid confusion (Heines, 1984). For example, information about functions of keys might always be at the bottom of the display. Color can also be employed to emphasize this difference. Subject matter content might be displayed in yellow and directions in white.

Special Features

Roles of color.   Color can serve numerous instructional purposes but its effectiveness is very much a function of its relationship to other instructional variables. In a review of the uses of color in learning and instruction, Dwyer and Lamberski (1982-83) report that research has yielded inconclusive results about its instructional value. Color can help organize displays and therefore reduce the amount of chunking the viewer needs to do (Haber & Wilkinson, 1982). If information is too complex for a learner to structure herself, or if a learner does not spontaneously code information, then color can be useful. Color can be motivating and increase attention (Heinich, Molenda, & Russell, 1985), but it does not necessarily increase comprehension (Tullis, 1981).

Realism.   Realistic visuals are not necessarily more effective than simplified ones for all types of objectives (Heinich, Molenda, & Russell, 1985; Dwyer, 1985). An increase in the degree of realism will not necessarily result in an increase in the amount of knowledge a student acquires. In fact, a complex, realistic visual may interfere with learning if a learner is unable to distinguish critical from irrelevant information. Figure 7.5 is an example of a visual that lacks realism, yet gets at the basic concept of a battery. A picture of a real battery would not provide this information.

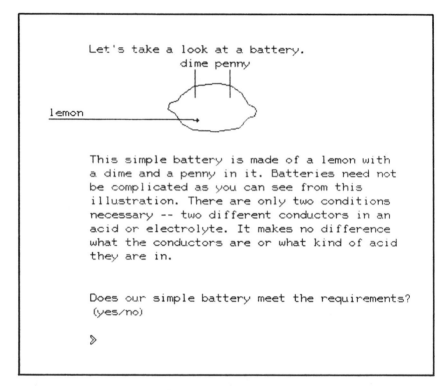

FIG. 7.5 Visual that presents a concept without realism. (From CAI lesson, Battery Principles by C. C. Dennis, Chanute Air Force Base, 1972. Reprinted by permission.)

COMPARISON OF CAI DISPLAYS AND PRINTED PAGES

CAI differs from printed materials in its potential for controlling the learning process and in its presentation capabilities (see Figure 7.6). The printed page controls scanning in a limited way by means of typographical cues, but CAI can exert even greater control. A CAI lesson can show as much or as little information at one time as the author chooses. The author can force a student to view the material in the order that the author intends. A computer can do a more extensive job than a printed page in getting viewers to selectively attend to important ideas. The author can limit the content that appears on the display. She can also selectively erase some parts of a display, leaving only the desired part for viewing.

The interactive capability of CAI enables the program not only to direct attention but also to ask questions to monitor students' attention.

Presentation capabilities of books and CAI are similar in two ways. (1)

FEATURE	CAI	PRINTED PAGE
Control of Learning Processes		
Scanning	Extensive control	Limited control
Selective attention	Extensive	Limited
Amount of information displayed	Learner or computer controlled	Controlled by page size
Interaction	Possible	Not possible
Presentation Capabilities		
Typographical cues	Available	Available
Illustrations	Available	Available
Resolution	Varies	Very good
Animations	Available	Not available
Realism	Possible	Limited
Inter—display continuity	Not smooth	Relatively smooth
Density of text	Variable	Uniform
Space available per display	Varies: from about 24 to 32 lines, 40-80 ch per line	Varies: from about 40 to 54 lines, 60–75 ch per line
Color	Widely available	Available but expensive to use extensively
Pacing presentation of a display	All at once or in sections	All at once

FIG. 7.6.   Comparison of CAI and printed page display capabilities.

Typographical cues are available in both. (2) Illustrations are possible in both. However, aside from their artistic and instructional merits, the quality of illustrations in CAI varies with the quality of the screen display. Fidelity is not as accurate on monitors with low resolution as with high.

The presentation capabilities in CAI are different from printed materials in several ways. Animations are available in CAI, but not on a printed page. The availability of interactive videodisc technology adds the capability of realism. Videodiscs are discussed further in the section, Interactive Videos, later in this chapter.

CAI is at a disadvantage to the printed page in matters of interdisplay continuity. Some amount of fragmentation seems to occur from one display to another. Sometimes students even fail to realize that there is a connection between displays.

In a book, the density of information per page is fixed; there are a fixed number of characters per line and a fixed number of lines per page. Almost every page is covered with this amount of text. In CAI, the amount of text on a display does not have to be uniform. Each conceptual unit can therefore be presented on a separate display, whether it requires one line or twenty. Of course a concept can be extended over several displays if necessary.

The amount of information on a computer display screen varies, but is often not more than 24 lines, with a range of 40 to 80 character per line. Page capacity in books varies from about 40 to 54 lines with 60 to 75 characters per line.

While color is available in printed materials, it is expensive to print and usually reserved for special purposes. Color is widely available and used in CAI. Although it has been shown that color improves performance under limited conditions, its full potential in CAI has not yet been explored. Even if color does not affect performance, it is pleasant and may make learning more enjoyable.

Finally, in books a reader may choose to read only parts of a page, but all of the information on the page is displayed simultaneously. The author of a CAI lesson can allow the learner to pace the display presentation.

Implications for CAI

The display advantages of CAI over printed materials make possible new instructional techniques. For example, a process can be displayed and simultaneously explained by creating the nonverbal displays interactively with verbal explanations. CAI can also exert more control over the learning process by step-wise presentation of information, that is, by presenting desired amounts of information and then allowing a learner to press a key when she is ready to continue.

Comments

Visuals can aid comprehension and retention but they do not do so automatically. As is the case in other aspects of learning and instruction, the value of visuals is not solely a function of the visuals themselves but rather a consequence of their relevance to the task at hand and their suitability for the intended learners.

Display techniques can and do affect learning, but the extent to which they do so depends on the relationship between the function of the display and the sophistication of the intended learners (Duchastel, 1982). As noted earlier, graphic organizers can be helpful, but they are not likely to facilitate learning if the text itself is well organized. Further, if learners are sophisticated enough to enlist their own strategies, graphic organizers will not add value.

An additional concern with respect to displays and visuals is learners' ability to interpret them. There is some evidence, for instance, that children under 12 years of age tend to interpret visuals by section. They tend to single out specific elements, whereas older students tend to abstract the mearning of the whole scene (Heinich, Molenda, & Russell, 1985). Learners need to learn how to interpret graphic information or complex displays, just as they need to learn to interpret text.

INTERACTIVE VIDEOS

Some kinds of knowledge and skills cannot be adequately taught by verbal text, diagrams, or photographs. To learn how to repair delicate equipment, for example, learners need to first observe the intricate manual techniques of an expert. To gain skill in handling interpersonal relationships such as interviews, learners need to observe how experts use an interviewee's verbal responses, facial expressions, and body movements to guide an interview. Students also need an opportunity to practice the techniques they have observed in real situations or in settings that simulate realism.

Benefits of Videos in Learning

Instructors can demonstrate technical skills but they must usually do so in group settings. It may be difficult for some students to see well, even in small groups. Furthermore it is not possible to simulate all facets of work environments, such as repair shops, or business offices, or hospitals in the classroom. Video devices such as films and videodiscs fulfill this need to see the details of the skills in the realistic setting.

Video presentations in combination with computers present information in one or more modes simultaneously. This includes video image, sound, and computer-generated text and graphics. Multimode presentations help students gain a more complete understanding of the topic being discussed. In a videodisc chemistry lesson, Smith, Jones, and Waugh (1986) display video images of chemical changes simultaneously with chemical equations. A music class gains a deeper understanding of an opera when they can see the musical notes and words of an opera superimposed on a film of the stage action.

In an early scene in one videodisc lesson (IBM, 1987), a man working in a manufacturing plant turns around and says to the viewer, with the hum of the plant in the background, "So you want to know what manufacturing is all about. You've come to the right place." The information content exceeds that which can be presented by an instructor, printed material, or computers alone. The motivational and attention-gaining impact also exceed that possible via other media.

Comparison of Video Devices

Four different video technologies are used in instruction. Films and television have been available for some time. Videotapes and videodiscs are more recent technology. They share some features that are beneficial to learners, but the videodisc is the most versatile for instruction.

Films and television.   Both films and television can present the kinds of real life or simulated situations described above. However, they are generally not satisfactory media for individualized instruction because they promote passive learning. Films do not include instructional messages and questions that can enhance information processing. They do not require overt and meaningful responses from learners. In that way they are like printed material. The information is there, but it is entirely up to the learner to select that which is critical and to remember it. Learners cannot interact with simulations on films or television, so they cannot benefit from making decisions and observing the consequences of their actions. There is no branching; there is no feedback; there is no individualization.

Videotapes.   Videotapes present the same kinds of information as films and television. In addition, they have an important instructional advantage over television in that videotapes can be integrated with CAI. A videotape can be placed under computer control just like the rest of a CAI lesson. The computer lesson can stop the tape, ask questions, wait for a student's response, and then provide feedback. Students can be required to become active learners.

A major disadvantage of videotapes is that information is accessed linearly. To view a section of the tape near the end, the tape must wind through all of the preceding footage. Although this can be done in a fast forward mode, it requires an unacceptable amount of time for instructional purposes. Thus branching, an important part of individualized instruction, is essentially unavailable.

Videodiscs.   Videodiscs have all of the advantages of videotapes and one additional critical feature—random access to any frame within a few seconds. Extensive branching is possible. In a tutorial lesson a student can select the frame or frames he wishes to see and can access them within an acceptable length of time. In an art appreciation course, for example, a student does not have to view a collection of paintings in a prespecified order but can see them by artist, subject matter, or any other system he chooses. In a patient management lesson, a student can see the consequences of her decisions immediately as the program branches to the appropriate sequence of frames.

Computer text and displays can be superimposed on the video to add supplementary information. Critical information can be added and emphasized. Particularly important for CAI is the capability of posing questions and requiring overt responses. Feedback and remediation can be provided.

Another advantage of videodiscs is that they can be placed under the direct control of either the lesson or the learner. A user can play a videodisc at various speeds of audio and video. He can slow down or speed up a process, but this may cause distortion of the audio.

Examples of Videodisc Instruction

Videodiscs are employed in academic instruction and in computer-based training. They can be applied in both direct and indirect instruction.

Chemistry. Although CAI simulations of chemistry laboratories have been used in chemistry education, they lack the necessary realism and graphic detail (Smith, Jones, & Waugh, 1986). Smith and his colleagues found that interactive videodisc lessons can replace selected laboratory experiments, and can promote understanding of concepts as well as, if not better than, traditional laboratory experiences. One of the advantages of interactive videodisc lessons in chemistry is that students can be exposed to equipment that is too expensive or too delicate for them to use. Another advantage is that it is possible to present experiments that are too fast, take too much time, or are too hazardous for students to run themselves.

Smith and his colleagues prepared approximately 10 hours of interactive videodisc laboratory simulations and evaluated them with 103 college students enrolled in a general chemistry course. One group of students was required to complete the interactive videodisc lessons in place of laboratory work. Another group was required to complete a traditional laboratory experiment on the same material. A third group was required to complete the videodisc lessons before the traditional laboratory experiment.

Students who participated in the regular laboratory experiment were required to write laboratory reports. Those who studied the videodisc lesson in addition to the traditional laboratory wrote better reports than those who did only the traditional laboratory. The differences were both statistically and practically significant. "Students who had not used the videodisc lessons were more likely to use rote citation of examples from the laboratory manual to explain their observations even when their explanations were in direct contradiction to their reported observations" (p. 120).

Students who participated in the videodisc lessons outperformed those who participated only in the traditional laboratories on a short paper and pencil quiz. Surprisingly, there were no significant differences between the two videodisc groups. The researchers attribute the advantage of the videodisc lessons over the experimental laboratory to the fact that the lessons are individualized and interactive. Students get individualized, immediate feedback that is not possible in large introductory courses. The opportunity to relate theoretical concepts to observations enhances students' understanding of chemical concepts and principles.

These results should not be taken to mean that all laboratories should be replaced by videodisc lessons. Clearly the manipulative skills experienced in the laboratory cannot be acquired through videodisc simulations. However, the simulations can assist in learning the intellectual skills, such as making observations and collecting and analyzing date.

Medicine.   In the health sciences, videodiscs help bridge the gap between theory and practice. A lesson for nurses, for example, contains a scenario of a young man who has a fractured leg as a result of an automobile accident (Ittelson, Land, Leedom, & Persaud, 1989). The patient develops four different complications about which the student nurse must make decisions. An important part of the task is to observe and judge the patient's condition. Is he gasping for breath? Is he sweating profusely? Other than in real life, it would be difficult to convey to the student nurse the impact or the urgency of these conditions and to give her the opportunity to judge the situation.

The lesson is presented in two modes. A student can watch an expert nurse care for the patient or else make her own decisions. At each decision point a student can get information about why an action was taken. If a student chooses an incorrect step, she gets immediate feedback with explanations.

Technical training.   Interactive videodiscs provide an important medium for technical training in industry and in the military. Eventually, trainees need to maintain real equipment and they need to practice on the actual equipment to get the highest degree of fidelity. The equipment is often very sophisticated and highly complex, and not designed to be used for training. When used in the training environment, students induce so many failures in the equipment that the cost of maintenance is very high. Interactive videodiscs offer a high-fidelity simulation of maintenance tasks as an adjunct or even as an alternative to training on the actual equipment.

Integration of interactive video lessons into existing programs for maintenance training on a radar system has significantly improved trainee performance. In general, trainees take less time to do the tasks and do them with greater proficiency. They can also perform hazardous tasks that were previously unachievable. Improved student retention, reduced costs for actual equipment and trainers, and reduced maintenance costs are additional benefits (Clark, 1988).

Videodisc Is a Tool

It is not the videodisc per se but rather appropriate use that adds new dimensions to instruction and learning. Good lessons are a combination of understanding instructional design, programming, and video (Smith, Jones, & Waugh, 1986). Successful applications engage students actively and overtly in the learning process. They provide individualized, informative feedback. The video capability assists learning.

SUMMARY

Pictures, diagrams, and illustrations aid comprehension by organizing and chunking information. They provide information in a different mode than verbal text and as such afford an alternative mode for learning. Visuals can supplement verbal information as well as present information that is difficult, if not impossible, to present verbally. Visual material can also aid retention.

Videodiscs add sophisticated visuals and present information simultaneously in more than one mode. They add realism and an opportunity to engage in experiences that are essential to learning but otherwise too dangerous or too costly for novice learners. Like computers, videodiscs are tools and not methods of instruction. As with other aspects of CAI, displays and videodiscs interact with learner characteristics, the task, the goals, and appropriate use of the computer.

Displays and interactive videos are among many features that enhance individualization in CAI. The many facets of individualized instruction are discussed in Chapter 8.

Chapter 8

ADAPTIVE CAI

CAI was defined in Chapter 1 as "computer-presented instruction that is individualized, interactive, and guided." It is individualized in the sense that the computer serves as a tutor for one individual. A major thesis of this volume and its companion (Steinberg, 1984) is that it is both possible and desirable to create CAI lessons that adapt to each individual's learning needs.

Individualized and Adaptive Instruction

The words, individualized and adaptive, are frequently used interchangeably. The general idea is that each student should be allowed to learn in the way that is best for him or her. There are some subtle differences between the terms, particularly in CAI.

Individualized instruction. Individualized instruction may simply mean that students study alone rather than in pairs or groups. It is most frequently defined more broadly to mean that the subject matter is individualized in one or more ways that promote learning. Students advance through a lesson at their own pace. Slower students can take the time they need and can get help when they need it. Each student begins instruction at a level commensurate with his knowledge. A knowledgeable student is not bored by content he already knows and a novice is not frustrated. The sequence of instruction and the difficulty level may also be adjusted to each student's level.

Adaptive instruction. Adaptive instruction combines all of the characteristics of individualized instruction with an additional dimension that good tutors provide. It is instruction that tries to adapt to a student's processes of learning. Adaptive instruction seeks to understand why a learner is having difficulty. It tries to determine whether the problem is one of omission or commission, whether the learner lacks an important subconcept or misunderstands it. Computers have the computational capacity to individualize and to adapt CAI lessons. The difficulty in generating adaptive lessons lies not in computational power but in the difficulty of making models of students' understanding.

NONCAI INDIVIDUALIZED INSTRUCTIONAL SYSTEMS

The idea of individualized instruction is not unique to CAI. Programs of individualized instruction were applied in traditional classrooms before the advent of computers. Although those systems were not adaptive in as many aspects of instruction as CAI, they do have implications for CAI.

Programmed Instruction: Individualized Pacing

Programmed instruction is individualized instruction that is based on an application of Skinner's principles of operant conditioning (cf. Chapter 2). It was Skinner's contention that because these principles involve both active responding and immediate reinforcement, it is impossible to apply them in group-paced classrooms. In the classroom, only one student at a time is called on to respond to the teacher's questions, so only that student can be reinforced. Other students need not respond actively. Even if they do "think" the answers, the instructor has no way of reinforcing each of them. Students do engage actively in individual tasks such as workbooks, but they are not immediately reinforced for every response. Teachers do not grade workbooks until after students complete entire blocks of responses.

In programmed instruction, students work individually at their own pace through a sequence of frames, which include frequently inserted questions to promote active responding. Answers to questions are available immediately. Teaching machines can require overt responses and can give immediate feedback, and are therefore useful tools for implementing programmed instruction. Unlike teaching machines, programmed texts cannot fully implement behavioral principles. Because answers to questions are provided in the text, students are free to look them up before they respond overtly.

A limitation of noncomputer-based programmed instruction is that all students follow the same linear sequence. Crowder (1960) believed that instruction should provide multiple paths through a lesson. Each student's sequence of instruction should be based on a history of her responses. Unfortunately, Crowder's attempts to implement this idea in written form were not practical because the programs frequently became too bulky.

In CAI, both individualized pacing and multiple paths are feasible. Nonlinear lessons need not be limited to multiple-choice questions as they sometimes were in print medium. Branching can be implemented on the basis of responses to constructed as well as multiple choice questions. Computers are a wonderful vehicle for implementing programmed instruction.

A number of systems of individualized instruction developed in the sixties derived from behavioral principles. Two systems are reviewed here.

Keller's PSI

Keller's (1968) Personalized System of Instruction (PSI) served as a model of individualized instruction for college level courses. Using programmed instruction, students move through the course at their own pace, according to their ability and the amount of time they have. Proctors administer tests and score them immediately. Students must master each unit of instruction before proceeding to the next. Performance criteria are set with the expectation that most students will attain them.

Although programmed instruction is the major technique in a PSI course, lectures and demonstrations are also employed. The purpose of these activities is to motivate rather than to serve as a source of critical information. Students also interact with peers or proctors. A consequence of all this interaction is an "almost unavoidable tutoring, and a marked enhancement of personal social aspect of the educational process."

Self-discipline.   Performance is mastery-based, so students just have to do the assignments and pass the tests to get an A or a B. Almost all of them do so. If students get lower grades, it is because they fail to complete the required work. Some drop out because they apparently do not "regularize" their study habits.

Evaluation.   The Personalized System of Instruction has been implemented in college courses in a wide range of subject areas and in both introductory and nonintroductory courses. A meta-analysis of 75 comparative studies of teaching methods (Kulik, Kulik, & Cohen, 1979) showed that PSI usually produced student achievement that was superior to instruction by lectures. Students were enthusiastic about the course and did not perceive it as controlling. They did not spend significantly more time in

PSI courses, nor did they show a higher dropout rate than in traditional courses.

Implications of CAI.   The issues of self-discipline and of environmental implementation are equally important in CAI. If PSI were implemented using computers as the vehicle for both programmed instruction and tests, proctors would not be needed for grading. Would the absence of the personal contact with proctors diminish the likelihood of students completing the course? There is a decided contrast between the low dropout rate in PSI courses and the high dropout rate in the early TICCIT mathematics project, which was also a full-course individually directed program (Chapter 3). To what factors can this difference be attributed? To differences in student populations? To differences in the requirement to interact with proctors? To the possibility that the proctor was perceived by students to be keeping a watchful eye?

It is not unreasonable to suggest that personal interactions played an important role in motivation to complete PSI courses. The knowledge that they had to report to a proctor for tests may have served as a subtle support to the self-discipline needed to complete such courses. It is also possible that students found it very useful to be able to discuss reasons for the mistakes they made on the tests. There is indirect evidence that the personal contact was also important in the CAISMS project (Chapter 4). In that project students not only answered computer-based questions about their reading assignments, but were expected to sign up for a given number of discussion groups dealing with topics they had completed rather than attend large group lectures.

It may very well be that if an entire course is to be presented via CAI, it is more likely to have a low dropout rate if the overall course also includes activities that require interpersonal interaction such as discussion groups. In fact, if the target learners are not likely to be well motivated or self-disciplined, supplementary interpersonal interaction may be critical to successful completion of the CAI course.

Individually Prescribed Instruction

Individualized systems of education were also developed at the elementary and secondary school levels during the 1960s. These programs stemmed from a general shift in educational philosophy, away from an earlier view that education was for selected individuals who could benefit from it. The new philosophy was that education should enable each child to develop to his maximum potential. A research and development effort particularly relevant to CAI is Individually Prescribed Instruction (IPI), which focused on diagnosis and development of curriculum materials in reading and arithmetic (Glaser & Rosner, 1975). The curriculum followed Skinner's principles in some ways: instruction was individualized, performance oriented, and systematically designed to follow well-defined sequences of behavioral objectives. Instructional sequences were developed for every topic, level, and skill, and presented in workbooks of exercises. The workbooks, however, were not programmed instruction. Answers were not provided. Performance was graded by a teacher or a "grader" after students completed them.

The developers did not want students to have to repeat what they already knew, but they did want each student to have the appropriate prerequisite knowledge. Therefore, students were tested to determine their starting point in the curriculum. Each student's learning was continually monitored by means of unit pretests. Results of pretests determined which objectives to assign a student within a given unit. Posttests were parallel to pretests and assessed mastery of those objectives. Students advanced according to their performance, criteria of competence, and available instructional alternatives. A consequence of this method, according to Hsu and Carlson (cited in Hambleton, 1974), is that students spent a considerable amount of time taking tests. It is not clear whether the system accurately assessed mastery when students took a posttest a second time. They may have passed it more as a result of practice than of actually mastering the objectives.

The developers intended that students would participate in both small and large group discussions in addition to working individually. In the arithmetic curriculum, discussions and other activities were needed to help students integrate their knowledge. One of the shortcomings of the individualized booklets was that while they enabled students to achieve the individual behavioral objectives, they did not help the students to become aware of the relationships between topics.

Unfortunately the programs were not always implemented in the way intended. Teachers lacked the training to develop the needed supplementary instruction. Many found it difficult to be constantly aware of where in the curriculum each of 25 or 30 students was working and did not hold group discussions.

Implications for CAI.   One of the components of a framework for CAI is the nature of environmental implementation (cf. Chapter 2). Experience with IPI shows that a critical aspect of that implementation is adequate training for instructors who will take part in a major curriculum shift or an innovative technology. For IPI, the task was to train teachers to shift their orientation from group-paced to individualized settings. In CAI, the task is to get teachers to shift their perception of their role in instruction and to help them learn how to do so. If the CAI materials are individualized drills, teachers need to learn how to use the time that they no longer need to spend turning out worksheets. If the lessons are innovative and depart from traditional instructional practices, teachers need to learn how to integrate them into the curriculum. They need time to study CAI lessons so they become familiar with the content.

NonCAI individualized systems set a fixed criterion for acceptable performance, say 85%, for all units of instruction. In a hierarchically structured sequence, as in IPI, students may not need such a high level of proficiency for each new skill. Some units might require less proficiency than others. Bright students might be able to acquire some subordinate topics while learning higher level ones. CAI has the potential for varying the criteria for mastery according to the structure of the content and an individual learner's ability.

In both nonCAI and CAI programs, a common method of monitoring students' achievement is through pretests and posttests. If tested too frequently, a student's performance may measure a practice effect rather than real understanding, as occurred in the IPI curriculum.

INDIVIDUALIZED AND ADAPTIVE CAI LESSONS

Programmed instruction is individualized in that it enables students to work at their own pace but the programs are linear. Every student studies the identical materials in the identical sequence. Individualized systems such as IPI are more individualized in that they add placement and branching capabilities. However, mastery is based on a fixed percentage of correct answers. In addition, once they begin a unit of instruction, students do a preset number of exercises at a fixed difficulty level.

CAI has the capacity to individualize in more sophisticated ways. To a certain extent it can also adapt to a student's understanding.

Drills

A CAI drill can individualize the amount of practice by employing any number of different criteria to assess learning. Assessment can be based on a succession of responses rather than on a single response. The mastery criterion might be a fixed number of successive correct answers, say three in a row, or it might be a certain percentage correct in the last set of ten exercises.

Selection of items for a drill can be adapted to each learner. Drills can be written to provide extra review on items that are difficult for a student. If the goal is to bolster self-confidence, drills can include many items that the student can answer successfully.

Informational feedback can help a student discriminate between items that previously confused him. In a drill about state capitals, for instance, a student might give the name of a state capital but for the wrong state. When asked for the capital of Missouri he might answer, "St. Paul." Feedback would point out that St. Paul is indeed a capital, but of Minnesota and not Missouri. If the response is St. Louis, the feedback would point out that St. Louis is in Missouri, but it is not the state capital.

Tutorials

It was stated in Chapter 5 that a student's responses to well chosen questions help a good tutor to diagnose misconceptions and enables the tutor to help the student overcome them. A good CAI lesson also embeds such questions and provides informative feedback that is attuned to the nature of the misunderstanding.

Feedback in CAI can also be developed at several levels of information and adjusted to the needs of each learner. A simple hint is adequate for some learners; more detailed information may be necessary for others. The amount of assistance given to a learner can be phased out as learning progresses.

More than one type of explanation can be provided in a lesson. A learner who needs remediation can be branched to alternative instruction. It may be a different way of explaining the topic or it might be a reminder of prerequisite knowledge and how it applies to the topic under discussion. Perhaps the alternative explanation gives more examples or adds some visual information. The point is that multiple instructional paths can be arranged to adapt not only to the sequence of topics but also to each learner's needs for remedial or supplementary instruction.

A CAI lesson can also be adapted to very specific kinds of help. For example, a reading lesson can allow a student to point to a word he cannot read or cannot understand, and the program can either pronounce it for him or present a definition.

To generate these kinds of adaptive lessons, authors or other members of the development team need experience teaching the given subject matter to the target population on a one-to-one basis. Developers need to know the kinds of misunderstandings that often occur so that they can generate diagnostic questions and provide suitable feedback. This kind of information cannot be obtained from instruction by lectures. It is gleaned from interaction with individual students and supplemented from the results of trials of lessons when they are under development.

Decision Making, Simulations, Exploratory Tasks

In decision-making and simulation tasks, each student can see the consequences of her actions. In that sense the program adapts the results to each learner's decisions. In exploratory tasks, the lesson can make suggestions to guide each student to the extent that she needs guidance.

Learning Styles

Students vary in their learning styles. In concept and rule learning, some students like to learn a rule before they see the examples. Others prefer examples and then the rule, while still others might like rule, examples, and rules again before doing practice exercises. CAI lessons can give students the option of selecting any of these learning styles (e.g., TICCIT).

As noted in Chapter 7, some students prefer to control the flow of learning themselves, while others prefer structured computer control. A CAI lesson can adapt to both preferences.

Motivators

Motivators can vary within a lesson and adapt to characteristics of each learner. Some may like music and others not. The lesson can let each learner decide for herself. Each student's performance score, or a record of her progress, can be made available when and if the learner wants to see it.

Disclaimers

It is not the claim here that all CAI lessons are adaptive in the ultimate sense. Some lessons individualize extensively, some very little. Many lessons available today do not take advantage of the adaptive potential of computers at all.

Nor is it the contention that all lessons need to be totally adaptive. The extent of adaptiveness varies with the goals of the lesson, the learners, and the subject matter. If the goal is to provide a self-testing drill, and students can learn from their own mistakes, it may not be necessary to repeat missed items more frequently than learned items. If the target population is a group of slow learners, then it would seem to be important to provide an adaptive drill. If the goal is to reach the majority of a rather homogeneous group of students and the subject matter is not very complex, extensive branching may not be necessary.

The preceding discussion should not be construed to mean that all instruction should be individualized. Although individualization has many benefits as noted earlier, interaction with peers and with mentors also plays a significant role in learning.

MATHEMATICAL/STATISTICAL ADAPTIVE CAI SYSTEMS

Mathematical and statistical approaches to instructional design are based on mathematical or probabilistic theories and models of learning and instruction. The specific models are different but they do have some common characteristics. All of the models estimate a student's performance before instruction and continue to estimate ability throughout the lesson. Instruction is then adapted, based on this assessment, and with respect to the learning outcomes set by the model (Park & Tennyson, 1983).

Potential Benefits

The major benefit of these approaches is their potential for individualizing instruction above and beyond appropriate initial placement and self-pacing. Theoretically, a good model can provide instruction at an appropriate level of difficulty and subject matter content and thus enable students to pursue truly different instructional paths. Appropriate sequencing and adjustment of difficulty level allows the more able students to take bigger steps in instruction or to do more challenging tasks. In addition, ideally, an individualized system of instruction diagnoses the reasons for each student's deficiencies and generates instruction designed specifically to help students overcome them.

Mathematical Models of Learning

Atkinson's (1976) approach to individualizing instruction was to develop a mathematical model for acquiring a specific skill and then to use this model to specify the optimal sequence of instruction. The model for item selection was based on an estimate of the student's ability and an estimate of item difficulty. The student's ability was determined from his complete response history. Estimates of item difficulty were made from an analysis of the performance of all students who had studied the lessons. The program modified itself automatically as more students completed the course and the data from their response histories showed defects in the instructional strategy (and thus indicated how the formula should be revised).

Applications of mathematical models.   The Stanford University Institute for Mathematical Studies in Social Sciences began a program for research and development in CAI in 1963 with an instructional program in elementary mathematical logic (Suppes, Macken, & Zanotti, 1978). The first implementation of CAI in an elementary school was in arithmetic in 1965. Since that time, the programs have been extensively expanded and are currently commercially available through Computer Curriculum Corporation. The mathematical models have been applied to arithmetic and reading drills and are intended to be supplementary instruction. The goal is to optimize instruction for each individual. Two of the early CAI programs based on mathematical models of learning are reviewed next to illustrate the concept.

Stanford Reading Program. The Stanford reading program addressed mainly decoding (sounding out) skills. The curriculum was divided into eight strands ranging from how to interact with the program to letter identification, sight word recognition, spelling patterns, and so on. The program decided which items and which instructional format to select within a given strand. Depending on a student's responses to previous items, the program decided when to shift from one strand to another. For example, in the sight word strand, one set of exercises involves copying a work like *pen*. Another set of exercises involves recognizing a word in a set of three words (pen, net, egg). The decision to shift from the sight word to the spelling pattern strand depended on a student's performance in sight words. The program also controlled for a student's progress within a strand compared to other strands because the developers perceived students' need to learn items from one strand in conjunction with the same items in another.

Fletcher and Atkinson (cited in Atkinson, 1972) compared 50 pairs of students who received 15 minutes daily of CAI with a control group that studied reading in the classroom during that time. At the end of first grade, the CAI group showed a five month gain over the control group and at the end of second grade the difference was about 4.9 months.

These differences between CAI and standard groups may have been a consequence of individualized practice rather than of CAI per se. If a reading teacher could interact individually with each student 15 minutes a day, the same results might have occurred. However, Atkinson questions the ability of a teacher to be as effective as the computer in making instructional decisions for so many students over an extended period of time.

In another study Atkinson (1976) applied a mathematical model of foreign language learning to optimize learning German vocabulary. The goal was to maximize students' performance on a delayed test. He compared three instructional alternatives: (1) items presented in random order; (2) items selected by the learner; and (3) items selected by a response-sensitive strategy programmed into the computer (based on a trial-by-trial analysis of each student's response history).

Results showed that performance during learning was best for students who saw items in random order, then for students under learner control, and poorest for students under the response-sensitive strategy. However, on the delayed test results were just the reverse. Those who had studied under the response-sensitive strategy scored 79% compared to 58% for learner controlled and 38% for random conditions.

Lessons learned. Experiences with these individualized systems are more examples of the contention that it is not the computer per se but how it is used that affects learning. To the extent that computers can serve as a tool for implementing individualization and for tasks in which individualized instruction is superior to group instruction, CAI can significantly improve students' performance, and in some cases, retention.

Question. Instruction based on these mathematical models is supposed to be supplementary rather than mainline instruction. One would expect it to be integrated with those activities. None of the published research provides information about the integration of this system of CAI with other learning activities.

Tennyson's Bayesian Model

Tennyson and his colleagues have done numerous CAI studies of instruction based on a Bayesian probabilistic model of instruction and on a model of concept learning (Park & Tennyson, 1983). Like other individualized systems, their system is based on a continuous estimate of each student's understanding and therefore of his learning needs. This system differs from traditional branching procedures in that it takes into account not only the structure of the learning task but also the learner's processing needs (Park, 1984). Concept learning, to which Tennsyon applied the Bayesian model, is thought to be a two-stage process in which a learner first forms a prototype of the concept and then develops skills to classify instances and noninstances of the concept. This adaptive program might determine, for example, that a student's responses indicate a failure to discriminate between two concepts. The program then selects items that promote discrimination, based on a previously developed strategy for sequencing examples.

For instance, when acquiring the concept of a triangle, a student might first think of a triangle as a three-sided, closed figure with equal sides and a horizontal base. Gradually, he learns that other three-sided closed figures are also triangles, regardless of lengths of sides or orientation. He also learns that closed figures with more than three sides are not triangles. If a program were teaching the concept of a triangle, it might determine that a student was having difficulty discriminating between a triangle and a trapezoid. The program would then select examples to facilitate discrimination between triangles and nontriangles.

Tennyson's system is still in the research stage and is not widely applied in real instructional settings. It is important because it expands the idea of instructional design to include not only an analysis of content structure but also an analysis of the psychological processes of learning. The computer is then used as a tool to implement and test the instructional model.

Conclusions

Each of the models presented is based on the assumptions of a given theory of learning or measurement. They are therefore only generalizable to specific instructional situations. This means that applications are limited to specific types of learning tasks. The mathematical models are limited mainly to memory tasks or those which follow a fixed procedure. The Bayesian models are limited to concept learning.

Probabilistic models are best estimates. As such, they can be accurate for only a given percentage of the students. They cannot determine appropriate instruction for every student. In some instances, such as lessons for mature learners, it may be just as beneficial to simply give students advice about the sequence and number of examples and let them decide whether to take advantage of this information. Of concern, too, is the effect on learning, motivation, and self-image of students who fall outside the range of the model.

For many concepts, it may not be necessary to have such a complex adaptive system. There may be easier ways to learn many concepts than the one given by this system. Furthermore, if all concepts are taught in the same way, students may become bored and lose motivation.

Finally, a considerable amount of data are needed to adjust the formulas for estimating learning. This means that many students must do the lessons under less than adequate conditions before the programs are reasonably adaptive.

SUMMARY

CAI lessons can be designed to individualize many aspects of learning and instruction. An entire course can be individualized by presenting all lessons via CAI. Two factors that seem to influence the likelihood of students completing such courses are personal contacts with instructors and students' self-discipline.

Mathematical and statistical models of learning have been employed to develop sophisticated systems for individualized CAI. The models are limited to particular tasks and subject matter. They are generalizable only to specific instructional situations.

Adapating to learners' understanding is a major goal of the developers of intelligent tutoring systems (ITS). The next chapter discusses ITS and compares them to CAI.

Chapter 9

ARTIFICIAL INTELLIGENCE AND INSTRUCTION: INTELLIGENT TUTORING SYSTEMS

Millions of dollars have been appropriated during the last 15 years to develop intelligent tutoring systems (ITS). The impetus for this development came from the confluence of an urgent educational need and advances in computer and cognitive sciences.

Rapid progress in science and technology has created a need for people who can solve complex problems and operate and maintain sophisticated equipment. To help people accomplish these tasks, instruction in qualitative reasoning and decision-making skills is essential. The hope is that computer systems can be developed in the manner of human tutors to provide the needed instruction.

Research in two areas provided the information needed to develop intelligent computer tutors. Cognitive scientists were learning about the problem-solving processes of experts and how novices' and experts' thought processes differ. Computer scientists were developing computer systems that could solve problems and aid in decision making in complex fields such as medicine and finance. These exciting advances in computing are taking place in the field known as artificial intelligence.

ARTIFICIAL INTELLIGENCE

Artificial Intelligence is a branch of computer science in which the goals, according to Winston (1979), "are to make computers more useful and to understand the principles which make intelligence possible" (p. 1). The goal of some researchers is to program computers to do intellectual tasks, while the goal of others is to program computers to accomplish those tasks by emulating human beings. In either case, by learning how to design intelligent computers, researchers hope to learn something about human learning processes.

Components of Intelligent Behavior

Reasoning skills, knowledge, and experience are all essential elements of intelligent behavior. Also important is knowing when, where, and how to apply this knowledge and experience.

Rules of reasoning.   One of the tools of intelligent behavior is a set of general rules of reasoning. Using such rules, early researchers in artificial intelligence created computer programs that could solve many problems. Their work was based on the idea that while individuals differ somewhat in the way they solve problems, they do display a common set of basic strategies (Newell & Simon, 1972). One such strategy is known as means-end analysis. It involves assessing the difference between one's current state of knowledge about a problem and the state of knowledge needed to solve it. This assessment is then used to decide what action to take to reduce the difference between these two states of knowledge.

Knowledge.   One of the lessons learned from this early experience and from research in cognitive science is that though necessary, general reasoning skills and heuristics (rules of thumb) are not sufficient for solving problems. Intelligent behavior is also crucially dependent on knowledge about a subject (Feigenbaum & McCorduck, 1983). Indeed, there is no such thing as expertise without knowledge (Simon, 1980). Knowledge is defined here in a broad sense and includes knowledge gained from experience as well as from factual information. To solve problems in knowledge-rich domains, such as medical diagnosis, experts apply extensive domain-specific knowledge, much of it acquired through experience solving problems in the given domain.

Knowing when and how to apply knowledge.   A person certainly needs both general reasoning skills and a considerable body of domain-specific knowledge to solve problems in a particular field. However, all of this knowledge is insufficient if the problem solver does not know when and where to apply it. It does a player little good to know the rules in chess if he does not recognize situations where those rules can be successfully employed. It is of little value to know a geometry theorem (e.g., the altitude of an isosceles triangle divides the base in half) if a student does not recognize situations in which this theorem can be used in a geometry proof or in applied problems. Thus intelligent behavior encompasses not only information and experience but also knowledge about when and how to apply it.

Expert Systems

Recognizing the importance of knowledge, researchers in artificial intelligence began to shift their focus of research to developing knowledge-based systems. These systems are commonly referred to as expert systems.

Examples of expert systems are MYCIN and its improved version, NEOMYCIN. MYCIN helps physicians diagnose bacterial infections in the blood and suggests appropriate treatment. The physician supplies important information about the patient to the expert system, such as patient history and laboratory results. The program reasons about the disease and comes up with a diagnosis. A physician can initiate a dialogue with the system and ask why it arrived at a particular diagnosis.

Relevance to learning. Research in expert systems investigates many of the same issues as research in learning: how knowledge is organized, how it is stored, and how it is retrieved. Given the techniques of expert systems it becomes possible to use computers to test theories of human learning. An additional benefit is that researchers have to define their theories precisely before they can program computers to test them.

INTELLIGENT TUTORING SYSTEMS

The technology of expert systems is being applied to instruction to develop computer systems that tutor. These systems are called intelligent CAI (ICAI) or intelligent tutoring systems (ITS) because they employ the techniques of artificial intelligence (Fletcher & Zdybel, 1979). This does not mean that if a system is called an ITS it is necessarily designed intelligently. Even if a system behaves intelligently from a computing or scientific perspective it may not be intelligent from an instructional point of view (Camstra, 1986). Some intelligent tutoring systems do not actually tutor, but rather diagnose errors or provide supplementary practice in a standard curriculum.

Key ideas. Early intelligent tutoring systems differ in many respects but they do share two key ideas. One is that students learn not only by answering questions posed by instructors but also by asking questions. Therefore students as well as computer/tutors should be able to initiate dialogues. This concept is referred to as mixed initiative dialogues.

A second key idea is that a tutor should formulate a model of the learner's understanding of a topic and adapt instruction accordingly. To achieve this goal these systems compare a learner's strategies with those of an expert or else they represent the subject matter knowledge as a set of rules and then diagnose students' misconceptions of the rules (Sleeman, 1982).

System architecture.   To implement their key ideas, researchers in ITS structure information in the computer in a particular way. This structure is called the system architecture. Information is stored in the computer in three separate components rather than in a single component, as is usually the case in CAI. Each separate body of information is called a data base. Subject matter knowledge is stored in one data base, a model of the learner in another, and the instructional or tutoring component in a third data base. A management system operates on these data bases, drawing on the subject matter and student model data bases to make instructional decisions. This structure of knowledge in the computer enables the system to decide which questions to ask. It then generates questions as needed rather than selecting questions from a pre-existing pool. The architecture also enables the system to respond to student-generated questions.

Diversity among systems.   Techniques of expert systems have been applied principally to problem-solving tasks or tasks for which there is no unique predetermined set of rules or procedures. These techniques have been implemented in such diverse fields as medical diagnosis, electronics, mathematics, and the operation of complex systems.

Expert systems technology has been employed for many different purposes. Among the goals are diagnosis of students' errors, (Burton, 1982; Johnson & Soloway, 1985), a test of Socratic dialogue as an instructional technique (Stevens, Collins, & Goldin, 1982), use of an expert system for instruction (Clancey, 1982; Raghavan & Katz, 1989), training in troubleshooting (Brown, Burton, & DeKleer, 1982), and test of a theory of learning (Anderson, Boyle, & Reiser, 1985).

Brief discussions of systems that represent a variety of goals and subject matters are presented next. The purpose is to give you the "flavor" of research in ITS. (See Wenger, 1987, for an extensive review and analysis of ITS).

SCHOLAR

SCHOLAR (Carbonell, 1970) was the first system to incorporate mixed initiative dialogues.

Purpose and Features.   The purpose of SCHOLAR was to review learners' factual knowledge of the geography of South America. The intelligence of the system lay in the fact that it could generate questions ad hoc like a human tutor. It did not need a prespecified pool of questions, such as "What is the capital of Brazil?" from which to select questions. The system could also respond to students' questions about South American geography.

Lesson learned. SCHOLAR was remarkable in its time as a computing achievement, but it had no teaching strategy. The computer system picked topics for questions essentially in random order. It had no systematic way of checking or assessing a learner's knowledge.

SOPHIE: Learning by exploring in mixed initiative mode

The purpose of the three SOPHIE systems (Brown, Burton, & de Kleer, 1982) was to teach electronics troubleshooting. The goal was to train people to be expert troubleshooters. The hope was that students would gain a good enough conceptual grasp of electronics to be able to generate their own troubleshooting strategies. Another goal was to be able to learn new information from the manual when faced with the task of troubleshooting unfamiliar equipment.

Pedagogical plan. The underlying philosophy is that a student learns best from extensive practice in an interactive environment. In a laboratory setting, a student applies his factual knowledge to problem solving. He can see the consequences of his actions and thus learn from his experience. To promote learning, an intelligent system provides a coach to critique the student's strategies and to call his attention to connections and relationships between principles just learned and current problems.

SOPHIE II was a collection of four components, each designed to facilitate some aspect of the kinds of knowledge needed to troubleshoot in electronics. One component was a simulated laboratory and a "canned" expert troubleshooter. A second component was a limited coach. The remaining two components were computer-based games and written material.

In the simulated laboratory, the student could insert a fault into the circuit and watch the computer expert troubleshoot it. The expert explained its strategy as it went along, and engaged the student in the process by asking him to make qualitative predictions about what would happen before the expert actually implements the step (e.g., taking a measurement).

In another component the student practiced troubleshooting and the computer served as an automated laboratory instructor. The computer critiqued the student's ideas, drew attention to effects that illustrated principles he had just learned, and helped him learn from his mistakes. The coach could also answer some of the student's questions.

Lessons learned.   A number of characteristics of users made it difficult to implement the mixed initiative dialogue. Students phrased questions in so many different ways that the computer system was not always able to understand their first phrasing. When the computer system asked the students to rephrase their questions, many had great difficulty and some were simply unable to do so. Furthermore, students used abbreviations and ambiguous references in the context of the dialogue. Sometimes they asked questions that were beyond the system's capability to answer.

The intent was for the SOPHIE coach to provide guidance without too much restriction. To accomplish this goal the system needed three features: (1) to allow considerable student initiative; (2) to make significant inferences about the circuit on the basis of the student's measurements; and (3) to explain those inferences. SOPHIE II was good at explaining its deductions, but it allowed very little student initiative and was unsuccessful at making inferences from students' inputs (Brown, Burton, & de Kleer, 1982).

WEST

Computer coaching has also been investigated for lessons for precollege students. WEST is an example of an ITS coach for an arithmetic game.

Educational computer games can be exciting and motivating. They can also provide a rich, informal environment for learning. Unfortunately this potential for learning frequently goes unfulfilled. Students can play a game and have a wonderful time but not discover any of the underlying principles. One way to overcome this problem is to provide a computer coach to guide the student. It is no easy task to design a coach that accomplishes this goal and at the same time maintains students' interest. In fact it is such a subtle task that many aspects still resist solution (Burton & Brown, 1982).

Purpose.   Burton and Brown designed a coach for the game, How the West Was Won, an arithmetic board game developed by Bonnie Anderson on the PLATO system. Two players take turns moving pieces across the board, which is represented as trails through towns in the old West (see Figure 9.1). Players move by constructing an arithmetic expression from three numbers randomly generated by the computer and then computing it. The distance they can move their pieces is equal to the value of the arithmetic expression they create from the random numbers and the four basic operators, $+$, $-$, $\times$, and $/$. For example, if the computer generates

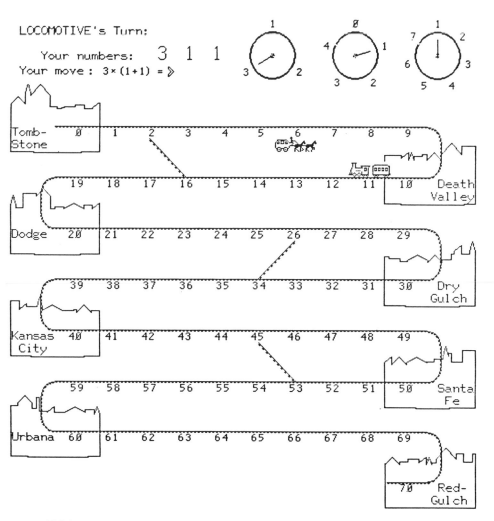

FIG.9.1. Display from *How the West Was Won*. (From CAI lesson by B. Seiler. Copyright 1976 by Board of Trustees of the University of Illinois. Reprinted by permission.)

the numbers 2, 3, and 1, a player can choose to move $3 \times (2+1) = 9$ spaces or $3 - 2 + 1 = 2$ spaces. Numerous combinations are possible. The goal is to be the first one to reach a town at the end of the trail, 70 spaces from the start. Certain moves have advantages. For example, landing on a town moves a player to the next town, 10 spaces along the way. The objective is for a player not only to use arithmetic facts but also to develop strategies to optimize moves. A player who is just two spaces from a town might choose

$3-2+1=2$ to land on the town and advance 10 spaces to the next town for a total of 12 spaces rather than move the 9 spaces that result from the expression $3 \times (2+1) = 9$.

The philosophy of the computer coach was to guide discovery learning. The idea was that if a student made a move that was not good strategy, she would notice it and that she would correct it herself if she had enough information to do so. One task for the coach, then, was to provide such information. Sometimes this was difficult to do, so the coach had to simply point out something that could be improved. The coach had to be a diagnostician and an advisor. In addition, the coach had to decide when to interrupt and also what to say when it did so. As noted earlier, if the advice was to accomplish its goal, it had to be accepted by the players while at the same time not destroy their interest.

Model. The paradigm underlying the coach was called "Issues and Examples." The skills the student was expected to learn were called the issues. The computer program had to recognize that a student did or did not use a particular skill (issue), and then decide whether the student was weak in it. The idea was for the coach to suggest a better move and an explanation at the time the issue was relevant to the current state of play.

Initially, the major effort in designing the coach was to determine how to model the student and to decide when to intervene and offer advice. The developers did not have enough time to generate adequate explanations. Explanations were simply prestored in a procedure attached to each issue, and only discussed single issues at that.

Principles. To avoid the situation of a player being hostile or ignoring the program's advice, the coach's comments must be both relevant and memorable. Among the practical implications is that the coach should give advice on issues on which a student is weak. When giving an example of a better move, the outcome should be a dramatically better than the one resulting from the student's move. Let the student repeat her turn in order to incorporate the issue and to decrease her antagonism to the advice. To increase chances of learning the authors recommend four levels of helps or hints: isolate the weakness, tell what moves are possible, why a particular move is optimal, and how to make that move.

Lessons learned. In this system, unlike mixed initiative systems, the student is in total control. This raises some special problems for diagnosing poor strategies and for giving advice. Suppose that a student makes a particular move and that the program notes that there was a better move. If the better move is based on several concepts, how can the computer determine which of these concepts the student failed to include, resulting in the inferior move? The program could ask questions to probe for information, but doing so would destroy the game environment. Students are not always consistent; they might not use a particular move because they are tired and just want to do the easiest thing possible. How is the program to know that such moves are not weaknesses in understanding and that it should therefore not give advice?

Sometimes a student uses a different strategy than the expert. A student might simply not want to make a "better" move because it does not fit with his strategy. The computer needs to look at a series of moves rather than just the last one to determine whether the student does indeed have a viable alternative strategy. This may be difficult when the set of possible strategies is extensive.

Finally, a student's strategy may be based on a different goal than that of the expert. He may not care so much about winning the game as about bumping his opponent (sending the opponent back to the beginning by landing on the same space).

Trial.   An experiment with elementary school children showed that children who were coached learned to use certain patterns of arithmetic expressions with parentheses that were not learned by uncoached children. Coached children expressed more enjoyment in playing the game than did uncoached. The report did not state the number of children or the duration of the experiment.

GUIDON and GUIDON 2: Tutoring medical diagnosis

GUIDON (Clancey, 1983) is an intelligent tutoring system that teaches medical diagnosis. The knowledge base used for developing GUIDON is MYCIN.

Features.   GUIDON's teaching knowledge is separate from the medical knowledge so it can be used in conjunction with more than one knowledge base. The teaching knowledge is a rule-based system with a rule structure similar to that of MYCIN. GUIDON gives the student basic data about a patient and the student tries to diagnose the case. The student carries on a dialogue with the computer, making inquiries and receiving data about the situation. GUIDON keeps a record of what can be known from the data it has provided the student and it uses this information to evaluate the student's partial solutions. The system may decide on the basis of its evaluation to intervene and provide help for the student. The overall philosophy is to allow either learner or tutor to initiate questions and discussion.

Lessons learned. Two basic assumptions that are built into the tutor are major sources of its shortcomings (Clancey, 1983). The first assumption is that a student's knowledge is a subset of MYCIN, the expert diagnostician. GUIDON tries to understand a learner solely on the basis of MYCIN's rules. If the student is basing his questions on incorrect rules, GUIDON cannot help him because it "is unable to formulate these rules and address them correctly" (p. 13). The other shortcoming is the assumption that there is a unique set of reasoning steps for every deduction. If a student's diagnostic strategy is different from MYCIN's, GUIDON will reject his reasonable hypotheses because GUIDON has only MYCIN's reasoning as a basis for judging.

While the representation of the teaching knowledge worked well, MY-CIN's representation of the subject knowledge was not satisfactory for teaching purposes. The students did not always understand or remember MYCIN's rules. MYCIN's expertise as a diagnostician is not in question. It is considered to be as good as that of faculty members at Stanford's School of Medicine but it represents "compiled expertise, molded into a machine-efficient framework" (Wenger, 1987, p. 271). MYCIN does not make explicit the strategies and knowledge structures that are built into its rules. The organization and representation of this expert's knowledge base are different from that required to tutor students. NEOMYCIN was designed to make the implicit design knowledge explicit, to separate out the knowledge from the diagnostic strategy and to add knowledge to justify the rules.

GUIDON 2 is based on NEOMYCIN. The goals of GUIDON 2 programs are different from those of GUIDON. Rather than judge and evaluate a medical student's diagnosis, a goal of this work is to explain explicitly the diagnostic reasoning processes used by the expert system. Another innovation in GUIDON 2 is that it uses a graphical diagram as a means of communicating the reasoning processes. It also serves as a tool for discussion between teachers and students. The hope is that, given explicit models of reasoning processes and tools for communicating these processes, students will learn how to emulate an expert and be able to construct a model of a case.

PROUST: Error diagnosis

The purpose of PROUST is to identify nonsyntactic (conceptual rather than format) errors in Pascal computer programs written by novices and to provide them with help to correct the misconceptions that caused the errors (Johnson & Soloway, 1985). Beginning students demonstrate tremendous variability in the programs they generate. Their programs usually have numerous errors, many of which seem bizarre. This is because beginners make errors in both what they intend to do and in how they do it, that is, in how they write the code. For example, a person might intend to write code that tells the computer to read a value, but she incorrectly writes code that tells the computer to increment the value. The intention is correct, but the implementation incorrect.

The conventional way for computer tutors to diagnose errors is to make a model or models of correct programs and to look for students' deviations from them. Such programs consider only students' errors and fail to consider their intentions. The developers of PROUST argue that to do an adequate job of diagnosing errors, a tutor should understand a student's intentions as well as how she implements them.

Features. When given a description of a problem, PROUST generates many ways of representing it. PROUST tries to analyze a student's program by matching it to one of the many conceptualizations in its intention-space. PROUST tells the student the likely source of the errors, based on what it thinks the student was intending to do. An example of PROUST output is, "It appears that you were trying to use line 12 to read the next input value. Incrementing NEW will not cause the next value to be read in. You need to use a READ statement here, such as you used in line 7" (p. 163).

Trial. In an initial test with a class of novice programmers, students were asked to program a modified averaging problem. PROUST was able to provide a full analysis of 79% of the programs that were syntactically correct and correctly analyzed 94% of the errors in these programs. Subsequent analyses indicated that "PROUST can facilitate on-line debugging, help students correct certain classes of bugs that otherwise remain unresolved, and contribute to improved performance on a related in-class examination" (Sebrechts, LaClaire, Schooler, & Soloway, 1986, p. 238).

Geometry Tutor: ITS based on a learning theory

Expert systems to tutor proofs in high school geometry and to tutor LISP programming were developed to test Anderson's ACT* (ACT star) theory of cognition (Anderson, Boyle, & Reiser, 1985).

Cognitive and consequent instructional principles. Four of the main features of Act* form the basis of the cognitive principles in the design of the system. One is that the student is represented as a production set, a set of if-then, (called condition-action) pairs. This enables the system to have explicit models of how a successful student solves a problem and how a student using the system is solving it.

Another feature of ACT* theory is that problem-solving behavior involves goals. An important task for a tutor is to communicate the goal structure to the learner. In geometry, the goal structure of an ideal student is to make inferences forward from the information given and backward from the desired situation until the two meet. Traditional geometry instruction does not provide this information explicitly. The geometry tutor makes the goal structure explicit by representing it as a proof graph (see Figure 9.2).

Minimizing the load on working memory is another key feature of ACT* theory. Computer tutors can relieve some of the load by keeping track of partial information and representing it visually. They can also reduce the load on working memory by providing immediate feedback on errors. If a student takes an incorrect step, and then proceeds on that basis, she will eventually hit an impasse. To correct the error, the student must keep in working memory all of the steps in the process. That may be an impossible task. The Geometry Tutor relieves this situation by providing immediate feedback to errors and by forcing the student to correct them immediately.

Still another principle is based on the concept of knowledge compilation. The principle is that problem solving should be taught in context. Productions (condition-action pairs) are only acquired during the process of problem solving. Another principle is that students "should be encouraged to produce the right abstract encoding" but it is not clear how that principle is implemented.

Experience. The Geometry Tutor depends on students' understanding the proof graph. How to use the graph is not self-evident, so students require an hour of instruction with the graphical notations, using arithmetic (not geometry) in order to understand the conventions of the graph.

The tutor is intended to supplement classroom instruction. It teaches students how to apply subskills in proofs. One skill is to provide supportive evidence for every statement. Another is to apply the following process: First state the goal; next state a premise, then the rule, and finally the conclusion from the rule. The premise is the starting point or basis for the current step in the proof. Suppose that at one point a student wants to show that two angles in a figure are congruent. She points to her premise, a set of vertical angles in the accompanying figure. She then states the rule that vertical angles are congruent, and then the conclusion that the two angles are congruent.

The system is restrictive in that a student must follow the process exactly and must use the rules or theorems exactly as stated in the system. In addition, a student cannot proceed if she makes an error. If she does not know how to go on, she can ask for help. However, the help messages are

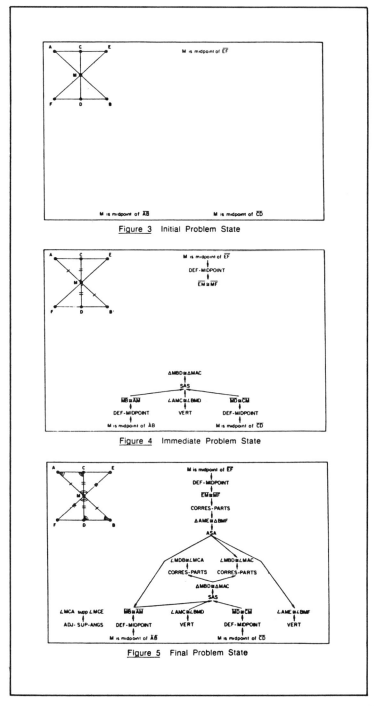

Figure 3 Initial Problem State

Figure 4 Immediate Problem State

Figure 5 Final Problem State

FIG.9.2. Example of some steps in a proof graph. *Note.* From "The Geometry Tutor" by J. R. Anderson, C. F. Boyle, and G. Yost in *Proceedings of the Ninth International Joint Conference on Artificial Intelligence* (pp. 1–7), 1985, San Mateo, CA: Morgan Kaufmann Publishers. Copyright 1985 by J. R. Anderson. Reprinted by permission.)

stated so formally that it is not clear that they are meaningful to high school students.

The Geometry Tutor is now available on microcomputer systems for classroom use. The LISP tutor, also based on ACT* theory, is being used successfully in classes in at least one university.

Lessons Learned

Two major ideological contributions of ITS to computer-presented instruction are (1) the concept of errors as bugs and (2) the importance of generating qualitative models of learners in order to adapt instruction.

Errors as bugs. In ITS, students' errors are thought of as misconceptions (bugs) rather than mistakes. It is not the mistake or wrong answer per se that is significant but the underlying misconceptions. An important task for the tutor is to try to understand why a student makes an error. Suppes (1984) comments that "The explicit emphasis on bugs and their detection has been one of the most important contributions of artificial intelligence to the general theory of cognitive processes" (p. 300).

Modeling learners. Much has been learned about modeling learners but much remains to be learned. In error diagnosis it is difficult to determine whether an error is simply a slip due to fatigue or carelessness, or is truly a misunderstanding. Further complicating the matter is the finding that some students' bugs are sometimes unstable. Students may demonstrate different bugs at different times (Tatsuoka, 1984; Tatsuoka & Eddins, 1985).

For instructional purposes a system must not only identify errors but also understand what caused them and how critical they are. In many ITS systems, responses to errors are not based on such an understanding. Some systems respond to errors by retrieving from a database prespecified responses designed for each error. Human tutors, on the other hand, use additional information to decide whether and how they should intervene. Littman, Pinto, & Soloway (1985) have identified the following five issues and recommend that they be incorporated into an intelligent tutoring system: (1) How critical the bugs are; (2) What category the bugs fall into; (3) What caused the bugs; (4) What tutorial goals are appropriate for tutoring the bugs; and (5) What tutorial interventions would achieve the tutorial goals.

Modeling students by comparing their strategies to those of experts is not entirely satisfactory because students' strategies are not mere subsets of experts'. To make inferences about a learner's strategies, a tutor needs an extensive response history. A student's most recent response is insufficient in and of itself.

Experts use many different strategies to accomplish a task, so intelligent tutoring systems need more than one conceptual framework for comparison purposes. However, many systems incorporate only one. That makes it difficult to determine whether a student is wrong or merely using a different strategy from the one in the system (Sleeman & Brown, 1982).

Mixed initiative dialogues. A major problem in attempts to implement mixed initiative dialogues is that the syntax and phrasing of students' questions are often so poor that the computer systems are unable to interpret them. In addition, when students ask questions, it becomes difficult for the system to provide a structure to generate a smoothly flowing dialogue. It is hard to generate a system that can figure out how to order the presentation, how to decide which issues to focus on, and when to shift focus (Bates, Brown, & Collins, 1979).

Another problem is that the system does not necessarily know how to answer every question students ask. In the WHY system, for example, some questions may be outside the knowledge capacity of the system (Bates, Brown, & Collins, 1979).

Experience in CAI has shown that novice and immature students do not necessarily know how to ask questions. S. Smith (personal communication, 1988) created a CAI chemistry lesson in which the computer selected a chemical and the goal for the students was to ask questions to determine which chemical it was. Smith found that students did not know what questions to ask. The lesson was not satisfactory even when he modified it by giving helpful suggestions. Students found typing a chore when they had to enter several words. The problem is no different in ITS.

Recent Trends

Based on experiences with early systems, researchers in ITS are modifying the scope or the goals of their research. Anderson and his colleagues, for example, try to avoid the limitations of communication in natural language by working in relatively circumscribed domains of high school geometry, LISP programing language, and now algebra.

Because much remains to be learned about modeling learners, some ITS researchers are concentrating less on evaluating learners' work and turning more of their attention to understanding learners' intentions and to helping them learn how to learn. Clancey is moving away from evaluating students' diagnostic procedures to modeling good procedures. He is also developing a graphic tool so that experienced physicians will be better able to communicate their reasoning processes and so that students will have a tool for communicating and for generating good reasoning processes. Similarly, Soloway and his colleagues are examining students' errors in terms of their intentions (Sebrechts, LaClaire, Schooler, & Soloway, 1986).

COMPARISON OF ITS AND CAI

CAI lessons present many kinds of instruction, based on various theories of learning and instruction (or none at all). Lessons are written for implementation on diverse systems, for diverse student populations. There is also great diversity among intelligent tutoring systems. It is therefore impossible to make general statements that are characteristic of every system. The following comparisons should be considered as an attempt to paint the general picture in broad strokes.

Goals of Researchers

The goals of ITS are to understand cognition and learning processes and to explore the application of the techniques of expert systems to instruction. Developers of ITS are primarily researchers in the fields of computer science, psychology, and linguistics. They study internal processes in learning. Their research emphasizes methods of representing information in the computer, making qualitative models of learners, and applying natural language techniques.

The goals in CAI are to use computer technology to present instruction and to solve educational problems (see Figure 9.3). Developers of CAI programs are mainly instructional designers, instructors, subject matter experts, and developers of training programs. They focus on improving learning and instruction and tend to emphasize the external processes in learning. There is an increasing trend toward incorporating findings from cognitive science and toward attending to internal as well as external processes in learning.

Target Populations

While some ITS programs are intended for elementary (e.g., coach for WEST) and secondary school (e.g., Geometry Tutor) students, most programs are for post secondary (Brandon, 1988). No programs for exceptional students are as yet commercially available.

CAI lessons are available for students of all ages and all educational levels, from preschool through post secondary. Lessons have been created for exceptional students, for hearing and physically impaired, for gifted and retarded students, as well as for average populations.

Goals for Learners

A major goal of ITS is the acquisition of reasoning skills in the given domain. Selection of subgoals, that is, sequence and component skills, are generated ad hoc during the course of instruction.

CAI lessons cover a full range of goals, including the acquisition of rote knowledge, verbal and computational skills, rule application, technical skills, and problem solving. Subgoals are predetermined.

CHARACTERISTICS	CAI	ITS
Goals Of Researchers	Present instruction Solve educational problems	Understand cognition Apply expert system technology to instruction Test theories of learning
Target Populations	Preschool through post secondary Special populations	Mainly post secondary
Goals For Learners	Ranges from rote information to reasoning/problem solving	Reasoning/problem solving
	Subgoals predetermined	Subgoals generated ad hoc
Tasks	Ranges from simple to complex	Relatively complex
Instruction		
Theoretical Basis	Instructional theories Cognitive theories Empirical data Intuition	ACT* theory Empirical data Intuition
Techniques	Direct instruction, Indirect instruction Tutorials, drills, simulations, games	Mixed initiative dialogues Tutorials, simulations, games
Modeling Learners	Mainly quantitative Some qualitative	Qualitative and quantitative
Environmental Implementation	Real classrooms	Mainly laboratories

FIG.9.3. Comparison of ITS and CAI.

Tasks

The tasks in ITS entail relatively complex skills. The tasks involve procedures for which there is usually no unique set of predefined steps. They include both visual and verbal materials.

Tasks in CAI, on the other hand, encompass a full range of skills, from simple to complex, rote memory, concept and rule learning, and problem solving. Some tasks are algorithmic; they can be achieved by following a fixed set of steps. Others are heuristic. Tasks are visual, verbal, or both.

Instruction

The instructional strategies of some intelligent tutoring systems are based on cognitive theories of learning (Geometry and LISP tutors). However, many are based on the developers' intuition or sense of artistry. In general, the strategies implemented in ITS lack empirical validation of their underlying assumptions (Frase, 1987; Montague, 1987; Suppes, 1984). Developers have, for the most part, ignored the knowledge gained from the considerable body of instructional design literature and the growing body of research in CAI (Park & Seidel, 1987). There is presently reason to believe that that situation is improving.

Developers of CAI lessons vary in the extent to which they apply learning and instructional theories. Most employ validated instructional models (e.g., behavioral, concept learning) and/or their experience teaching the subject matter to the intended student population. Some make direct application of instructional research in a given subject such as reading comprehension. Some lessons are carefully crafted from a computing perspective but are clearly totally ineffective as instruction. Others are based on intuition or pure artistry.

Subject matter.   ITS deals primarily with those aspects of subjects that require a high level of reasoning rather than rote memorization. These subjects include mathematics, electronics, medical diagnosis, computer programming, operating large sophisticated physical systems, climate, and economics.

CAI lessons are available in many subject matter areas, including the humanities (e.g., languages), the arts (e.g., music), the professions (e.g., medicine), the social sciences (e.g., economics, psychology), mathematical and computer sciences, physical and biological sciences (e.g., chemistry, physics, genetics), and technical fields (e.g., airport control).

Pedagogical techniques.   In ITS, the flow of instruction is structured by both learner and computer system. Either one can initiate interactions or dialogues. Instruction is presented in the form of tutorial dialogues, simulations, and games.

CAI lessons employ a broad spectrum of techniques. Control of instruction varies widely from total computer control to total learner control. Many lessons are expository. Interactions are initiated and controlled by the computer. The lessons tell and they ask. CAI lessons are also drills, simulations, or games. Park and Seidel (1987) point out that games are employed for different purposes in CAI and ITS.

ITS and CAI must make some of the same critical decisions. Both types of computer/tutor must decide when to intervene and what to say when they do so. In a sense, these kinds of instructional decisions are predetermined in ITS as well as in CAI. Although the ultimate decision is made ad hoc, this decision is based on a body of if-then rules that are predetermined.

Modeling Learners

The importance of adaptive instruction is recognized by developers of both CAI and ITS. Both have made strides in adapting instruction, but neither has yet solved all of the problems. The differences between the two are mainly due to methods of implementation.

Learning processes are the primary focus of ITS models. ITS systems try to emulate human tutors by setting instructional goals and subgoals ad hoc, based on both a qualitative and quantitative assessment of the learner's understanding. ITS systems model learners by techniques such as matching students' production rules to those of experts or by looking for systematic errors.

Modeling a learner carries with it an implicit assumption that a student has an internal model of the skills he is using to perform a task (Suppes, 1984). It is not clear that this assumption is valid in all situations. A student may solve a problem by trial and error and have no model at all. A student may begin to solve a problem by trial and error and not develop a model until after he has some experience with a problem.

CAI usually models learners quantitatively by predesigned algorithms. The tendency is to focus on the subject matter structure. Models of learners are based on measures such as the percentage of correct responses or the mathematical probability that the student has acquired the designated knowledge. Assessment in CAI is qualitative in lessons that employ diagnostic questions to determine the depth of learning and the nature of misunderstanding.

Learning styles. Students vary in their preference for learning style. Some learners prefer explicit instruction while others prefer to figure things out for themselves. Steinberg and Baskin (1985) found that some learners felt that the computer's tight control of learning caused them to make errors whereas other students found the highly structured instruction helpful. Steinberg and Baskin propose that an individual may be better able to solve a problem using his own preferred style even though it is neither the most efficient for the given task nor the preferred style of experts in the domain. At present, neither CAI nor ITS accommodates individual differences in learning styles.

Design Process

Regardless of a lesson author's knowledge of a subject and of her experience teaching the subject, she cannot be sure that a lesson will be effective until she tests it with the intended students. Intelligent tutoring systems are by their very nature complex systems to produce and take many person-years of effort. Some forms of testing are carried on while a system is being developed because it is difficult, if not impossible, to make major changes after the system is completed.

One of the problems encountered in designing ITS is the difficulty of capturing the expertise of subject matter specialists. Experts often are unable to explain their problem-solving behavior. Their tacit knowledge is hard to elicit.

In CAI, it is feasible to test and revise instruction relatively frequently during development. When developing lessons in modules, unanticipated and undesirable results can be discovered, and the lesson revised before it is finished and before it is too difficult to make the needed changes.

Environmental Implementation and Evaluation

In ITS, success is usually measured by how well the system handles computing capability features, such as error analysis. We really do not know how well most ITS systems accomplish their instructional goals. Developers of these systems rarely provide evidence of instructional effectiveness. Some provide results after testing their system with only a handful of subjects, usually with a limited number of tasks. Systems are usually tested under laboratory conditions. It is not known if the positive results gained in the laboratory will also be demonstrated in real world situations.

The goal of many ITS systems is to understand cognition and learning processes. It may therefore seem unreasonable to criticize their failure to evaluate instructional effectiveness. However, because developers claim that they are developing tutoring systems, they have a responsibility to demonstrate not only the intelligence of their computer system but also the effectiveness of their instruction. Some progress is being made in that direction. Anderson's LISP and Geometry tutors are used in regular classrooms. Versions of Smithdown, an ITS lesson that helps students learn economics reasoning, have been tested and evaluated with college and high school students (Raghavan & Katz, 1989).

CAI lessons are studied in classrooms in all educational settings, including elementary schools, professional schools, and industrial, military, and governmental training programs. Success in CAI is measured by how well a lesson accomplishes its goal, that is, by how well students perform. The need to evaluate is recognized, though not always carried out. There are many successful implementations of CAI in real world classrooms. It is true that CAI has been underway for perhaps a decade longer than ITS and there has been more opportunity for evaluation.

APPROPRIATE APPLICATION OF COMPUTERS TO INSTRUCTION

In general, ITS and CAI differ in goals, subject matter, and target populations. The power of ITS systems is not needed, nor was it ever intended, for all instructional goals. It seems most reasonable to generate instruction in the manner of ITS when the subject matter is complex and/or relatively unstructured, assuming that it is possible to overcome some of the major hurdles to effective instruction.

While rote memorization and straightforward acquisition of knowledge are obviously best implemented in CAI, they are by no means the only kinds of goals that can be presented in CAI. CAI is also appropriate for complex tasks, particularly where there is experience teaching the subject matter to the target population, or where the subject matter is relatively well structured.

Effective instruction does not happen merely by applications of computer technology, whether CAI or ITS. CAI, like ITS, must be intelligent. The intelligence in instruction lies not in the architecture of the system, nor in the intelligence of the computer code. Intelligence lies in the ability of computer-presented instruction to achieve its goals for learners in a way that is palatable and acceptable to them.

SUMMARY

The potential of ITS is great, and a considerable amount of progress has been made over the past two decades since the first program was produced. A few instructional programs are available for classroom use, but a considerable amount of work remains to be done before instructional applications become widely available.

In the final analysis, the purpose of ITS and CAI is to improve the quality of learning and instruction for all people. To assess progress toward that goal, formal plans for evaluation are essential. Evaluation is the subject of Chapter 10.

Chapter 10

EVALUATION

Evaluation in CAI often refers to lesson review. Potential buyers evaluate lessons for their overall quality, their applicability to a curriculum, their cost, the equipment needed, and so on.

Evaluation also serves other purposes in CAI design. One purpose is to assist in lesson development; a second is to determine how well a lesson accomplishes its goals. A third purpose, although outside of the design procedure, is to maintain lessons, such as to correct errors that appear only after hundreds of uses.

Because the topic of evaluation is discussed in the last chapter of this book, one might assume that evaluation is merely the last step in instructional design. This is incorrect. Quite the contrary. Evaluation is part of an iterative cycle of designing, evaluating, and revising, and is carried out in all phases of lesson development.

Evaluation is not a casual process. Formal plans are made for evaluation when the initial plans for a lesson are being formulated. The importance of making formal plans is dramatically illustrated by events in a project described by Spitzer (1982). A large government agency developed print and audiotape instructional materials to orient new employees as well as experienced personnel who were moving into new positions. Little systematic planning went into the development of instruction, and no plans for evaluation were included. When put into practice, the training materials did not work. Among the numerous reasons cited for this failure were that the trainees did not like listening to audiotapes and that instruction was too elementary for the intended learners. The designers wanted to make sure that they catered to everyone, so they used silly cartoon characters. The net

194

effect was that the lessons, "insulted the trainees and demeaned the job." Some of the problems could have been avoided by using a systematic design procedure; many could have been resolved by ongoing evaluation before the materials were completed.

In business and government, the limitations of time and money often force developers of computer-presented training to skip or condense steps in the ideal procedures for instructional design. Nevertheless, all instructional designers, academics (Briggs & Wager, 1981; Dick & Carey, 1985; Gagné & Briggs, 1974; Tennyson, 1976) as well as practitioners in business/industry (Arwady, 1983; Kearsley, 1983; Simpson, 1985; Spitzer, 1982), agree that two aspects of evaluation are essential: formative for evaluating lessons and summative for evaluating learners. Developers of CAI also agree that maintenance evaluation is essential to correct errors and to keep content current.

EVALUATING LESSONS: FORMATIVE EVALUATION

Formative evaluation is the process of systematically trying out materials as you write them. Although there is little formal research to document its significance (Dick, 1977), experience with materials for all media and for projects big and small demonstrates the importance of formative evaluation. Developers of Individually Prescribed Instruction (Glaser & Rosner, 1975) prepared new lessons in draft form and tested them with a few children before revising or discarding them. Similarly, developers of expert systems (Feigenbaum & McCorduck, 1983) and intelligent tutoring systems (Sleeman, 1982) find it necessary to do formative evaluations.

Formative evaluation is particularly important in CAI because once a lesson is completed it may be very difficult or very time consuming to make major revisions in the computer program. Authors who are not familiar with the computer as an instructional medium may find unexpected effects. Formative evaluation provides the opportunity to investigate the application of various features without expending an inordinate amount of time.

Purpose. The purpose of formative evaluation is to make the lesson as effective as possible. Measuring students' learning is not the objective, although some measures of learning are taken. Evaluating a lesson as it is being developed enables authors to detect content errors and technical errors in programming. Formative evaluation shows deficiencies that were present in the initial plans before the materials were written (Gagné & Briggs, 1974). Data collected uncover ambiguities and gaps in presentations and validate the sequence and flow of instruction. Field tests provide information for bringing instruction into harmony with the target learners and with the environment in which the lesson will be implemented.

Precomputer trials.   In some circumstances it is useful to draft and evaluate precomputer versions of instruction. The author prepares the instructional materials in print form. She then plays the role of the computer as she tests the material with a typical student. This preliminary investigation helps the author determine whether an idea for innovative instruction is feasible or appropriate for computer presentation. There is no point to investing time programming a lesson if there is considerable uncertainty about its utility. Precomputer evaluation is also helpful when an author lacks experience teaching the particular subject or students. "Dry runs" provide insights about how the lesson will interact with the intended students.

Procedures.   All lessons are developed in modules or units. The modules are then joined to form a first draft of the whole lesson. There are differences of opinion about the need to evaluate individual modules before evaluating the first draft. Systems procedures for instructional design, which are not media-specific (e.g., Gagné & Briggs) begin formative evaluation with the first rough draft of the entire lesson. Developers of computer-based instruction and computer-based training (Arwady, 1983; Kearsley, 1983; Simpson, 1985; Steinberg, 1984; Walker & Hess, 1984) recommend evaluating at least some modules before completing the lesson.

Evaluating prototype modules is valuable if an author wishes to decide which of several presentations is most likely to be effective. Evaluating and revising prototypes is also efficient because once these prototypes are polished, little revision will be necessary when they are generalized to other units of instruction.

Module evaluation is also helpful when it is not possible to predetermine all aspects of interactions of learners with computer instruction. Students may, for instance, find it difficult to follow the directions. A question may be interpreted differently by students than intended by the author.

After the modules are completed, they are linked together with introductory and concluding displays to become the first draft of the lesson. This draft is evaluated before the lesson is polished to reveal deficiencies in the lesson as a whole. The goal is to validate content accuracy, completeness, and smoothness of flow. There is no point to polishing a lesson, say redesigning a display, before determining that the display is necessary and will be included in the final version. Evaluation of the first draft also helps to determine whether there is enough instruction. (This evaluation is not helpful for determining if there is too much instruction. That is the reason why designers are advised to write "lean." It saves both student's and designer's time to add material if necessary rather than include too much initially.)

Field tests. Testing with target students in the environment in which lessons will be used is called field testing. It is sometimes desirable to field test a few modules to evaluate the learning environment and to make design decisions, such as the use of audio. Audio is feasible only in a quiet environment or if earphones are available. In many classrooms, CAI is only one of several learning activities. Classroom noise might interfere with CAI lessons; and sound from one terminal might interfere with sound from another. The effect of certain kinds of content may need to be determined. For example, some kinds of graphics may be distracting rather than helpful (Roblyer, 1982).

Field testing a rough draft of a CAI lesson is also important. If there is not enough time to test a lesson at the development site and also in the field, Arwady (1983) recommends field testing. He gives an example of how disastrous consequences were avoided by field testing a training package for a small business environment before the final version was completed. The goal was to train personnel to operate computers when they had free time while conducting a regular day's activities. Since the developers were aware that there would be constant interruptions of other duties such as answering the phone, they modularized the lesson. The idea was to allow trainees to work through program segments as often as necessary. However, the field test with operators convinced the lesson developers to also allow learners to return to the beginning of each individual module, no matter how short, if interruptions were substantial.

It is not reasonable to field test a rough draft of a lesson with a large group of learners until after it is pilot tested with a few individuals. After gross errors are discovered and removed, a lesson can be tested with large groups.

Who evaluates. Lesson developers evaluate modules informally as they are developed to eliminate obvious errors or to make decisions about whether the result is really what they intended. This process is similar to that of an author who revises a sentence or a paragraph until she thinks it communicates her intention.

Formal evaluation by other individuals is also essential. An author cannot always see her own mistakes, just as when proofreading a manuscript she may overlook errors. In addition, individuals tend to fall into habitual ways of testing a lesson and may fail to test all possibilities. It is therefore helpful to ask subject matter experts and some colleagues to test the rough draft of the lesson.

A major goal of formative evaluation is to understand the problems students might have with the lesson. The only ones who can provide that information are individuals from the target population. One-to-one tryouts of materials with representatives of the target population are critical. A satisfactory evaluation includes average students and at least one who is above average, and one who is below. They are likely to take different paths through a lesson, and thus a lesson will be more thoroughly tested. Bright students are more likely to articulate their opinions about a lesson than others. Small groups and subsequently an entire class of intended learners are the final participants in formal formative evaluation.

Evaluation measures. The data collected during formative evaluation are both quantitative and qualitative. Quantitative data, which can be gathered by the computer system, include students' responses to questions, time to respond, the number of attempts to get the correct answer for each question, scores on quizzes, time to respond to individual questions, and time to complete the lesson.

Qualitative data are gathered by unobtrusively observing students while they are studying. Students' body motions and spontaneous remarks provide evidence of unusual events, exciting and confusing, good and bad. Oral interviews on completion of the lesson assist in determining the reasons for these reactions. Questionnaires, written for the computer lesson, reflect students' attitudes. On some systems, learners have the option of making comments about the lesson on the computer system while they are studying it.

EVALUATING LEARNING: SUMMATIVE EVALUATION

Summative evaluation takes place after the lesson is complete and is being used with the target population in the intended environment. The purpose is to determine whether the lesson is achieving its goals. It is essentially an evaluation of the group of learners.

Methods of assessment. The most common method of assessing achievement is by end-of-lesson tests. Paper and pencil tests are also used to measure performance. The number of students who successfully complete a lesson, the time it takes, and the dropout rate are also important measures. Reasons why students drop out can be ascertained from interviews and questionnaires.

Documentation. Documentation of the data collected in summative evaluations provides important information for others who might want to use the lessons. Performance scores and a description of the learners who participated in the summative evaluation are valuable information. Average time needed to complete the lesson is also important if a lesson will have to fit into a limited time schedule.

Unfortunately, documentation of this sort rarely accompanies computer lessons. A reasonable explanation is that summative evaluations are rarely implemented. We do not ask for summative evaluations of books and other instructional materials, so why should we expect it of CAI? Summative evaluations of books and print materials are not feasible because results would be confounded with the instructor variable. There is also the possibility of such confounding with CAI materials, but it is likely to be minimal. Documentation of summative evaluations can increase the probability that consumers will select CAI lessons appropriately and thus increase the likelihood of effectiveness.

Comparisons to Other Media

Some researchers evaluate CAI lessons by making media comparisons. These studies (Kulik, Bangert, & Williams, 1983; Niemic & Walberg, 1987; Orlansky & String, 1981) typically show that students have positive attitudes toward CAI and that learning time is reduced. Performance is either the same or somewhat better in CAI.

Comparison studies, however, are not really a comparison of the media but rather of the material presented by the media (Hagler & Knowlton, 1987). Although many studies document the superiority of learning as a consequence of CAI, few studies document clearly that the superiority is due to characteristics unique to CAI (Avner, Moore, & Smith, 1980).

Studies that compare CAI with classroom instruction are really comparisons of individualized and group-paced instruction rather than comparisons of computers and instructors. Comparisons of CAI practice with traditional homework are also invalid because they compare different instruction. Computer-controlled drills with feedback are not the same as self-instruction. Furthermore, the amount of practice might be considerably different when computer-presented than when done as homework (Hagler & Knowlton, 1987). In fact, reports that the performance of classes who do CAI drills is superior to those who do not may simply be a reflection of more instruction rather than the superiority of the drills. The superiority of CAI may be due to novelty effects if the lessons are short.

MAINTAINING LESSONS

Like equipment, CAI lessons need to be maintained. Sometimes programming errors occur under unusual circumstances. It may take hundreds of users before they are discovered. Once discovered, however, they need to be corrected. Other elements that require maintenance or accommodation are subject matter content and characteristics of the target population.

Lessons may include dated information. New research in medical practice, for example, may necessitate updating a lesson. Statistical data as in economics or demographic studies require revision as current data become available.

Characteristics of students using a lesson may change over time. They may have a better background and require less introductory information. Attitudes toward certain features of a lesson may differ from attitudes of previous students. Motivators may need to be modified.

Lessons are maintained so that they will continue to make appropriate use of the computer and be consistent with the target population, the goals, the task, and the study environment.

SUMMARY

The purpose of CAI is to improve the quality of learning and instruction. To assess progress toward that goal, formal plans for evaluation are essential. Lessons need to be evaluated as they are being developed. Students' achievement needs to be measured to determine whether the lessons helped them achieve the goals. Lessons need to be maintained even after they are completed and in actual classroom use.

REFERENCES

Alderman, D. L., Appel, L. R., & Murphy, R. T. (1978, April). PLATO and TICCIT: An evaluation of CAI in the community college. *Educational Technology*, pp. 40-45.

Allen, B. S. & Merrill, M. D. (1985). System -assigned strategies and CBI. *Journal of Educational Computing Research, 1*(1), 3-21.

Alpert, D. & Bitzer, D. L. (1970, March 20). Advances in computer-based education. *Science, 167*, 1582-1590.

Amarel, M. (1983). The classroom: An instructional setting for teachers, students and the computer. In A. C. Wilkinson (Ed.), *Classroom computers and cognitive science* (pp. 15-29). New York: Academic Press.

Anderson, J. R. (1980). *Cognitive psychology and its implications*. San Francisco: Freeman.

Anderson, J. R. & Bower, G. H. (1973). *Human associative memory*. New York: John Wiley & Sons.

Anderson, J. R., Boyle, C. F., Farrell, R., & Reiser, B. J. (1985). *Cognitive principles in the design of computer tutors* (Tech. rep.). Pittsburgh, PA: Carnegie Mellon University, Advanced Computer Tutoring Project.

Anderson, J. R., Boyle, C. F., & Reiser, B. J. (1985). Intelligent tutoring systems. *Science, 228*, 456-467.

Anderson, R. C. (1977). The notion of schemata and the educational enterprise: General discussion of the conference. In R. C. Anderson, R. J. Spiro, & W. E. Montague (Eds.), *Schooling and the acquisition of knowledge* (pp. 415-431). Hillsdale, NJ: Lawrence Erlbaum Associates.

Anderson, R. C. & Biddle, W. B. (1975). On asking people about what they are reading. In G. Bower (Ed.), *Psychology of learning and motivation* (Vol. 9). New York: Academic Press.

Anderson, R. C. & Faust, G. W. (1973). *Educational psychology*. New York: Dodd, Mead, & Company.

Anderson, R. C. & Kulhavy, R. W. (1972). Learning concepts from definitions. *American Educational Research Journal, 9*, 385-390.

Anderson, R. C., Kulhavy, R. W., & Andre, T. (1971). Feedback procedures in programmed instruction. *Journal of Educational Psychology, 62*, 148-156.

201

Anderson, T., Biddle, W. B., Surber, J. R., & Alessi, S. M. (1975). An experimental evaluation of a computer based management study system. *Educational Psychologist, 11* (3), 184–190.

Arwady, J. W. (1983, October). Corporate training and development. *Educational Technology*, pp. 32–34.

Atkinson, R. C. (1972). Ingredients for a theory of instruction. *American Psychologist, 27*, 921–931.

Atkinson, R. C. (1976). Adaptive instructional systems: Some attempts to optimize the learning process. In D. Klahr (Ed.), *Cognition and instruction* (pp. 81–115). Hillsdale, NJ: Lawrence Erlbaum Associates.

Ausubel, D. P. (1968). *Educational psychology: A cognitive view*. New York: Holt, Rinehart, & Winston.

Ausubel, D. P., Novak, J. D., & Hanesian, H. (1978). *Educational psychology* (2nd ed.). New York: Holt, Rinehart, & Winston.

Avner, R. A. (1975). *The evolutionary development of CAI evaluation approaches*. Paper presented at the Annual Meeting of the American Educational Research Association, Washington, D. C. (ERIC Document Reproduction Service No. ED 105 897)

Avner, R. A. (1979). Production of computer based materials. In H. F O'Neil, Jr. (Ed.), *Issues in instructional development* (pp. 133– 180). New York: Academic Press.

Avner, R. A. (1987). *A quarter century of computer-based education*. Keynote address presented at the Nordic Conference on Computer Aided Instruction, Stockholm, Sweden.

Avner, R. A., Moore, C., & Smith, S. (1980). Active external control: A basis for superiority of CBI. *Journal of Computer-based Instruction, 6*(4), 115–118.

Barbatsis, G. S. (1978). The nature of inquiry and analysis of theoretical progress in instructional television from 1950–1970. *Review of Educational Research, 48*(3), 399–414.

Barnes, B. R. & Clawson, E. U. (1975). Do advance organizers facilitate learning? Recommendations for future research based on an analysis of 32 studies. *Review of Educational Research, 45*(4), 637–659.

Bates, M., Brown, G., & Collins, A. (1979). Socratic teaching of causal knowledge and reasoning. *Proceedings of the annual convention of the Association for the Development of Computer-based Instructional Systems* (Vol. 1, pp. 104–119). Bellingham, WA: Association for the Development of Computer-based Instructional Systems.

Beck, I. L. & McKeown, M. G. (1986). Instructional research in reading: A retrospective. In J. Orasanu (Ed.), *Reading comprehension: From research to practice* (pp. 113–134). Hillsdale, NJ: Lawrence Erlbaum Associates.

Beck, I. L., Roth, S. F., & McKeown, M. G. (1984). *Syl-la search III teacher's manual*. Allen, TX:Developmental Learning Materials.

Bloom, B. S. (Ed.). (1956). *Taxonomy of educational objectives: Handbook I: Cognitive Domain*. New York: David McKay.

Brandon, P. R. (1988, October). Recent developments in instructional hardware and software. *Educational Technology*, pp. 7–12.

Bransford, J. D. (1979). *Human cognition*, Belmont, CA: Wadsworth.

Bransford, J. D. (1982). *Comparisons of successful and unsuccessful learners*. Paper presented at the Annual Meeting of the American Educational Research Association, New York.

Bresler, L. (1989). *Computer-mediated communications in a high school*. Paper presented at the Annual Meeting of the American Educational Research Association, San Francisco, CA.

Briggs, L. J. (1970). *Handbook of procedures for the design of instruction*. Pittsburgh, PA: American Institutes for Research.

Briggs, L. J. & Wager, W. W. (1981). *Handbook of procedures for the design of instruction* (2nd ed.). Englewood Cliffs, NJ: Educational Technology Publications.

Broadbent, D. E. (1958). *Perception and communication*. New York: Pergamon Press.

Brown, A. L. (1977). Development, schooling, and the acquisition of knowledge about knowledge. In R. C. Anderson, R. J. Spiro, & W. E. Montague (Eds.), *Schooling and the acquisition of knowledge* (pp. 241–253). Hillsdale, NJ: Lawrence Erlbaum Associates.

Brown, A. L. (1978). Knowing when, where, and how to remember. A problem of metacognition. In R. Glaser (Ed.), *Advances in instructional psychology.* Hillsdale, NJ: Lawrence Erlbaum Associates.

Brown, A. L., Armbruster, B. B., & Baker, L. (1986). The role of metacognition in reading and studying. In J. Orasanu (Ed.), *Reading comprehension: From research to practice* (pp. 49–75). Hillsdale, NJ: Lawrence Erlbaum Associates.

Brown, A. L., Bransford, J. D., Ferrara, R. A., & Campione, J. C. (1982). Learning, remembering, and understanding. In J. H. Flavell and E. M. Markman (Eds.), *Cognitive development: The handbook of child psychology.* New York: John Wiley & Sons.

Brown, J. S., Burton, R. R., & de Kleer, J. (1982). Pedagogical, natural language and knowledge engineering techniques in SOPHIE I, II, and III. In D. Sleeman & J. S. Brown (Eds.), *Intelligent tutoring systems* (pp. 227–282). London, England: Academic Press.

Burton, R. R. (1982). Diagnosing bugs in a simple procedural skill. In D. Sleeman & J. S. Brown (Eds.), *Intelligent tutoring systems* (pp. 157–183). London, England: Academic Press.

Burton, R. R. & Brown, J. S. (1982). An investigation of computer coaching. In D. Sleeman & J. S. Brown (Eds.), *Intelligent tutoring systems* (pp. 79–98). New York: Academic Press.

Call-Himwich, E. & Steinberg, E. R. (1977). *Myths and reality: Essential decisions in computer-based instructional design.* (MTC Report No. 18). Urbana, IL: University of Illinois, Computer-based Education Research Laboratory. (ERIC Document Reproduction Service No. 152 239)

Camstra, B. (1986). AI in computer-based training. *Interactive Learning International, 3*(4), 27–30.

Carbonell, J. (1970). AI in CAI: An artificial-intelligence approach to computer-assisted instruction. *IEEE Transactions on Man-Machine Systems, 11*(4), 190–202.

Carlson, S. B. (1985). *Creative classroom testing.* Princeton, NJ: Educational Testing Service.

Carter, J. F. (1977). Comments on Chapter 6 by Meyer. In R. C. Anderson, R. J. Spiro, & W. E. Montague (Eds.), *Schooling and the acquisition of knowledge* (pp. 201–208). Hillsdale, NJ: Lawrence Erlbaum Associates.

Case, R. (1975). Gearing demands of instruction to the developmental capacities of the learner. *Review of Educational Research, 45*, 59–87.

Case, R. (1978). A developmentally based theory of instruction. *Review of Educational Research, 48*, 439–469.

Case, R. & Bereiter, C. (1984). From behaviourism to cognitive development: Steps in the evolution of instructional design. *Instructional Science, 13*(2), 141–158.

Chernoff, H. (1973). The use of faces to present points in k-dimensional space graphically. *Journal of the American Statistical Association, 68*, 361–368.

Clancey, W. J. (1982). Tutoring rules for guiding a case method dialogue. In D. Sleeman & J. S. Brown (Eds.), *Intelligent tutoring systems* (pp. 201–225). London, England: Academic Press.

Clancey, W. J. (1983). GUIDON. *Journal of Computer-Based Instruction, 10*(1 and 2), 8–15.

Clark, H. H., Jr. (1988, July/August). Air force likes training on a "silver platter." *Instructional Delivery Systems,* pp. 32–33.

Collins, A. & Stevens, A. L. (1983). A cognitive theory of inquiry teaching. In C. M. Reigeluth (Ed.), *Instructional-design theories and models: An overview of their current status* (pp. 247–278). Hillsdale, NJ: Lawrence Erlbaum Associates.

Crowder, N. A. (1960). Automatic tutoring by intrinsic programming. In A. A. Lumsdaine & R. Glaser (Eds.), *Teaching machines and programmed learning.* Washington, DC: National Education Association.

Damarin, F. & Damarin, S. K. (1983). Response sets: Implications of research on psychological testing for interactive computer-based instruction. *Journal of Computer-Based Instruction, 9,* 124–130.

Dansereau, D. F. (1985). Learning strategy research. In J. Segal, S. Chipman, & R. Glaser (Eds.), *Thinking and learning skills: Relating instruction to basic research* (Vol. 1, pp. 209–239). Hillsdale, NJ: Lawrence Erlbaum Associates.

De Klerk, L. F. W., Jr. & De Klerk, L. F. W., Sr. (1978). The effect of knowledge of correct results per item on verbal learning and retention. *Instructional Science, 7,* 347–358.

Dick, W. (1977). Summative evaluation. In L. J. Briggs (Ed.), *Instructional design principles and applications.* Englewood Cliffs, NJ: Educational Technology Publications.

Dick, W. & Carey, L. (1985). *The systematic design of instruction* (2nd ed.). Glenview, IL: Scott, Foresman and Company.

Duchastel, P. C. (1982). Textual display techniques. In D. H. Jonassen (Ed.), *The technology of text: Principles for structuring, designing, and displaying text* (Vol. 1, pp. 167–191). Englewood Cliffs, NJ: Educational Technology Publications.

Dwyer, F. M. (1985). Visual literacy's first dimension: Cognitive information acquisition. *Journal of Visual Verbal Language, 5,* 7–15.

Dwyer, F. M. & Lamberski, R. J. (1982–83). A review of research on the effects of the use of color in the teaching-learning process. *International Journal of Instructional Media, 10,* 303–328.

Elder, C. L. & White, C. S. (1989). A world geography database project: Meeting thinking skills head on. *The Computing Teacher, 17*(3), 29–32.

Faust, G. W. (1974). Design strategy and the TICCIT system. *Viewpoints, 50,* 91–101.

Feigenbaum, E. A. & McCorduck, P. (1983). *The fifth generation.* Reading, MA: Addison-Wesley.

Flavell, J. H., Beach, D. H., & Chinsky, J. M. (1966). Spontaneous verbal rehearsal in memory tasks as a function of age. *Child Development, 37,* 283–299.

Flavell, J. H., Friedrichs, A. G., & Hoyt, J. D. (1970). Developmental changes in memorization processes. *Cognitive Psychology, 1,* 324–340.

Fletcher, J. D. & Zdybel, F. (1979). Intelligent instructional systems in training. *Proceedings of the Annual Meeting of the Association for the Development of Computer-based Instructional Systems* (Vol.1, pp. 68–83). Bellingham, WA: Association for the Development of Computer-based Instructional Systems.

Frase, L. (1987, May). Untitled presentation. In S. Chipman (Chair), *Instructional principles for ICAI.* Panel discussion conducted at the Third International Conference on Artificial Intelligence and Education, Pittsburgh, PA.

Frederiksen, J. R., Warren, B. M., & Roseberry, A. S. (1985a). A componential approach to training reading skills: Part 1. Perceptual units training. *Cognition and Instruction, 2*(2), 91–130.

Frederiksen, J. R., Warren, B. M., & Roseberry, A. S. (1985b). A componential approach to training reading skills: Part 2. Decoding and use of context. *Cognition and Instruction, 2*(3 & 4), 271–338.

Frederiksen, N. (1984). Implications of cognitive theory for instruction in problem solving. *Review of Educational Research, 54*(3), 363–407.

Friend, J. & Milojkovic, J. D. (1984). Designing interactions between students and computers. In D. F. Walker and R. D. Hess (Eds.), *Instructional Software* (pp. 143–150). Belmont, CA: Wadsworth.

Fuller, R. G. (1982, September). Solving physics problems-how we do it. *Physics Today, 35,* 43–47.

Gagné, R. M. (1977). *The conditions of learning* (3rd ed.). New York: Holt, Rinehart, and Winston.

Gagné, R. M. (1985). *The conditions of learning* (4th ed.). New York: Holt, Rinehart, and Winston.

Gagné, R. M. & Briggs, L. J. (1974). *Principles of instructional design.* New York: Holt, Rinehart, and Winston.

Gagné, R. M. & Briggs, L. J., & Wager, W. W. (1988). *Principles of instructional design* (3rd ed.). New York: Holt, Rinehart, & Winston.

Gay, G. (1986). Interaction of learner control and prior understanding in computer-assisted video instruction. *Journal of Educational Psychology, 78*(3), 325–327.

Gillingham, M. G. (1988). Text in computer-based instruction: What the research says. *Journal of Computer-Based Instruction, 15*(1), 1–6.

Glaser, R. (1978). The contributions of B. F. Skinner to education and some counterinfluences. In P. Suppes (Ed.), *Impact of research on education: Some case studies* (pp. 199–265). Washington, DC: National Academy of Education.

Glaser, R. & Nitko, A. J. (1971). Measurement in learning and instruction. In R. L Thorndike (Ed.), *Educational Measurement* (2nd ed.). Washington, DC: American Council on Education.

Glaser, R. & Rosner, J. (1975). In H. Talmadge (Ed.), *Systems of individualized education.* Berkeley, CA: McCutchan.

Glynn, S. M., Britton, B. K., & Tillman, M. H. (1985). Typographical cues in text: Introduction. In D. H. Jonassen (Ed.), *The technology of text: Principles for structuring, designing, and displaying text* (Vol. 2, (pp. 192–209). Englewood Cliffs, NJ: Educational Technology Publications.

Goetzfried, L. & Hannafin, M. J. (1985). The effect of locus of control of CAI control strategies on the learning of mathematics rules. *American Educational Research Journal, 22*(2), 273–278.

Gray, S. H. (1987). The effect of sequence control on computer-assisted learning. *Journal of Computer-Based Instruction, 14*(2), 54–56.

Greeno, J. G. (1985, March). Advancing cognitive science through development of advanced instructional systems. In P. Resta (Chair), *Advanced computer applications in education: The next generation of research.* Symposium conducted at the Annual Meeting of the American Educational Research Association, Chicago.

Gronlund, N. E. (1982). Constructing achievement tests (3rd ed.). Englewood Cliffs, NJ: Prentice-Hall.

Gropper, G. L. (1974). *Instructional strategies.* Englewood Cliffs, NJ: Educational Technology Publications.

Gropper, G. L. (1983). A behavioral approach to instructional prescription. In C. M. Reigeluth (Ed.), *Instructional design theories and models: An overview of their current status* (pp. 101–161). Hillsdale, NJ: Lawrence Erlbaum Associates.

Gropper, G. L. (1988, April). How text displays add value to text content. *Educational Technology,* pp. 15–21.

Haber, R. N. (1970). How we remember what we see. *Scientific American, 222*(5), 104–112.

Haber, R. N. & Wilkinson, L. (1982, May). Perceptual components of computer displays. *IEEE CG&A,* pp. 23–35.

Hagler, R. & Knowlton, J. (1987). Invalid implicit assumptions in CBI comparison research. *Journal of Computer-Based Instruction, 14*(3), 84–87.

Hambleton, R. K. (1974). Testing and decision-making procedures for selected individualized instructional programs. *Review of Educational Research, 44*(4), 371–400.

Hamilton, R. J. (1985). A framework for the evaluation of the effectiveness of adjunct questions and objectives. *Review of Educational Research, 55*(1), 47–85.

Hannafin, M. J. & Hughes, C. W. (1986). A framework for incorporating orienting activities in computer-based interactive video. *Instructional Science, 15,* 239–255.

Hartley, J. & Davies, I. K. (1976). Preinstructional strategies: The role of pretests, behavioral objectives, and advance organizers. *Review of Educational Research, 46*(2), 239-265.

Hartley, J. R. & Lovell, K. (1984). The psychological principles underlying the design of computer-based instructional systems. In D. F. Walker & R. D. Hess (Eds.), *Instructional software*, (pp. 38-56). Belmont, CA: Wadsworth.

Hatasa, K. (1986). *Japanese Hiragana, Parts 1 and 2* [Computer program]. West Lafayette, IN: K. Hatasa, Department of Foreign Languages, Purdue University.

Hawk, P., McLeod, N. P., & Jonassen, D. H. (1985). In D. H. Jonassen (Ed.), *The technology of text: Principles for structuring, designing, and displaying text* (Vol. 1, pp. 158-185). Englewood Cliffs, NJ: Educational Technology Publications.

Heines, J. M. (1984). *Screen design strategies for computer-assisted instruction*. Bedford, MA: Digital Press.

Heinich, R., Molenda, M., & Russell, J. D. (1985). *Instructional media and the new technologies*. New York: John Wiley & Sons.

Henney, M. (1983). The effect of all-capital vs. regular mixed print. *AEDS Journal, 16*(4), 205-217.

Hofstetter, F. T. (1981). Computer-based aural training: The GUIDO System. *Journal of Computer-Based Instruction, 7*(3), 84-92.

IBM. (1987). *Fundamentals of discrete manufacturing* [Interactive videodisc program]. Atlanta, GA: IBM Videodiscs.

Ittelson, J. C., Land, L., Leedom, C. L., & Persaud, D. (1989, September/October). Computer-assisted interactive video instruction in nursing. *Journal of Nursing Staff Development*.

Jaeger, M. (1988, March). Zaps, booms, & whistles. *The Computing Teacher*, pp. 20-22.

Johnson, W. E. & Soloway, E. (1985). *Intention-based diagnosis of programming errors* (Report No. 19). New Haven, CT: Yale University, Department of Computer Science.

Jones, M. (1978). TICCIT application in higher education: evaluation results. *Proceedings of the Annual Meeting of the Association for the Development of Computer-based Instructional Systems* (pp. 398-419), Dallas, TX. Bellingham, WA: Association for the Development of Computer-based Instructional Systems.

Kearsley, G. P. (1983). *Computer-based training*. Reading, MA: Addison-Wesley Publishing.

Kearsley, G. P. & Hillelsohn, M. J. (1982). Human factors considerations for computer-based training. *Journal of Computer-Based Instruction, 8*(4), 74-84.

Keller, F. S. (1968). Goodbye, teacher. *Journal of Applied Behavior Analysis, 1*, 79-89.

Kieras, D. E. (1982). A model of reader strategy for abstracting main ideas from simple technical prose. *Text, 2*, 47-81.

Krahn, C. G. & Blanchaer, M. C. (1986). Using an advance organizer to improve knowledge application by medical students in computer-based clinical simulations. *Journal of Computer-Based Instruction, 13*, 71-74.

Kulhavy, R. W. (1977). Feedback in written instruction. *Review of Educational Research, 47*, 211-232.

Kulhavy, R. W. & Anderson, R. C. (1972). Delay-retention effect with multiple choice tests. *Journal of Educational Psychology, 63*, 505-512.

Kulik, J. A., Bangert, R. L.,& Williams, G. W. (1983). Effects of computer-based teaching on secondary school students. *Journal of Educational Psychology, 75*(1), 19-26.

Kulik, J. A., Kulik, C. L. C., & Cohen, P. A. (1979). A meta-analysis of outcome studies of Keller's personalized system of instruction. *American Psychologist, 34*, 307-318.

Lambrecht, M. E. (1986, October). Computer-assisted instruction: A vehicle for effective learning. In B. Thomas (Ed.), *Proceedings of Instructional Computing in Nursing Education Conference* (pp. 133-139). Cedar Rapids, IA.

Lamos, J. P. (1984). Programmed instruction to computer-based instruction: The evolution of instructional technology. In R. K. Bass & C. R. Dills (Eds.), *Instructional development:*

The state of the Art, II (pp. 169–176). Dubuque, IA: Kendall/ Hunt.

Landa, L. N. (1983). The algo-heuristic theory of instruction. In C. M. Reigeluth (Ed.), *Instructional design theories and models: An overview of their current status* (pp. 163–211). Hillsdale, NJ: Lawrence Erlbaum Associates.

Lederman, B. J. (1975). Analyzing algebraic expressions and equations. *Journal of Computer-Based Instruction, 1*, 80–83.

Lehmann, H. (1968). The systems approach to education. *Audiovisual Instruction, 13*, 144–148.

Leibowitz, A. Z. (1985). User-friendly methods of judging. *Journal of Computer-Based Instruction, 12*(3), 69–70.

Lepper, M. R. (1985). Microcomputers in education. *American Psychologist, 40*(1), 1–18.

Lepper, M. R. & Chabay, R. W. (1985). Intrinsic motivation and instruction: Conflicting views on the role of motivational processes in computer-based education. *Educational Psychologist, 20*(4), 217–230.

Leron, U. (1985, February). LOGO today: Vision and reality. *The Computing Teacher*, pp. 26–32.

Lesgold, A. M. (1983). A rationale for computer-based reading instruction. In A. C. Wilkinson (Ed.), *Classroom computers and cognitive science* (pp. 167–181). New York: Academic Press.

Linn, M. C. & Dalbey, J. (1985). Cognitive consequences of programming instruction: Instruction, access, and ability. *Educational Psychologist, 20*(4), 191–206.

Littman, D. C., Pinto, J., & Soloway, E. (1985). *An analysis of tutorial reasoning about programming bugs* (Tech. report). New Haven, CT: Yale University, Cognition and programming project, Department of Computer Science.

Mager, R. F. (1975). *Preparing instructional objectives* (2nd ed.). Belmont, CA: Pitman Learning.

Malone, T. W. (1981). Toward a theory of intrinsically motivating instruction. *Cognitive Science, 4*, 333–369.

Malone, T. W. & Lepper, M. R. (1987). Making learning fun: A taxonomy of intrinsic motivations in learning. In R. E. Snow & M. J. Farr (Eds.), *Aptitude, learning, and instruction: III. Conative and affective processes* (pp. 223–253). Hillsdale, NJ: Lawrence Erlbaum Associates.

Markle, S. M. (1978). *Designs for instructional designers*. Champaign, IL: Stipes.

Marshall, N. & Glock, M. D. (1978). Comprehension of connected discourse: A study into the relationships between the structure of text and information recalled. *Reading Research Quarterly, 14*(1), 10–56.

Mayer, R. E. (1975). Information processing variables in learning to solve problems. *Review of Educational Research, 45*(4), 525–541.

Mayer, R. E. (1979). Can advance organizers induce meaningful learning? *Review of Educational Research,49*(2), 371–383.

McDermott, L. C. (1984). Research on conceptual understanding in mechanics. *Physics Today, 37*(7), 24–32.

McKeachie, W. J. (1974). The decline and fall of the laws of learning. *Educational Researcher, 3*(3), 7–11.

Merrill, M. D. (1984). What is learner control? In R. K. Bass & C. R. Dill (Eds.), *Instructional Development: The state of the art, II* (pp. 221 242). Dubuque, IA: Kendall/Hunt.

Merrill, M. D. & Boutwell, R. C. (1973). Instructional development: Methodology and research. In F. N. Kerlinger (Ed.), *Review of research in education* (Vol. 1, pp. 95–131). Itasca, IL: F. E. Peacock.

Merrill, M. D. & Tennyson, R. D. (1977). *Teaching concepts: An instructional design guide*. Englewood Cliffs, NJ: Educational Technology Publications.

Meyer, B. J. F. (1977). The structure of prose: Effects on learning and memory and implications for educational practice. In R. C. Anderson, R. J. Spiro, & W. E. Montague (Eds.), *Schooling and the acquisition of knowledge* (pp. 179-200). Hillsdale, NJ: Lawrence Erlbaum Associates.

Meyer, B. J. F. (1985). Signaling the structure of text. In D. H. Jonassen (Ed.), *The technology of text: Principles for structuring, designing, and displaying text* (Vol. 2, pp. 64-89). Englewood Cliffs, NJ: Educational Technology Publications.

Miller, G. A. (1956). The magical number seven, plus or minus two: Some limits on our capacity for processing information. *Psychological Review, 63*, 81-97.

Montague, W. E. (1981). *After years of instructional research do we know more tham grandma did about how to teach people?* Paper presented at the Annual Meeting of the American Educational Research Association, Los Angeles.

Montague, W. E. (1987, May). Untitled presentation. In S. Chipman (Chair), *Instructional principles for ICAI*. Panel discussion conducted at the Third International Conference on Artificial Intelligence and Education, Pittsburgh, PA.

Moran, T. P. (1981). An applied psychology of the user. *Computing Surveys, 13*(1), 1-11.

Moursund, D. (1983-84, December-January). LOGO frightens me. *The Computing Teacher*, pp. 3-4.

Nadler, G. (1981). *The planning and design approach*. New York: John Wiley & Sons.

Nesbit, J. C. (1985). Approximate string matching in response analysis. *Journal of Computer-Based Instruction, 12*(3), 71-75.

New directions in English: Evidence and evaluation. (1973). New York: Harper & Row.

Newell, A. & Simon, H. A. (1972). *Human problem solving.* Englewood Cliffs, NJ: Prentice-Hall.

Niemic, R. & Walberg, H. J. (1987). Comparative effects of computer-assisted instruction: A synthesis of reviews. *Journal of Educational Computing Research, 3*(1), 19-37.

Obertino, P., Fillman, L., Gilfillan, J., Silver, D., & Yeager, R. (1977). *Elementary reading on PLATO IV.* Urbana, IL: University of Illinois, Computer-based Education Research Laboratory.

Olson, D. R. (1985). Computers as tools of the intellect. *Educational Researcher, 14*(5), 5-7.

Orlansky, J. & String, J. (1981). *The performance of maintenance technicians on the job* (Final Report). Arlington, VA: Institute for Defense Analysis.

Paivio, A. (1974). Language and knowledge of the world. *Educational Researcher, 3*(9), 5-12.

Papert, S. (1980). *Mindstorms.* New York: Basic Books.

Park, O. C. (1984). Example comparison strategy versus attribute identification strategy in concept learning. *American Educational Research Journal, 21*(1), 145-162.

Park, O. C. & Seidel, R. J. (1987, May). Conventional CBI versus intelligent CAI: Suggestions for the development of future systems. *Educational Technology*, pp. 15-21.

Park, O. C. & Tennyson, R. D. (1983). Computer-based instructional systems for adaptive education: A review. *Contemporary Educational Review, 2*, 121-135.

Pearson, P. D. & Fielding, L. (1982). Listening. *Language Arts, 59*, 617-629.

Perez, E. C. & White, M. A. (1985). Student evaluation of motivational and learning attributes of microcomputer software. *Journal of Computer-Based Instruction, 12*(2), 39-43.

Raghaven, K. & Katz, A. (1989, August). Smithtown: An intelligent tutoring system. *T.H.E. Journal*, pp. 50-53.

Reder, L. M. (1980). The role of elaboration in the comprehension and retention of prose. A critical review. *Review of Educational Research, 50*(1), 5-53.

Reigeluth, C. M., Merrill, M. D., & Bunderson, C. V. (1978). The structure of subject matter content and its instructional design implications. *Instructional Science, 7*, 107-126.

Reigeluth, C. M. & Stein, F. S. (1983). The elaboration theory of instruction. In C. M. Reigeluth (Ed.), *Instructional-design theories and models: An overview of their current status* (pp. 335-381). Hillsdale, NJ: Lawrence Erlbaum Associates.

Reilly, S. S. & Roach, J. W. (1986, January). Designing human/computer interfaces: A comparison of human factors and graphic arts principles. *Educational Technology*, pp. 36-40.

Resnick, L. B. (1976). Task analysis in instructional design: Some cases from mathematics. In D. Klahr (Ed.), *Cognition and instruction* (pp. 51-80). Hillsdale, NJ: Lawrence Erlbaum Associates.

Resnick, L. B. (1981). Instructional Psychology. *Annual Review of Psychology, 32*, 659-704.

Richardson, J. J. (1981). The limits of frame-based CAI. *Frontiers of Thought: Proceedings of the Association for the Development of Computer-based Instructional Systems* (pp. 88-94), Atlanta, GA. Bellingham, WA: Association for the Development of Computer-Based Instructional Systems.

Rigney, J. W. (1978). Learning strategies: A theoretical perspective. In H. F. O'Neil, Jr. (Ed.), *Learning Strategies* (pp. 165-205). New York: Academic Press.

Rigney, J. W. & Lutz, K. A. (1976). Effect of graphic analogies of concepts in chemistry on learning and attitude. *Journal of Educational Psychology, 68*(3), 305-311.

Roblyer, M. D. (1981). Instructional design versus authoring of courseware: Some crucial differences. *AEDS Journal, 14*, 173-181.

Roblyer, M. D. (1982, July). Courseware. *Educational Technology*, pp. 29-30.

Roid, G. H. & Haladyna, T. M. (1982). *A technology for test-item writing*. New York: Academic Press.

Romiszowski, A. J. (1981). *Designing instructional systems*. London: Kogan Page.

Roper, W. J. (1977). Feedback in computer-assisted instruction. *Programmed Learning & Educational Technology, 14*(1), 43-49.

Rothbart, A. & Steinberg, E. (1971, January). Some observations of children's reactions to computer-assisted instruction. *The Arithmetic Teacher*, pp. 19-21.

Rothkopf, E. Z. (1966). Learning from written instructive materials: An exploration of the control of inspection behavior by test-like events. *American Educational Research Journal, 3*, 241-249.

Rubincam, I. & Olivier, W. P. (1985). An investigation of limited learner-control options in a CAI mathematics course. *AEDS Journal, Summer*, 211-226.

Rumelhart, D. E. & Norman, D. A. (1981). Analogical processes in learning. In J. R. Anderson (Ed.), *Cognitive skills and their acquisition* (pp. 335-359). Hillsdale, NJ: Lawrence Erlbaum Associates.

Samuels, S. J. (1970). Effects of pictures on learning to read, comprehension, and attitudes. *Review of Educational Research, 40*(3), 397-407.

Sasscer, M. F. (1984). *The myths: The system comes with courseware: Creating your own course materials is easy*. Paper presented at the meeting of the American Association of Community and Junior Colleges.

Sassenrath, J. M. M. & Yonge, G. D. (1969). Effects of delayed information feedback and feedback cues in learning and retention. *Journal of Educational Psychology, 60*, 174-177.

Schallert, D. L. (1980). The role of illustrations in reading comprehension. In R. S. Spiro, B. C. Bruce, & W. F. Brewer, (Eds.), *Theoretical issues in reading comprehension* (pp. 503-524). Hillsdale, NJ: Lawrence Erlbaum Associates.

Schank, R. C. (1982). *Reading and understanding: Teaching reading from the perspective of Artificial Intelligence*. Hillsdale, NJ: Lawrence Erlbaum Associates.

Schloss, P. J., Sindelar, P. T., Cartwright, G. P., & Schloss, C. N. (1986). Efficacy of higher cognitive factual questions in computer assisted instruction modules. *Journal of Computer-Based Instruction, 13*(3), 75-80.

Schloss, P. J., Wisniewski, L. A., & Cartwright, G. P. (1988). The differential effect of learner control and feedback on college students' performance in CAI modules. *Journal of Educational Computing Research, 4*,(2), 141–150.

Schneider, W. (1985). Training high-performance skills: Fallacies and guidelines. *Human Factors, 27*(3), 285–300.

Schneider, W. & Shiffrin, R. M. (1977). Controlled and automatic human information processing: I. Detection, search, and attention. *Psychological Review, 84*, 1–66.

Schoenfeld, A. H. (1987). Cognitive science and mathematics education. In A. H. Schoenfeld (Ed.), *Cognitive science and mathematices education.* Hillsdale, NJ: Lawrence Erlbaum Associates.

Sebrechts, M. M., LaClaire, L., Schooler, L. J., & Soloway, E. (1986). Towards generalized intention-based diagnosis: GIDE. In R. C. Ryan (Ed.), *Proceedings of the National Educational Computing Conference.*

Seiler, B. A. & Weaver, C. S. (1976). *Description of PLATO whole number arithmetic lessons* (Tech. Report). Urbana, IL: University of Illinois, Computer-based Education Research Laboratory.

Shiffrin, R. M. (1975). The locus and role of attention in memory systems. In P. M. A. Rabbit & S. Dornic (Eds.),*Attention and performance V* (pp. 168–193). New York: Academic Press.

Shiffrin, R. M. & Schneider, W. (1977). Controlled and automatic human information processing: II. Perceptual learning, automatic attending, and a general theory. *Psychological Review, 84*, 127–190.

Shneiderman, B. (1982). System message design: Guidelines and experimental results. In A. Badre & B. Shneiderman (Eds.), *Directions in human/computer interaction.* Norwood, NJ: Ablex Publishing Corporation.

Siegler, R. S. (1976). Three aspects of cognitive development. *Cognitive Psychology, 4*, 481–520.

Simon, H. A. (1980). Problem solving and education. In D. T. Tuma & F. Reif (Eds.), *Problem solving and education: Issues in teaching and research* (pp. 81–96). Hillsdale, NJ: Lawrence Erlbaum Associates.

Simon, H. A. & Chase, W. G. (1973). Skill in chess. *American Scientist, 61*(4), 394–403.

Simpson, H. (1985). *Design of user-friendly programs for small computers.* New York: McGraw Hill.

Skinner, B. F. (1953). *Science and human behavior.* New York: The MacMillan Co.

Skinner, B. F. (1961, November). Teaching machines. *Scientific American*, pp. 3–13.

Skinner, B. F. (1986). Programmed instruction revisited. *Kappan, 68*(2), 103–110.

Sleeman, D. (1982). Assessing aspects of competence in basic algebra. In D. Sleeman & J. S. Brown (Eds.), *Intelligent tutoring systems* (pp. 185–199). New York: Academic Press.

Sleeman, D. & Brown, J. S. (1982). Introduction. In D. Sleeman & J. S. Brown (Eds.), *Intelligent tutoring systems* (pp. 1–11). New York: Academic Press.

Slottow, H. G. (Ed.). (1977). *Final Report: Demonstration of the PLATO IV computer-based education system.* Urbana, IL: University of Illinois, Computer Based Education Research Laboratory.

Smith, S., Chabay,R., & Kean, E. (1980). *Introduction to general chemistry* [Computer program]. Urbana, IL: S. Smith,Chemistry Department, University of Illinois.

Smith, S. G., Jones, L. L., & Waugh, M. L. (1986). Production and evaluation of interactive videodisc lessons in laboratory instruction. *Journal of Computer-Based Instruction, 13*(4), 117–121.

Snelbecker, G. E. (1974). *Learning theory, instructional theory, and psychoeducational design.* New York: McGraw-Hill.

Spitzer, D. R. (1982, February). Training technology. *Educational Technology*, pp. 37–38.

Steinberg, E. R. (1975). *The evolutionary development of PLATO courseware.* Paper presented at the Annual Meeting of the American Educational Research Association,

Washington, D.C. (ERIC Document Reproduction Service No. ED 105 888)

Steinberg, E. R. (1977). Review of student control in computer-assisted instruction. *Journal of Computer-Based Instruction, 3*(3), 84–90.

Steinberg, E. R. (1980a). Evaluation processes in young children's problem-solving. *Contemporary Educational Psychology, 5,* 276–281.

Steinberg, E. R. (1980b). *Experience vs two kinds of feedback in CAI problem solving* (Tech. Report). Urbana, IL: University of Illinois, Computer-based Education Research Laboratory. (ERIC Document Reproduction Service No. ED 194 076)

Steinberg, E. R. (1984). *Teaching computers to teach.* Hillsdale, NJ: Lawrence Erlbaum Associates.

Steinberg, E. R. & Anderson, B. C. (1973, December). Teaching tens to Timmy. *The Arithmetic Teacher,* pp. 620–625.

Steinberg, E. R., Avner, R. A., Call-Himwich, E., Francis, L., Himwich, A., Klecka, J. A., & Misselt, A. L. (1977). *Critical incidents in the evolution of PLATO projects* (MTC Report No. 12). Urbana, IL: University of Illinois, Computer-based Education Research Laboratory. (ERIC Document Reproduction Service No. ED 148 298).

Steinberg, E. R. & Baskin, A. B. (1985). Instructional design for problem solving based on the study of problem solving behavior. In Steinberg, E. R. (Ed.), *Designing computer based instruction for problem solving* (Tech. report). Urbana, IL: University of Illinois, Computer-based Education Research Laboratory.

Steinberg, E. R., Baskin, A. B., & Hofer, E. (1986). Organizational/memory tools: A technique for improving problem solving skills. *Journal of Educational Computing Research, 2*(2), 169–187.

Steinberg, E. R., Baskin, A. B., & Matthews, T. D. (1985). Computer-presented organizational/memory aids as instruction for solving Pico-Fomi problems. *Journal of Computer-Based Instruction, 12*(2), 44–49.

Steinberg, S. H. (1966). *Five hundred years of printing.* Baltimore, MD: Penguin Books.

Sterling, C. H. & Kittross, J. M. (1978). *Stay tuned.* Belmont, CA: Wadsworth.

Sternberg, R. J. (1986, March-April). Inside intelligence. *American Scientist,* pp. 137–143.

Stevens, A., Collins, A., & Goldin, S. E. (1982). Misconceptions in students' understanding. In D. Sleeman & J. S. Brown (Eds.), *Intelligent tutoring systems* (pp. 13–24). New York: Academic Press.

Sticht,T. G. (1984). Listening and reading. In P. D. Pearson (Ed.), *Handbook of reading research.* New York: Longman.

Stifle, J. E. (1975). *The evolutionary development of CAI hardware.* Paper presented at the Annual Meeting of the American Educational Research Association, Washington, D.C. (ERIC Document Reproduction Service No. ED 105 868)

Striley, J. (1988, August/September). Physics for the rest of us. *Educational Researcher,* pp. 7–10.

Sturgis, P. T. (1969). Verbal retention as a function of the informativeness and delay of informative feedback. *Journal of Educational Psychology, 60,* 11–14.

Sturgis, P. T. (1972). Information delay and retention: Effect of information feedback and tests. *Journal of Educational Psychology, 63,* 32–43.

Suppes, P. (1984). Observations about the application of artificial intelligence research to education. In D. F. Walker & R. D. Hess (Eds.), *Instructional software: Principles and perspectives for design and use* (pp. 298–308). Belmont, CA: Wadsworth.

Suppes, P., Jerman, M., & Brian, D. (1968). *Computer-assisted instruction: Stanford's 1965–66 arithmetic program.* New York: Academic Press.

Suppes, P., Macken, E., & Zanotti, M. (1978). The role of global psychological models in instructional technology. In R. Glaser (Ed.), *Advances in instructional psychology* (Vol. 1). Hillsdale, NJ: Lawrence Erlbaum Associates.

Suppes, P. & Morningstar, M. (1972). *Computer-assisted instruction at Stanford, 1966–68: Data, models, and evaluation of the arithmetic programs.* New York: Academic Press.

Surber, J. R. & Leeder, J. A. (1988). The effect of graphic feedback on student motivation. *Journal of Computer-Based Instruction, 15*(1), 14–17.

Swinton, S., Amarel, M., & Morgan, J. (1978). *The PLATO elementary demonstration: Educational outcome evaluation. Final Report* (ESS PR 78-11). Princeton, NJ: Educational Testing Service.

Tatsuoka, K. K. (1984). Changes in error types over learning stages. *Journal of Educational Psychology, 76*(1), 120–129.

Tatsuoka, K. K. & Eddins, J. E. (1985). Computer analysis of students' procedural "bugs" in an arithmetic domain. *Journal of Computer-Based Instruction, 12*(2), 34–38.

Tennyson, R. D. (1976, September). The role of evaluation in instructional development. *Educational Technology,* pp. 17–24.

Tennyson, R. D. (1980). Instructional control strategies and content structure as design variables in concept acquisition using computer-based instruction. *Journal of Educational Psychology, 72,* 525–532.

Tennyson, R. D. (1981). *The interactive effect of cognitive learning with computer attributes in the design of CAI.* Paper presented at the Annual Meeting of the American Educational Research Association, Los Angeles.

Tennyson, R. D. & Park, O. C. (1980). The teaching of concepts: A review of the literature. *Review of Educational Research, 50*(1), 55–70.

Tennyson, R. D. & Rothen, W. (1979). Management of computer based instruction: Design of an adaptive control strategy. *Journal of Computer-Based Instruction, 5*(3), 63–71.

Thomas, K. J., Stahl, R. J., & Swanson, C. C. (1984). Developing textual materials: What research says to the practitioner. In R. K. Bass & C. R. Dills (Eds.), *Instructional development: The state of the art, II* (pp. 203–220). Dubuque, IA: Kendall/Hunt.

Tiemann, P. W. & Markle, S. M. (1985). *Analyzing instructional content: A guide to instruction and evaluation.* Champaign, IL: Stipes.

Travers, R. M. W. (1984). Human interface processing. In R. K. Bass & C. R. Dills, *Instructional development: The state of the art, II* (pp. 111–125). Dubuque, IA: Kendall/Hunt.

Trimby, M. J. & Gentry, C. G. (1984). State of ID systems approach models. In R. K. Bass & C. R. Dills (Eds.), *Instructional development: The state of the art, II* (pp. 80–93). Dubuque, IA: Kendall/Hunt.

Tufte, E. R. (1983). *The visual display of quantitative information.* Chesire, CT: Graphics Press.

Tullis, T. S. (1981). An evaluation of alphanumeric, graphic, and color information displays. *Human Factors, 23*(5), 541–550.

Van Matre, N. (1980, September). *Computer-managed instruction in the Navy: Research background and status* (NPRDC TR 9-80-33). San Diego, CA: Navy Personnel Research and Development Center.

Walker, D. F. & Hess, R. D. (1984). Evaluation in courseware development. In D. F. Walker & R. D. Hess (Eds.), *Instructional software: Principles and perspectives for design and use* (pp. 204–215). Belmont, CA: Wadsworth.

Waller, R. (1982). Text as diagram: Using typography to improve access and understanding. In D. H. Jonassen (Ed.), *The technology of text: Principles for structuring, designing, and displaying text* (Vol.1, pp. 137–166). Englewood Cliffs, NJ: Educational Technology Publications.

Waugh, M. L. & Levin, J. A. (1988/89). Telescience activities: Educational use of electronic networks. *Journal of Computers in Mathematics and Science Teaching, Winter,* 29–33.

Wenger, E. (1987). *Artificial intelligence and tutoring systems.* Los Altos, CA: Morgan Kaufmann.

White, B. Y. (1984). Designing computer games to help physics students understand Newton's Laws of Motion. *Cognition and Instruction, 1*(1), 69–108.

Williams, R. G. & Haladyna, T. M. (1982). Logic operations for generating intended questions (LOGIQ). In G. H. Roid & T. M. Haladyna (Eds.), *A technology for test-item writing* (pp. 161–186). New York: Academic Press.

Wilson, L. S. (1984,Winter Quarter). Presenting TICCIT: State-of-the-art computer-based instruction. *Training Technology Journal*, pp. 26–32.

Winn, W. & Holliday, W. (1982). Design principles for diagrams and charts. In D. H. Jonassen (Ed.), *The technology of text: Principles for structuring, designing, and displaying text* (Vol. 1, pp. 277–299). Englewood Cliff, NJ: Educational Technology Publications.

Winston, P. (1979). *Artificial intelligence*. Reading, MA: Addison-Wesley.

Wittrock, M. (1979). The cognitive movement in instruction. *Educational Researcher, 8*, 5–11.

Woodward, J., Carnine, D., & Gersten, R. (1988). Teaching problem solving through computer simulations. *American Educational Research Journal, 25*(1), 72–86.

Wyles, B. (1984). *The myth: Computer-assisted instruction (CAI) translates qualitative skills and demands that the humanists among us become "technocrats."* Paper presented at the meeting of the American Association of Community and Junior Colleges.

Yerushalmy, M. & Houde, R. A. (1986). The Geometric Supposer: Promoting learning and thinking. *Mathematics Teacher, 79*, 418–422.

AUTHOR INDEX

215

SUBJECT INDEX